P9-AFO-888

Praise for *Keeping Up With the Dow Joneses*

"Elegant, lucid, and incisive, *Keeping Up with the Dow Joneses* is an invaluable resource for political and intellectual challenges to captivity. Vijay Prashad's critique of globalization, local policing, welfare, and his mapping of resistance waged by women, the impoverished, the racialized, and incarcerated are fierce and fruitful."

—Joy James, editor of *Imprisoned Intellectuals*, author of *Resisting State Violence*

"Vijay Prashad draws a compelling bottom-up picture of the American political economy today. He shows the mesh between the stressed economic situation of working people and our increasingly repressive social policies. And he also points to the kinds of movement struggles that might disrupt this fundamentalist neoliberal regime."

—Frances Fox Piven, author of *Why Americans Still Don't Vote: And Why Politicians Want It That Way*

"Some people write eloquently. Some are wonderful researchers. Some think clearly, giving us new ideas with each new page. Vijay Prashad manages all three achievements, and does it with admirable passion, in his new book *Keeping Up With The Dow Joneses*. Essays on debt, prison, workfare, and movement struggle are all, in fact, really about how we can best understand our world in order to dramatically change it. It is a fine book belonging on every radical's bookshelf and beyond."

—Michael Albert, author of *The Trajectory of Change*

"Vijay Prashad's *Keeping Up With the Dow Joneses* provides the complete package —a detailed account of the ways in which class, race, and gender inequality have played out in the United States over the last twenty years, how they are related and get played out in a wide range of policies, and how groups are collectively resisting these pressures. Wrapped around the story of growth in low-wage, contingent workforce and the opposition to these efforts, Prashad provides careful and useful documentation on growing greed at the top and debt at the bottom, the criminalization of poverty and the corresponding growth

POINT LOMA NAZARENE UNIVERSITY
RYAN LIBRARY
3900 LOMALAND DRIVE
SAN DIEGO, CALIFORNIA 92106-2899

in for-profit prison industry, as well as the hell-bent intent to dissolve the safety net and force poor mothers into lousy jobs."

—Randy Albelda, co-author of *Glass Ceilings and Bottomless Pits: Women's Work, Women's Poverty* and co-editor of *Lost Ground: Welfare Reform, Poverty and Beyond*

"Prashad expertly analyzes the linkages between globalization, racism, and the prison industrial complex. What is particularly noteworthy about this book is that it does not just describe the problems we face, but provides a wide range of creative strategies for tackling what seem to be overwhelming obstacles in the fight for social and economic justice. In addition, he highlights the organizing work of people of color, particularly women of color, whose contributions in anti-globalization work are generally marginalized by other scholars."

—Andrea Smith, co-founder of Incite! Women of Color Against Violence

POINT LOMA NAZARENE UNIVERSITY
RYAN LIBRARY
3900 LOMALAND DRIVE
SAN DIEGO, CALIFORNIA 92106-2899

330.973
P911k
E
5104

Keeping Up With the Dow Joneses

Debt, Prison, Workfare

Vijay Prashad

South End Press
Cambridge, Massachusetts

POINT LOMA NAZARENE UNIVERSITY
WITHDRAWN
RYAN LIBRARY

Copyright © 2003 by Vijay Prashad
Cover design by Ellen P. Shapiro

First edition published in 2001 as *The American Scheme* by Three Essays Press in India.

Union printed in Canada.

Any properly footnoted quotation of up to 500 sequential words may be used without permission, as long as the total number of words quoted does not exceed 2,000. For longer quotations or for a greater number of total words, please write to South End Press for permission.

Library of Congress Cataloging-in-Publication Data

Prashad, Vijay.
  [American scheme]
  Keeping up with the Dow Joneses: debt, prison, workfare / Vijay Prashad.
    p. cm.
  "First edition published as 'The American Scheme' by Three Essays Press in India" —T.p. verso.
  "First appeared in a much briefer version…in New Delhi (Summer 2002)"—P. .
  Includes bibliographical references and index.
  Contents: Introduction: America—Debt— Prison—Workfare—Movement.
  ISBN 0-89608-690-9—ISBN 089608-689-5 (pbk.)
      1. United States—Economic conditions—2001- 2. United States—Economic conditions—1945- 3. Debt—United States. 4. Marginality, Social—United States. 5. Prisons—United States. 6. Public welfare—United States. 7. Welfare recipients—Employment—United States. 8. Social movements—United States. I. Title: Debt, prison, workfare. II. Title

HC106.83.P73 2003
305.5'6'0973—dc21

                                                      2003050587

South End Press, 7 Brookline Street, #1, Cambridge, MA 02139-4146
www.southendpress.org

07 06 05 04 03   1 2 3 4 5 6

TABLE OF CONTENTS

RESPECT

Keeping Up With the Dow Joneses first appeared in a much briefer version from Three Essays Press in New Delhi (Summer 2002) thanks to the initiative and hard work of Asad Zaidi. Without him I would not have thought to write a book about the US economy, about prisons, about welfare. Here I am, an Indian historian with a tendency to write about racism, and a scribbler on matters political, trying to write a book on so vast a topic. Ravi Ahuja asked me to explain contemporary trends in US economic life for *Marxistishe Blätter* in 2001 (and the title for the book comes from the essay for that volume: "Mit den Dow Joneses Mithalten: Sorgen und Kämpfe in den USA"). N. Ram (*Frontline* magazine in India), Krishna Raj (*Economic and Political Weekly* in India), Mike Albert (ZNET), Bob Wing (*ColorLines* magazine in the US) and Prakash Karat (*People's Democracy* in India) published bits and pieces of what has been totally refashioned in this text.

I received several needed tutorials on matters technical over the years from Jenni Gainsborough (of the ACLU, in 1995), from Alisa Solomon (of the *Village Voice*), from Libero Della Piana (at the time of *Race File*), from Merrilee Milstein (whose presentation on union density and the new AFL-CIO offered useful correctives to my impatience), from Miriam Ching Yoon Louie's *Sweatshop Warriors,* from the fact books and bibliographies and endless documents and briefs given by the Grass Roots Organizing for Welfare Leadership (GROWL) staff at the Center for Third World Organizing (CTWO). I learned endless amounts about the lives of the contingent class from conversations with Sudhir Venkatesh, Biju Mathew, Brian Steinberg, Joelle Fishman, Sudhanva Deshpande, and Johnny Williams. Mir Ali Raza gives me tutorials on business management. M. V. Ramana and I co-wrote an article on Mumia that helped with the section on the death penalty. Brinda Karat offered very useful shifts in the framework to make this book legible. Andy Hsiao, Justin Podur, Naomi Klein, Eric Mann, and Michael Albert helped me think about the globalization movement. Conversations with Gary Delgado, Linda Evans, Joy James, Raj Jayadev, Rinku Sen, and Mark Toney made the chapters closer to our truths. Work at Direct Action for Rights and Equality (DARE) in the mid-1990s introduced me to fiery organizers who taught me about life on the lam, life on the Man, and life in the can: Shakira Abdullah, Grace Brown, Shirley Craighead, Conteh Davis, Lisa Dupree, Ana Franco, Maria Guerrero, Alice Hicks, Dale Jackson, Simon Kue, Shannah Kurland, Sabrina Smith, Shirley Wilhelm, and a host of others. Extended interviews with Angela Chung (PUEBLO), Joelle Fishman (Campaign to End Child Poverty), Bonnie Macri (Jedi for Women), Dana Parades (CTWO), Sandra Robertson (Georgia Coalition Against Hunger), Janet Robideau (Indian People's Action), and Mark Toney (CTWO) provided the analysis for the chapter on workfare.

John Trumpour found *War Against the Planet*, tried to get it published in the US and introduced me to Tina Beyene at South End Press. Tina read these essays and enthusiastically shepherded this book to press. I am very grateful to her for her commitment to this project. The South End collective is an extraordinary place, with a wonderful crew whose hard work and humor helped get the book out.

My family is central to my life: mother, in-laws, siblings, aunts, uncles, and cousins. Jojo and Meera introduced me to America many years ago, making me a part of their home and teaching me about its wonderful, complex people. Without that, I wouldn't be me. Nor would I be me without Leela, and Rosy. When I started to draft the magazine articles and essays into a book, I kept thinking about what sort of America I wanted my beloved Zalia Maya to enjoy—I hope the contradictions move in favor of humanity in her lifetime. This book is dedicated to her and to her many cousins.

The main argument about the structural adjustment of the United States came from Elisabeth Armstrong in a spirited discussion at our barsati in New Delhi more than a decade ago. As the Indian government willingly joined hands with the International Monetary Fund (IMF) bureaucrats in 1991, she emphasized that we not take an overly nationalist view of the process, but keep the class question in focus. This book is a set of elaborations on the ideas she presented then and later, on the US and on India. She read the entire manuscript, pointed out several embarrassing gaffes, reframed the introduction, and made this book half decent. Always in your debt.

Writers crave solitude. But those who write about things political would be starved without ceaseless contact with the movement. This is also a movement book, so let's move on.

This one is for Salig, Sonita, Gautam, Samir, Gaurav, Ayesha, Ishan, Vivan, Saira, Zalia, and the baby from Pacifica.

"But now," says the Once-ler, "Now that you're here,
the word of the Lorax seems perfectly clear
UNLESS someone like you cares a whole awful lot,
Nothing is going to get better, it's not."

—Dr. Seuss, *The Lorax,* 1971

AMERICA

In America you are not
Required to offer food
To the hungry, or shelter
To the homeless, or to visit
The lonely—in fact, one
Of the nicest things about
Living in America is that
You really don't have to
Do anything for anybody.

—Homeless poet, Seattle, Washington, 1999

There are many Americas. America has its poor as much as its rich, its indigent and forgotten population tucked away in segregated zones, ridiculed by racism and the frustration of being poor in the richest country on earth. The poor in America are not so because of any inner failure, because of a lack of hard work or of genetic deficiency. Any contact with those who live in the straits of poverty will show that they work hard, but get nowhere, that one or two may rise into the managerial strata and stand like a beacon for the rest, but these role models are always a few, proud but marginal. There are many who have also given up, gone off the grid of social mobility, taken refuge in illegal economies or else in the warm embrace of social networks.

Both Americas, the domestic hardships for a considerable population and the American fantasy, are maintained by yet another entity: the America of global corporations and the taxpayer funded military force. The brand "America" is like Clorox corporation: it sells both toxic bleach (Clorox) and salad dressing (Hidden Valley Ranch). If the salad dressing came with the Clorox label, we wouldn't buy it. If "America" came with images of poverty and of military domination, it would fail as fantasy. The brand "America," therefore, denies that it reinforces poverty and suffering, and says that all that is outside itself, an excrescence, a result of bad luck or bad genes, or else of bad men who force the US to bomb them.

Keeping Up With the Dow Joneses is about people. It is about those who live in the US, who are American, and yet who do not benefit from the fantasy of America. It is about the six million people who are in the vise of the prison complex, the six million more who have been thrown off the welfare rolls since 1996, the uncounted millions who toil in terrible entry-level jobs whose only solace is their neighbors and families, the bits and pieces of joy that can be eked out in the throes of economic uncertainty. Even as we gasp at the devastation wrought for the lives of these millions, keep in mind the virtuoso ways in which these millions seek pleasure and leisure, how they reconstruct their humanity. Father Gene Boyle, a priest who works with the strawberry workers in California, warns us, "We live in a time when people are working too hard and are still in poverty. And communities and neighborhoods are crumbling because of it. We have to bring this into the daylight."

"The American welfare state was supposed to be dead, victim of the free-market economy and its success in creating a job for anybody who wanted one," wrote journalist David Leonhardt in late 2002.[1] While the unemployment rate rose in 2002, it still seemed awfully low for the general crisis being reported from the basement of US society. Food kitchens and homeless shelters cried out that they had reached capacity, and community organizations fulminated over the forgotten America—the working poor. Republicans talked about an across-the-board (regressive) tax cut, Democrats talked about a targeted tax cut for the "middle-income families," but no one with influence seemed to speak for those who had no job, no prospects, nothing. The unemployment rate, Leonhardt gently reminded *New York Times* readers on a September Sunday, is unreliable. It does not count those who give up looking for work, it does not count those who collect disability payments, and it does not count those who are in jail. Those who collect disability now number 5.4 million (twice the 1990 figure), and the government spends more money on them than on Food Stamps or unemployment insurance. There are now two million Americans behind bars (again, twice the 1990 figure). Although there is no accurate count of those who have ceased to register themselves as unemployed, one study

Leonhardt cites found that 11 percent of men between the ages of 18 and 54 did not work in 2000. Since the official unemployment rate is now just below six percent, we can surmise that it is artificially low because of those on disability, in jail, and outside the system.

The rate of indigence in our society and the strong ethics of some of our people have engendered powerful social movements, such as those that oppose prisons and poverty, sexism and racism, homophobia and war. These powerful movements sometimes fight along the axes of their own oppressions, but often find common cause with each other. The latter, those who seek solidarity across the lines of one fight, acknowledge that even as the specific problems we face may be different, there is something that we share in our struggles. From Critical Race theorist Kimberly Crenshaw we learn that subordination does not operate on a "single axis framework" and that we need to struggle against the "complexities of compoundedness." Crenshaw offers the idea of "intersectionality" to understand the "multi-dimensionality" of subordination: a black woman has to deal with racism as well as sexism, and then she must deal with issues of class and sexuality. Nothing can be put between brackets for another occasion.[2]

If intersectionality is an adequate concept for the insistence that we see linkages between different concrete instances of subordination, how does an activist make sense of those links? It is not enough to say that those in poverty, in prison, on welfare, with disabilities, and others share something in common. If we are to make sense of the links in practice, we need to analyze our present condition to find union and to act on it. Prisons are not far from the welfare offices, but do we have a theory of our world to make sense of the links between them, to find the connections at a structural level? There are, of course, various programs of action that circulate in the American Left, and these are all useful documents that need to be read by all of us so that we can find constructive ways to bring all our struggles into the intersection of the system. It is my sense that the current conjuncture, under the framework of neoliberalism, emerged in the 1970s and 1980s in the aftermath of the slowdown in the US, and global, economy. US industry lagged behind Japanese and West German manufacturing, and in response, the US state conducted the structural adjustment of the economy.[3] When Ronald Reagan took over as president of the US, he intensified a process begun by his predecessors. As he accepted his party's nomination on July 17,

1980, in an already gutted Detroit, Michigan, Reagan said, "I believe it is clear our federal government is overgrown and overweight. Indeed, it is time for our government to go on a diet."

The strategy of Reagan in particular and of neoliberalism in general was not to shrink the government in total, it was to refocus the priority of government away from the creation of equity and toward the maintenance of law and order. The stagnation of wages from 1973 and the creation of contingent work are not accidents of history or stories of race failure, they are the natural outcomes of the strategy used by the US administrations from the 1970s onward. Chapter 1 (Debt) offers a summary analysis of the transformations in the US economy over the past three decades. Reagan's assault on America, his adjustment of America, produced a state in the neoliberal image.[4] Neoliberalism, in its American theater, can be summarized in the following four components.

Attenuation of the Social Welfare System

In 1916, M. K. Gandhi told an English audience, "The test of civilization is not the number of millionaires it boasts, but in the absence of starvation among the masses." Two decades later, in his presidential address, Franklin D. Roosevelt told his fellow Americans, "The test of our progress is not whether we add more to the abundance of those who have much. It is whether we provide enough for those who have little" (January 20, 1937). There was a time, therefore, when the world's leaders did not feel embarrassed to admit that the task of a state was to minimize inequality and to put the resources of the state to this end. The best of Gandhian socialism or of FDR's New Deal came to an end as Reaganism assaulted the welfare state.[5]

All the aspects of the state that tended toward the social good, such as healthcare, public education, income support, etc., faced the axe in this new regime. Funds spent on the creation of social equity, on the alleviation of inequality, and the creation of justice dwindled as the state's managers claimed to rule over large bureaucracies with bankrupt exchequers. The state dispensed with the provision of many basic needs, giving them out to the highest bidder in the process called "privatization." Such areas of social life once thought to be under the dispensation of the state, such as water or electricity supply, came into the private, or profit, sector. "There Is No Alternative," we heard from London, for instance, as the Conservative government slashed and burnt its way through Britain's considerable social welfare system.[6] In the United States, the government allowed inflation to whittle away at the disbursements to the poor until it dropped the axe in 1996 and ended "welfare as we know it." The new bill threw the poor to the wolves of destitution, either to the temporary workforce (to deflate wages) or else to the vice economy (and eventually to incarceration). The violence of workfare and its impact on the lives of the poor, of the temporary workforce, is detailed in Chapter 3 (Workfare).

The neoliberal managers talk about "fiscal conservatism," about "small government," about how our "belts must be tighter," about "sacrifice," and about the need to have "less waste" and a "less bloated government." Much of this is obfuscation, because the state has not shrunk its budget, only curtailed its expense on the creation of humane social policies. The target of the state's accountants is social welfare, not the massive expenditure on the state's police, prisons, and military.

Expansion of the Punitive Functions

Rather than fund social welfare, the state turned those funds over to the police and the military. The global military expenditure is estimated to be around $839 billion (based on adopted defense budgets, and not counting any secret expenditures to security forces).[7] From 1987 to 1998, the total declined as governments moved funds away from military uses to other, more productive uses. However, since 1998 and especially since 9/11, spending on armed forces has increased exponentially. The US military budget request for 2003 was $396.1 billion—almost half of the entire world's military expenditure.[8]

The career of General Barry McCaffrey provides a useful synopsis of Secretary of State (and retired General) Colin Powell's doctrine of "overwhelming force" as applied to every aspect of social life. From Andover to West Point, McCaffrey went twice to Vietnam, spoke out against racism and sexism within the military, and then took his 24th Infantry Division from Georgia to Kuwait to pulverize the Iraqi Republican Guard. Two days after the ceasefire, on March 2, 1991, the 24th Infantry Division launched an assault on the column of retreating troops and killed tens of thousands of Iraqis. After speaking to 200 US military personnel for his article, journalist Seymour Hersh notes that the assault "was not so much a counterattack provoked by enemy fire as a systematic destruction of Iraqis who were generally fulfilling the requirements of the retreat."[9] Called alternatively the Battle of the Causeway, the Battle of Rumaila, and the Battle of the Junkyard, the engagement would be better known as the Rumaila Massacre.[10] The army held four investigations of the conduct of the 24th Division, found that it had not acted inappropriately (although many generals felt this was a whitewash of the truth). McCaffrey retired from the army in January 1996. Taken by this resume, President Bill Clinton invited McCaffrey into the cabinet as director of the Office of National Drug Control Policy, to be the Drug Csar. McCaffrey then brought the Powell Doctrine of "overwhelming force" into play on the domestic scene (with an intensification of combat against street drug dealers) as well as against Colombia (the source for the drugs themselves). He was the crucial player in the US government's massive $1.574 billion package to the Colombian military to fight the "narco-terrorists" (but really the left-wing insurgency).[11] Overwhelming force is the order of the day.

Chapter 2 (Prisons) follows the growth of the prison economy in the US. With a rise in unemployment and underemployment, the state decided upon a strategy to deal with the surplus population through increased law and order in the cities. The Rockefeller drug laws from 1973 and the increased rates of incarceration are not a result of "crime," but of the turn to debt among the population, the turn to drug trafficking among some for survival, and the general withdrawal of social services by the state.

Expansion of Corporate Welfare

When the state insisted that its people go on a diet, it did not extend this provision to the world of the rich. The elected representatives slashed the income tax on the rich with the argument that this money would go toward investment in the productive capacity of the nation. In the 1980s, US firms got large tax rebates as an incentive for them to enhance their technological and productive operations, to make them more competitive against the Japanese and West Germans, for instance. However, in 1985, the House Ways and Means Committee's report (which became the Tax Reform Act of 1986) noted:

> Proponents of massive tax benefits for depreciable property have theorized that these benefits would stimulate investment in such property, which in turn would pull the entire economy into more rapid growth. The committee perceives that nothing of this kind has happened.[12]

The money went to firms that threatened departure from the US without the "incentives" to remain stateside and guarantee re-election for the representatives. The right-wing Cato Institute calculates that all forms of corporate welfare in the US total $75 billion per year.[13] Even this, a low figure, is extraordinary.

With less money to spend, the state claimed it could not afford social welfare, even as it continued to fund the military and the police. But, in these "lean times," neoliberal states across the planet continue to subsidize "free market" firms. On this score, as with so much else, the US is in the lead. One federal agency, the Export-Import Bank, for instance, disbursed $100 billion in international trade assistance to global corporations, far more than the US government gives out in food, disaster, and development relief. The main recipients of the Ex-Imp Funds are (in order of amounts pillaged from the treasury): Boeing, Halliburton, Fluor, General Electric, Petróleos de Venezuela, Northrup Grumman, Bechtel, the ABB Group, Siemens, Edward Bateman, Applied Materials, Lucent Technologies, Chevron Texaco, KLA-Tencor, and Phillips Petroleum. Furthermore, the Internal Revenue Service shows us that non–US based global corporations pay less US income taxes on business done in the US than comparable US-based global corporations; these same US-based corporations gain the same unequal benefits from countries outside the US in a universal quid pro quo of corruption and sleaze.[14] "This is naked corporate welfare," said Representative Ron Paul (Republican-Texas). "It never ceases to amaze me how members of Congress who criticize welfare for the poor on moral and constitutional grounds see no problem with the even more objectionable programs that provide welfare for the rich."[15]

Tax breaks to the rich and to global corporations act as an "entitlement" in the budget, because they lock in the gains to these sections of society without any annual discussion about their impact and usefulness. This tax on the budget has a regressive impact on the working poor for whom state services are crucial.

Promotion of Cultural Nationalism

If the state is less able or willing to provide resources toward the creation of equity, how do the representatives return to the people in a formal democracy and ask for re-election? Why would people keep a regime afloat if it promises nothing in return? The expenditure on the punitive side certainly takes care of a considerable amount of organized and unorganized dissent. Even the most formally democratic states rule with some measure of coercion and the prison/police offer enough reason to fear the state.

Consent, under neoliberalism, is bred through the promotion of cruel forms of cultural nationalism. This nationalism can be religious (Hindutva in India, Wahhabism in Saudi Arabia), secular (Ba'thism in Iraq, Fascism in France), or some measure in between. Most forms of cultural nationalism posit a golden age in the past that offers the nation the reason for its cohesive existence, and then urges people to return in some measure to that ethical standard. In the US, the national myth evinces a nostalgia for the early years of the Republic, when individual yeomen stood up to the tyrant George III, fought for liberty, and then instantiated their ethical horizon in the Constitution. The mythology undermines the political role of the "motley crew in the American Revolution," the sailors, enslaved Africans, and working class "mobs" whose struggles enabled the "Sons of Liberty" (Washington, Adams, Jefferson) to wrest control of the situation to their advantage.[16] Furthermore, the idea that individual yeomen created the wealth of the nation obscures the role of both slavery in the accumulation of values for the white landholders *and* the new state's protectionism for its industrial development (as laid out in Alexander Hamilton's 1791 *Report on Manufactures* and put into practice via such laws as the 1807 Embargo Act and in the War of 1812).[17] State support and theft of labor produced the resilient yeoman. Yet, the myth of the individual who pulls "himself" up by the bootstraps persists to torment those who came into history without its advantages—such as the descendants slaves. Therefore, the idea of "self-reliance" (or individualism), without the context of what kind of "self" produced wealth in the first place, operates in a racist manner and is a form of cruel cultural nationalism.

Even as individualism is the alibi for widespread racism in our polity, there are other forms of social oppression that work in tandem to forward the violent agenda of cultural nationalism. Misogyny and homophobia in equal parts allow heterosexual men to feign social power and to claim the mantle of bootstrap individualism.

These four elements form the core of the neoliberal state, and Clorox America fits the definition aptly. With an enormous military and police, with an eagerness to fund global corporations (with cash or tax breaks), with the assassination of social welfare, and then, with the manufacture of consent through a perverse mixture of individualism, patriotism, and consumerism—this is the character of Clorox America.

Keeping Up With the Dow Joneses follows the career of the several millions in this country who have been left out of upward mobility. The interest in those who work for low wages and those who cannot find work leads naturally to welfare and to prisons. Even as all those who are on welfare or in prison are hardly people of color, the structures of racism disproportionately send impoverished people of color to both. So this book offers a general introduction to the political economy of racism. For the urban poor in this country, all families, it seems, can fess up to at least one person on welfare or in prison: the contours of urban life for people of color are therefore between debt, prison, and welfare. To explore these three areas, then, is not arbitrary; it both follows from the reality of urban life and hews close to my own analysis of how neoliberalism guts the funds of civilization, and enhances the budget of repression.

"I AM NOT A LEADER"

At the corner of East Broadway and Grand Street in Manhattan sits a new public school called Shuang Wen. Meaning "Two Languages," the school teaches all subjects in English and Mandarin. While most of the pupils are children of the Chinese Diaspora, a tenth of the student body is black. "People would ask me, 'Why Chinese? Why not French? Why not Spanish,'" remembered one black parent. "I would ask them, 'Why not Chinese?'" Mandarin is not what draws these black parents to travel hours each day to bring their children to lower Manhattan. They are called by the informal network of friends who know that this is a quality public school that accepts children from all five boroughs of New York. The language training forces the children to work hard, and, in essence, teaches them work habits across the curriculum. Denise Gamble, one of the black parents, says that it is worth the long journey because "I just want my children to have a good education."[18]

In the early 1990s, a group of high school students in Providence, Rhode Island gathered together at the office of Direct Action for Rights and Equality (DARE) on Lockwood Street across from Classical High School. Angry at the racism of the police in the vicinity of the school and of the curriculum foisted upon them by their teachers, the students, mainly young women, wanted to do something. They knew that they wanted a good education and they knew it would not come to them by being idle. Over several afternoons they developed an analysis of their situation, they started a campaign, they forced DARE's staff and resources to adopt their agenda, and they launched $E=MC^2$ (Education=Multi-Cultural Curriculum). The youth organized their parents and their classmates, fought the school board, and finally, on October 5, 1996, introduced three new elective courses to their curriculum: Science, History, and Literature, all from an anti-racist perspective. For the youth the point was to "reclaim their own educational path, and in doing so, their future."[19]

People know what is good in education and what a good education is. The lengths to which working-class parents and youth go to secure education and to preserve schools are extraordinary. Families undergo long commutes and harsh struggles to ensure that children get the means to understand and transform their reality. Too often, those of us who are ensconced in our comfortable middle-class habits fail to see how important education is to the working class. Among teachers like myself, we frequently say that among those who are driven to learn, desperate to learn, the working-class students are often a surprising majority. The surprise is on our prejudices, not on the long traditions of hunger for ideas hoarded in the academies of the rich.

The gradual destruction of public education in the country certainly leads many, even among the working class, to hope for other solutions, perhaps places called charter schools, or else to struggle to make the schools more open, less racist. One reason for the fight-back is that the working class recognizes that it needs to preserve its resources to exercise intellectual leadership in both the reproduction of everyday life and in the struggles to transform the world. Given the constraints on life for the working class, it requires an immense amount of ingenuity to keep it together, to ensure that things go on. Working class women most often face the challenge because state support to maintain the family has collapsed in the last three decades, and the virtuoso efforts of these women enable life to continue. The knowledge of survival provides these women with the tools of resistance and transformation. They are, then, not only the leaders in the art of existence, but also, most crucially, intellectual leaders to change this America of inequality and injustice. They are our struggle intellectuals, our struggle leaders.

Keeping Up With the Dow Joneses is built on the analysis of women and children from the working class, many of color, most who live in polycultural neighborhoods. In 1988, Cecelia Rodriquez of La Mujer Obrera, a garment workers' organization in El Paso, Texas, wrote to the US Urban Rural Mission and asked them to fund a study of what community organizing meant to women of color. Many discussions, drafts, and reviews later, Rinku Sen of the Center for Third World Organizing in Oakland edited the final product, *We Are the Ones We Are Waiting For*. The 21 women whose words filled the final document underscore the role of these women as intellectual and struggle leaders. Shirley Sherrod of the Federation of Southern Cooperatives pointed out that even if working class women appear isolated in their everyday struggles, they "are the ones in their community always dreaming, always thinking we can do more [to] make life better where we are."[20] Ethel Long-Scott of Oakland's Women's Economic Agenda Project introduces us to a movement intellectual:

> One of our strongest leaders, she's a mother of six, she's a deep thinker. She's been really trying to figure out what does it take to get power and to change a situation. A great deal of this work involves a fairly intellectual pursuit. That means the willingness to sit down and think through a process. The other part is understanding how power is held in this country. Discipline is the other part of this plan to obtain the kind of information we need. We have all kinds of buddy systems set up. We have a book exchange between our networks and if somebody gets hold of a good historical piece, we share it. We don't back away from the fact that there has to be fundamental change. For us that's an ongoing effort, the whole community is a university for us. Everybody brings something to the table and there's potential. How do we get to that talent, that light of dignity? That's different from saying we've got to "rehabilitate" this person.[21]

Keeping Up With the Dow Joneses draws upon the documents and reports prepared by the organizations of mainly working class women as well as the work of social scientists. While the latter provided useful data and historical information, the former, the work of the women in struggle, provided sophisticated analyses of our current conjuncture. This book draws from that analysis and offers itself as a summary of the hundreds of testimonies and reports that emerged from years of struggle against the government. *Keeping Up With the Dow Joneses* is heavy on the numbers, but let these not stand in as a substitute for the framework developed by the women in struggle. The numbers help us make the analysis *true* in the eyes of those who are only swayed by governmental data and not by the everyday data of social life.

"Within the constrained choices that we make," writes feminist Elisabeth Armstrong, "there are libratory possibilities that are outside those constraints."[22] We need to recognize the parents who wake up early in the morning to take their children far across town so that they can get a good education, schooled in English and Mandarin (even as they have no historical tie to China), or the students from a battered part of America who struggle to make their curriculum more inclusive, to find the funds to get textbooks and to generate interest among their peers for knowledge. These are stories of people who want education to build the capacity for transformation. Within the constraints, they find the path to liberation. In this book, we will also take this route, searching for a better life while in Babylon.

Alice Hicks, a venerated member of the DARE family, used to say, "I am *not* a leader." She led by example in the fights against urban blight, job flight, and police might. She was a strong leader whose maxim "You make a difference" ennobled those around her to continue if the circumstances turned bleak. She was a leader, but her statement stressed her insistence that *everyone* mattered in the struggle to make democracy. As she said, "I am not a leader," she meant, "We are *all* leaders"—in the struggle, both in body and in mind.

1   David Leonhardt, "Out of a Job and No Longer Looking," *New York Times,* September 29, 2002.

2   Kimberly Crenshaw, "Mapping the Margins: Intersectionality, Identity Politics and Violence Against Women of Color," *Critical Race Theory: The Key Writings that Formed the Movement,* Ed. Kimberly Crenshaw, et. al., New York: The New Press, 1996.

3   Robert Brenner, *The Boom and the Bubble: The US in the World Economy,* London: Verso, 2002; Walden Bello (with Shea Cunningham and Bill Rau), *Dark Victory: The United States, Structural Adjustment and Global Poverty,* Penang: Third World Network, 1994. The point is elaborated in the next chapter.

4   Structural adjustment is of course the instrument used by organizations like the International Monetary Fund (IMF) to transform the world into a playground for global corporations. In 1981, the IMF's director Jacques de Lavosiere called for "sacrifices on the part of all: international financing will serve no purpose if spent on consumption as if there were no tomorrow" (*IMF Survey,* February 9, 1981). For a useful analysis, see Ron Phillips, "The Role of the IMF in the Post–Bretton Woods Era," *Review of Radical Political Economy,* summer 1983. Reagan went so far as to argue that the problems of developing countries stemmed from too much aid, that is, these countries used overextended credit for wasteful consumption (*IMF Survey,* October 12, 1981). The working people, it turned out, had to make all the sacrifices. Just so there is no misunderstanding, Clorox America is part of the nation-state, but this phenomenon is both larger and smaller than the state. It is larger in that elected US representatives seem to work at the service of global corporations and put the US military at their service. It is smaller in that it does not include all the people who live within the US, many of whom are as much survivors of the system as their brethren around the world. I have argued this in detail elsewhere: *War Against the Planet: The Fifth Afghan War, Imperialism and Other Assorted Fundamentalisms,* New Delhi: Leftword, 2002 and *Fat Cats and Running Dogs: The Enron Stage of Capitalism,* Monroe, ME: Common Courage Press, 2002.

5   Frances Fox Piven and Richard A. Cloward, *The New Class War: Reagan's Attack on the Welfare State and Its Consequences,* New York: Pantheon, 1982.

6   Bob Jessop, Kevin Bonnett, Simon Bromley and Tom Ling, *Thatcherism: A Tale of Two Nations,* Oxford: Polity Press, 1988.

7   Elisabeth Sköns, Evamaria Loose-Weintraub, Wuyi Omitoogun and Petter Stålenheim, "Military Expenditure," *SIPRI Yearbook 2002: Armaments, Disarmament and International Security,* Oxford: Oxford University Press, 2002.

8   The heaviest per capita expense on arms is in the states of West Asia, while the greatest economic burden (in terms of the military's share of

the gross domestic product) is in Africa. Neoliberal states around the world spend enormous amounts on the military, with expenditure on the domestic police and on prisons lagging not too far behind.

9   Seymour Hersh, "Overwhelming Force," *The New Yorker*, May 22, 2000.

10 In the summer of 1990, the Iraqi government accused the Kuwaitis of drilling laterally into the Iraqi oil fields of this very spot, Rumaila. This was the provocation for the Iraqi invasion of Kuwait.

11 I have summarized the tale in my book *Fat Cats and Running Dogs: The Enron Stage of Capitalism,* Maine: Common Courage Press, 2002, pp. 162–78, but also see Alma Guillermoprieto's lyrical book, *Looking for History: Dispatches from Latin America*, New York: Vintage, 2001, pp. 20–71.

12 House Ways and Means Committee, *Report on HR 3838, The Tax Reform Act of 1985*, Washington, DC: US Congress, 1985, pp. 145–46.

13 Stephen Moore and Dean Stansel, *Ending Corporate Welfare as We Know It*, Washington, DC: Cato Institute, 1995.

14 General Accounting Office, *Foreign and US-Controlled Corporations That Did Not Pay US Taxes, 1989–95*, Washington, DC: GAO, 1999.

15 Leslie Wayne, "A Guardian of Jobs or a 'Reverse Robin Hood?'" *New York Times*, September 1, 2002. More details in *Fat Cats*, pp. 34–36.

16 Peter Linebaugh and Marcus Rediker, *The Many Headed Hydra: Sailors, Slaves, Commoners and the Hidden History of the Revolutionary Atlantic*, Boston: Beacon Press, 2000, pp. 211–47.

17 On the role of slavery, see *Reckoning with Slavery: A Critical Study in the Quantitative History of American Negro Slavery*, ed. Paul David, Herbert Gutman, Peter Temin and Gavin Wright, New York: Oxford University Press, 1976, and Roger Ransom, *Conflict and Compromise: The Political Economy of Slavery, Emancipation and the American Civil War*, New York: Cambridge University Press, 1989.

18 Yilu Zhao, "New York School for Chinese Is a Magnet for Black Pupils," *New York Times*, November 2, 2002. Older Afro-Asian currents can hardly be ignored here. For more on this subject, see Vijay Prashad, *Everybody Was Kung Fu Fighting: Afro-Asian Connections and the Myth of Cultural Purity*, Boston: Beacon Press, 2001.

19 "DARE Youth Win Multi-Cultural Curriculum," *DARE to Win*, vol. V, issue II, Winter 1996, p. 1.

20 Rinku Sen, *We Are the Ones We Are Waiting For: Women of Color Organizing for Transformation*, Durham, NC: United States Rural Missions for the World Council of Churches, 1995, p. 8.

21 *We Are the Ones We Are Waiting For*, p. 32.

22 Elisabeth Armstrong, unpublished manuscript on the All-India Democratic Women's Association (AIDWA).

DEBT

Back on the streets I thought I wouldn't survive
So I'm bustin' my ass on this nine to five.
Flippin' patties all day when the place is hot
Gettin' paid peanuts, in the burger shop.
Now everybody wants to know the deal,
is this brother real
Can I feed my family off of a Happy Meal?
I remember the time when I was six
The American Dream was everybody gets rich
But yo, a fact for all to know
Four hundred years has passed, and we still po'
He ain't my Uncle,
but Sam know what he's talkin' about
If you wanna get paid, sell your people out.

—The Coup, "Kill My Landlord," 1993

In 1995, the members of the AFL-CIO took decisive action to renounce the heritage of "business unionism," of "concessionary bargaining," of a half century of leadership by two men wedded to the status quo (George Meany, head from 1954 to 1979, and Lane Kirkland, head from 1979 to 1995). Three sections of organized labor, about 40 percent of the union workforce, fought against the anointed successor of Kirkland: industrial unions (United Auto Workers (UAW), International Association of Machinists and Aerospace Workers, Steelworkers, and Mine Workers), service and public sector unions (American Federation of County, State, and Municipal Employees (AFSCME) and the Service Employees International Union (SEIU)), and the newly revived International Brotherhood of Teamsters. A reform slate made up of John Sweeney (SEIU), Linda Chavez-Thompson (AFSCME), and

Richard Trumka (UMW) won the election to the leadership of the AFL-CIO and pledged the union to organize with enthusiasm.[1] On the first day of the AFL-CIO meeting, Sweeney promised to "recreate a [labor] movement that will improve the lives of working people, not just protect them from current assaults. Our members need to see a labor movement that is a powerful voice on behalf of their interests and unorganized workers need to see a movement that can make their lives better."[2] Even those with a great deal of suspicion about the AFL-CIO could not but feel as if change was afoot. A labor force made buoyant by militant service workers (many of whom were, and are, immigrants) pushed the leadership to the Left. Sweeney, despite his own record steeped in business unionism, came from the union of the service workers, and he knew of the brave struggles of immigrant workers in southern California from the decade-long Los Angeles Justice for Janitors campaign from 1988 to the San Diego Drywall Strike of 1992.[3] With only a tenth of the workforce in unions and with wages stagnant since 1973, the AFL-CIO had to make some moves.

On January 24, 1995, before the AFL-CIO provided a measure of buoyancy to the progressive forces within the US, President Bill Clinton offered his state of the union address to the nation. Even as Clinton boasted of the six million jobs created under his watch, reality did not allow him to forget the inequality that tore the union apart. People are being "left out," he said, and "the rising tide is not lifting all boats."

> [People are] working harder for less. They have less security, less income, less certainty that they can even afford a vacation, much less college for their kids or retirement for themselves. We cannot let this continue. If we don't act, our economy will probably keep doing what it's been doing since about 1978, when the income growth began to go to those at the very top of our economic scale and the people in the vast middle got very little growth, and people who worked like crazy but were on the bottom then fell even further and further behind in the years afterward—no matter how hard they worked.

What did Clinton have in mind for the population? His recipe was uninspiring: "Work and responsibility over welfare and dependency." While he promised jobs instead of government cheese and the bank instead of Food Stamps, the Clinton administration failed to provide a road map for the impoverished toward the nirvana of what he called the "New Covenant." But even Clinton had to recognize that the state of the union's workers did not merit applause.

Pushed by its militant membership and by the broad social movements against capitalist globalization, the AFL-CIO under Sweeney/Chavez-Thompson/Trumka made gestures toward a progressive agenda. The labor movement questioned "free trade" and called for an amnesty for immigrants at the same time as it called out its members to oppose Third World debt and the debt of the working class within the US. These small acts engendered a sense of immense hope among the progressive sections of the labor movement, and the AFL-CIO's participation in the massive anti-capitalist protests from the 1999 Battle of Seattle onward provided a greater sense that things might change for the better.

On April 9, 2000, during a week-long protest against the IMF, Sweeney noted of Third World debt, "We want debt relief and we want it now." The IMF, he continued, must "stop pressuring countries to reform their economies in the wrong direction. They must allow countries to pursue different paths of development. We need a world where the market lifts us up instead of driving us down." Sweeney also noted, "Rich countries like the United States must provide money for development, and make certain it provides jobs and benefits and not more palaces and more tanks for the rulers." The rhetoric marked a departure for the AFL-CIO, particularly from its long history of protectionism, of overt assistance to imperialism, and of its concern for the wages of US workers above all other considerations.[4]

While Third World debt incensed Sweeney at the protests to shut down the IMF meetings, in November of 2000, he went to Johns Hopkins University in Baltimore to rail against the debt of US workers. After a brief overview of the booming stock market, Sweeney pointed the figure at America's other side.

> America's workers are putting in longer hours, especially mandatory overtime, and working second jobs for the gains they've enjoyed. Families are paying a price for lost time together. A record number of workers are now employed in temp jobs, with low wages, few if any benefits and no job security. All across our country, more households than ever before are getting by only by having both spouses away

from home and working, more workers are going into debt to make ends meet and personal bankruptcy filings doubled over the last decade. Something fundamental and dangerous is at work in our economy. The bright glow of Wall Street isn't lighting every corner of America. Even in this extraordinary age of prosperity, when the abundance of riches all around us should finally be lifting all workers and all families, millions of Americans are not getting ahead.

No progressive observer of the US economy can fail to be startled by the high level of debt borne by the bulk of the population. These are folk who borrow not for luxury, but for survival. These are folk who struggle to find one job that sustains them, since they work in multiple jobs that offer few hours, low pay, and no benefits. Our general survey of the US economy will not stay with the major indicators, but it will start with debt, deal with the sweatshop conditions for the bulk of the workforce, find out why the US is increasingly divided into two classes (the CEOs and the contingent), and what the contingent classes are doing to change the system. It is a tall order for a short chapter, but here goes...

ALL WE ARE WORTH

While September 11 was a defining event for America, it was not a defining event for the economy or the financial markets. That role belongs to the stock market bubble of the late 1990s that finally popped in March 2000. The equity bubble helped create other bubbles—most notably in the housing market and in consumer spending. There is good reason to believe that both the property and consumer bubbles will burst in the not-so-distant future. If they do, there is a realistic possibility that the United States, like Japan in the 1990s, will suffer a series of recessionary relapses over the next several years. Yet denial remains deep, just as it was when the Nasdaq composite index was lurching toward 5,000. Few want to believe that this economic expansion may be built on such a shaky foundation.

—Stephen S. Roach, Chief Economist, Morgan Stanley

Over the course of the past century, the US public has tolerated (and sometimes encouraged) the notion of consumer peer pressure.

With the advent of mass production and of advertising, the citizen was converted into the consumer whose entire destiny was to be governed by the goods in one's home. To capture this iron cage of consumerism, US slang produced the phrase "To keep up with the Joneses," those imaginary neighbors whose purchases ensured that the crisis of overproduction not be undone by the phenomenon of underconsumption. Buy, buy, buy; go into debt, and buy, buy, buy. The vast US market, buyer of the last resort, had to prime the pump of planetary capitalism.

Through the 1990s, as economies around the world felt the tsunami of the Kondratiev Wave, the US seemed marooned on its own island of prosperity. But there was an enigma that befuddled those who looked at the economy: while the financial indicators looked sound (despite some tumultuous fluctuation), income and wealth differentials increased to record highs. The rich got richer, the poor got poorer, but the economy looked perfectly healthy. If increased class division precluded the "Keep up with the Joneses" axiom, then the new slogan was "Keep up with the Dow Joneses," the only reliable standard for the American Dream that kept its upward ascent regardless of the reality of people's lives.

Invented in the 1890s by Charles Dow (the first editor of the *Wall Street Journal*), the Dow Jones Industrial Average is not the most representative index for the stock market—it is an average of 30 top-flight industrial stocks, whereas the Standard and Poor's 500 indexes 500 industrial, service, and financial stocks. Nevertheless, the Dow Jones, since the 1980s, has become the index of human reason. The ascent of the Dow since its invention has been extraordinary. From the base or starting value of 100 (in 1928), the index inched up to 1,000 (by 1966). In August 1982, investment in the stock market created a bull market—vast sums of money entered the New York Stock Exchange, astronomical numbers of stocks exchanged hands, and the index escalated upwards to 10,000 (by March 1999). During this phase (from 1983 to 1998), the Dow Jones rose by 1,333 percent. Optimists among stock analysts expect that the Dow will triple its value in the 21st Century, despite the decline below 10,000 in the year of 9/11 and Enron/WorldCom. By their account, the bulls will soon be running down Wall Street again.

Wall Street's stock market, inaugurated in 1791, is only one among the world's many exchanges. From the Japanese Nikkei to Kenya's Nairobi Stock Exchange, the phenomenon of stock markets has now come to dominate the planet. In 1996, a World Bank economist estimated that the total value of stocks listed in all the world's stock markets had reached $15.2 trillion (compared to $4.7 trillion in 1986).[5] Banks, pension funds, those with wealth, and a few others, take their money to the stock market, invest it in this or that share of a firm, then either wait out a dividend payment, or else freely trade the stock and make a profit based on the difference between their buying and selling price. Of course this is a highly simplified version of what has become a thoroughly complex world of financial transactions. The stock market universe has its own argot, filled with such phrases as "put options," "capacity utilization," "odd lot shorts," and "stopped out." The professionals at the market, who know the language of the trading floor, follow long lists of numbers and figures, indexes such as the Hang Seng of Hong Kong, the NASDAQ and Dow Jones of New York, the FTSE of London, the Nikkei 225 of Tokyo, the Sensex (or Sensitive Index) of Mumbai, and the Straits Times Index of Singapore. They pore over these figures like medieval scholars, while the rest of the population holds onto their brokers to help them make sense of the upward or downward ticks of the Big Board. These brokers and their bosses have constructed a bewildering series of financial instruments, such as derivatives, to draw in more money to expand the scope of the exchanges.[6] An astounding number of shares trade hands each day. At the New York Stock Exchange alone, 307.5 billion shares traded in 2001, with an average daily trade of $42.3 billion. Brokers and professionals who are in the know easily dominate a system that has come to be thoroughly undemocratic in its operation, even as it claims to be the bastion of financial democracy.

Certainly, the stock market allows anyone to invest in any publicly traded firm. From its early days three centuries ago till our own time, the stock market has elicited its own brand of ecstatic commentary that it is the instrument for democracy under capitalism.[7] Wall Street advertises its power to democratize ownership without revolution and forced redistribution. In this climate, George Soros, Ross Perot, and Donald Trump sell themselves as men of the people, simple businessmen who are not so very different from those small merchants who toil under the yoke of interventionist states. Until the collapse of the technology stocks and the slowdown in Silicon Valley, the techno-gurus of California took on that role for our time. First among them was Jim Clark, founder of the multi-billion dollar empire of Silicon Graphics, Netscape, and WebMD. "Somewhere in the process of equity sharing," he said, "is the basis for a new economy that distributes wealth far more diversely than at any other time in the history of business." Whereas the political system, namely the adult franchise, promised democracy at one time, now the stock market has taken on that role. As the *New York Times* columnist Thomas Friedman put it so indelicately to the prime minister of Thailand, "One dollar, One vote."[8] If the vote gives a citizen the same political rights as anyone else, much the same can be said of investment. Of course, Friedman neglects to tell us that those with more dollars have a greater command of the system, even of the shareholders meetings. During the entire bull market from August 1982 till the end of the 1990s, the top five percent of stockowners (by household wealth) owned 94.5 percent of all stock held by individuals. In other words, the stock market boom produced the illusion of equality when in fact it was another avenue for the maintenance (or even motor) of inequality.

A Congressional inquiry in mid-September 2002 offered the public one example of why the millions did not make the billions. Individual investors could not make the same money as these tycoons, Pulitzer Prize–winning business journalist Gretchen Morgenson reported, because "ahead of them in line at most big firms were grasping executives who had a far greater chance of bagging hot stocks because their companies were paying investment banking fees to the firms doing the doling."[9] How does the boondoggle work? The investment research firm, Sanford C. Bernstein & Co., published a report in 1999 on how initial public offerings (IPOs) are priced far below what they are worth. An IPO is the first sale of stock from a concern on the open market, what is also called "going public." In the early 1990s, private firms offered stock on the market as IPOs at about five percent below value. That is, whereas analysts expected the stock to trade at a certain price, the firm offered a below value price to boost demand for the stock. If the "aftermarket performance" or the first day's sale is good, then the stock analysts will talk up the firm and its share price will rise. By 1999, the IPOs began to come to the block a full 30 percent below value, much more than the five percent of only a few years before. Morgenson offers the Telecom world as an example of this scam. Between January 1999 and January 2001, the first day gain of Telecom shares was about $9.6 billion, which meant that the brokerage firms had this much "free money" to give out to their best customers.[10] Those customers who had the benefit of "private placement" could get access to the immediate 30 percent discount with little attendant risk. They were also privy to the "whisper numbers," the word on the Street that is unavailable to the bulk of the small players who use their local brokers or who trade via the Internet. Reports such as Morgenson's study on IPOs validate the statistical data. While almost half of US households own some stocks (whether through a retirement plan or otherwise), for 60 percent of households, their stocks amounted to only $4,000. The top one percent, those people who are given "free money," hold almost half of all stocks (47.7 percent), while the bottom 80 percent hold a minuscule 4 percent of all stock holdings.[11]

To keep up with the Joneses, the US public quixotically went into massive consumer debt. In January 2000, the Federal Reserve Board offered a look at the state of debt within US households. The authors of the Survey of Consumer Finances for 1998 wrote in their understated manner, "The median amount of debt increased for most of the demographic groups [classes], and many of the changes were large."[12] As debt increased among the population, the authors pointed out that while households seemed to borrow less for home purchases, they made up for it with "an increase in borrowing for investment purposes; in light of the rising stock market and strong business conditions, some of this borrowing may include borrowing to invest in equities or start a new business."[13] Few doubt the existence of debt among the US population, but what does not often get noticed is that the debt is borne disproportionately by the working class (among whom I include both the waged workers and those who are unemployed— the potential workers whose various labors keep the waged workers physically and spiritually afloat). Those households that made less than $10,000 carried the highest debt, while those who earned between $25,000 and $49,999 had the next highest debt rates. Once you move beyond the $100,000 range, the debt burden lifts enormously.[14] For those whose income is above $50,000 and who own property, the early years of the household mortgage are mainly paid off with tax-free money, so that this is an incentive and not a liability for them, whereas the rent paid by those who earn at the lower end is entirely an expense.[15] The report from the Federal Reserve also notes the increase in personal bankruptcy filing (particularly among those who earn at the low end of the income totem). Debt is a genuine concern when it puts a burden on the family's finances. The Federal Reserve concludes that the "debt burden" (the ratio of family debt payments to total family income) was 15.9 percent in 1989, but it rose to 17.6 percent in 1998. Again, "the most striking increases were among families with incomes of less than $10,000 and those in the 75-or-older group."[16] Like the countries of the global South, US households in 1995 spent a total of almost 17 percent of their after tax incomes on debt payment ($903 billion), an enormous upward redistribution of income.[17] Analysis of the data in the Survey of Consumer Finances shows us that the poorest 40 percent of the US public borrowed money to compensate for stagnant or battered incomes rather than to expend money on indulgences.[18] Only the richest 20 percent borrowed money principally to invest in the stock market, to suffer the occult movements of the Big Board as part of the small, but influential, investor class. The poor gained in one statistic, debt, which rose for the bottom 90 percent by over 11 percent while it fell for the richest one percent by 19 percent. This debt went toward the maintenance of some modicum of the American Dream amongst households long mortgaged to the will of the banks.

There is no government plan to help shoulder the debt of the yacht-less. Neither is there any government plan to regulate credit agencies so that they not prey on the desires of the multitude. Nor is there a plan to increase the financial literacy of students to replace, or else to supplement, the education they get in how to make money on stocks. Instead, we hear the rich disrespect hard workers, and blame them for their lack of "personal responsibility" and for their lack of "incentive."

In 1995, Pete Du Pont, heir to the vast Du Pont family fortune and Delaware's former congressman and governor, wrote, "The minimum wage turns out to be one of our leading killers—a killer of economic growth and opportunity among the young, the poor, and the minority community. It's time to stop it before it kills again."[19] This fulmination came just as the US government raised the minimum wage for the first time in over two decades, a rise in pay that was marginal and has not done near enough to overcome the inequities that tear the nation apart.

From then President Clinton to now President Bush, there is a consensus that things have never been better, despite 9/11, and that the brief recessions (under the watch of Bush's father, and then again in the immediate aftermath of 9/11) are over. For almost a third of the population who live under or near the poverty line, this provides little solace.[20] The previously unemployed may now be at work, but few ask them about their conditions at "work," about the number of part-time jobs they must hold to maintain a household, or about their lack of medical insurance. "Economic segregation in this country is so rigid that we literally don't know one another anymore," columnist Molly Ivins complained.[21] If we did, perhaps the hoopla about the return to prosperity would not be made so cavalierly.

For those who watch the US from afar (or during brief, well orchestrated holidays), it is hard to imagine the poverty within this haven of capital. Sated by Hollywood movies and by the smooth talk of US politicians, the world imagines that each US citizen must bear some title to the wealth of the nation. Within the US, however, there are few that have illusions about the nature of the economic miracle, of the Second Gilded Age whose Rockefellers and Carnegies are named Gates and Waltons. If Du Pont worried about the lack of incentive to the working people, he did not have to worry about the ample incentives provided to the CEOs and the one percent from which they hail. In the 1990s, corporate profits rose by 108 percent. Someone seems to be doing quite well, as indeed the pay of Chief Executive Officers (CEOs) rose during this decade by 481 percent. With the collapse of Enron and WorldCom, the business pages of the major newspapers began to resemble tabloids—rather than deal with the structural problems of Enron-type capitalism, they told us that the problem was CEO compensation.[22] Nevertheless, news of CEO excesses provides a useful window into the general inequality that pervades US corporations and US society. CEOs of the major corporations earned an average of $274 million as salaries (with stock options and other perks) in 2000, according to calculations done by *Fortune* magazine.[23]

No longer do CEOs simply take home a salary. The real bonus comes to them in stock options. When a corporation gives one of its employees the right to buy a given amount of its shares at a particular price within a specific time, that right is a stock option. The income tax code of 1950 allowed companies to pay their employees in stock options, but from the late 1950s to 1982, when the stock market produced unspectacular results, this was not a major line item in the CEO pay package. When the stock market began its boom, and when Congress created section 162 (m) of the tax code in 1993, to prevent a firm from taking a tax exemption for CEO salaries that exceed $1 million, corporations began to lace their compensation packages with stock options and other juicy perks. In 2000, Apple Computer's Steve Jobs walked away with $381 million, by far the largest compensation package, but this pales in comparison to the $872 million options grant that Apple gave him. In 2001, the top five executives of the 1,500 largest US firms earned a total of $18 billion in option profits, more than a fivefold increase since the early 1990s. Over the 1990s, the heads of these firms made a total of $58 billion.[24]

Another untaxed incentive to the CEO class comes in kind. General Electric's former CEO Jack Welch got his former firm to pay for free lifetime use of the company jet, use of an office and secretary, a large salary as consultant, courtside seats at the US Open, satellite TV at his four homes, use of a GE-owned apartment on Central Park West in Manhattan, laundry, wine, newspapers, meals, and other such *basic* needs.[25] Tyco International's former CEO Dennis Kozlowski not only gave 51 of his chosen employees $56 million in bonuses (and then, $39 million to pay for the taxes on those bonuses), but he flinched more than $60 million in personal expenses of his own. That amount included a $30 million house in Boca Raton, Florida, a $16.8 million apartment in Manhattan, a $1.32 million rental for a second apartment and $7 million on a co-op in Manhattan, $3 million to renovate the apartment that he bought in the City, and $11 million to furnish it. The furnishings include such choice items as a traveling toilet box ($17,000), a dog umbrella stand ($15,000), shower curtains ($6,000), a gilt metal wastebasket ($2,200) and a pincushion ($445).[26] The pincushion itself cost more than the weekly take-home pay of a minimum wage worker.

Do these incentives to the CEO class deliver rewards to the firms and, eventually, the shareholders? According to a major study by Harvard Business School's Rakesh Khurana, the compensation given to CEOs far outweighs their contribution to the firm: the rate of return for them is extraordinary.[27] Two studies of stock options, in addition, found that "the companies whose executives took more had no better returns in the following three years than those that took less. Worse, the firms whose corporate chieftains were most likely to take a bigger share had sub-par performance to begin with." Thus, "it seems clear that options have been seriously misused as a tool for motivating executives."[28] Despite the excellent work of United for a Fair Economy and its Responsible Wealth Project, despite the general anger at CEO compensation, and despite the economic insecurity of the multitude, little seems to be done to reform the system.[29] When the Welch scandal hit the public in September 2002, Robert J. Stucker, a lawyer at Vedder, Price, Kaufman & Kammholz who represents executives in contract negotiations, told the press, "I don't think there are any changes in the negotiations over severance packages. They're pretty much the same."[30]

Reforms that shake the foundation of neoliberal capitalism do not come, because the one percent works hard to lobby the US government who pass laws to their tune and not to the democratic sirens that occasionally emanate from the rest of America. *Fortune* magazine's Power 25 list of the most powerful lobbyists in Washington, DC, in 2000, is filled with the agents of the CEO class: American Association of Independent Business (no. 3), Chamber of Commerce of the United States of America (no. 7), National Beer Wholesalers Association (no. 8), National Association of Realtors (no. 9), National Association of Manufacturers (no. 10), National Association of Home Builders of the USA (no. 11), American Hospital Association (no. 13), Motion Picture Association of America (no. 16), National Association of Broadcasters (no. 17), Health Insurance Association of America (no. 19), National Restaurant Association (no. 20), Recording Industry Association of America (no. 22), American Bankers Association (no. 23), and the Pharmaceutical Research & Manufacturers of America (no. 24). Organs of the radical Right are strong in the Power 25 list, led by the National Rifle Association (no. 1), the American-Israel Public Affairs Committee (no. 4), and the National Right to Life Committee (no. 18). Only two organizations from the side of labor make the list, the AFL-CIO (no. 6) and the International Brotherhood of Teamsters (no. 25).[31] Following journalist Ken Silverstein, it is important to point out that Washington, DC, is a cheap city, as small campaign finance donations from the lobbyists buy immense boondoggles for corporations and the one percent. Silverstein offers as an example the behemoth Lockheed who paid a measly $5 million to lobby Congress in

1996, but "won approval for the creation of a new $15 billion government fund that will underwrite foreign weapons sales."[32] The government's tax codes that allowed, for example, firms to hide money in offshore havens like the Cayman Islands—these giveaways enabled the one percent to reap more benefits from their wealth, whereas the rest of the population found themselves at a loss. To create discipline among the population, President Clinton, in 1996, ended social welfare and asked those without work to find their own way in the thicket of a market already geared to benefit the rich. Obviously, an incensed US population took refuge in the populist anger of the 2000 presidential campaigns of John McCain and Ralph Nader and despaired by the Milquetoast of Al Gore in the face of the CEO onslaught.

In the three decades before 1900, US "robber barons" created the Gilded Age in which a few families (Rockefellers, Carnegies, Morgans, and Vanderbilts) made massive fortunes and enjoyed an era of "conspicuous consumption" (as sociologist Thorstein Veblen put it).[33] Most of this wealth was built by the rapacious use of resources, and by the withdrawal of the state from the affairs of the wealthy. President Abraham Lincoln levied the first tax on income in the United States in August 1861 as a means to finance the Union's war against the Confederacy. That tax, and the inheritance tax, ended in the early 1870s after the United States abandoned Reconstruction (which was the reason President Grant offered the continuation of the income tax). When the state abandoned a progressive income tax, despite the clamor from the farmer-backed Populist Party, the benefits accrued to those who had become or would become the robber barons.[34] Finally, these same robber barons used monopoly methods to secure their fortunes. The outcry from the public against these "trusts" (such as John D. Rockefeller's Standard Oil Trust) was considerable. Congress passed the Sherman Anti-Trust Act in 1890 to regulate mergers of firms and ensure that business combinations did not restrain commerce. The bill, long a bugbear of the bosses, did not, however, do its job. Not only did it lack an independent enforcement mechanism, it was also drafted in a vague manner. In 1940, Chief Justice Harlan Stone wrote of the Act, "The prohibitions of the Sherman Act were not stated in terms of precision or of crystal clarity and the Act itself does not define them. In consequence of the vagueness of its language, perhaps not uncalculated, the courts have been left to give content to the statute."[35]

If the novelist Edith Wharton worried about the "monstrous vulgarity" of the rich, the 1892 Populist Party complained that "the fruits of the toil of millions are boldly stolen to build up colossal fortunes for a few, unprecedented in the history of mankind, and the possessor of these, in turn, despise the Republic and endanger liberty."[36] The close relationship between money and government was tempered by the rise of organized labor and the socialists, and by the creation of a civic consciousness by an activist media (led by Ida Tarbells, Upton Sinclair, and Lincoln Steffens).

Ronald Reagan inaugurated the Second Gilded Age with his 1981 tax cut, which prompted a rise in unemployment and a polarization of wealth (when challenged on the figures in 1982, Reagan explained that "the statisticians in Washington have funny ways of counting").[37] According to historian Robert Brenner, the manufacturing capacity in the US had stagnated in the decades before Reaganism, battered by a failure to invest in the productive capacity due to a desire to recoup expensive investments in the 1950s and by the emergence of lean export-driven manufacturing from Japan and Germany. To reinvigorate US manufacturing, the US government relied upon the volume of credit released into the market to do the job, what in economic theory is called monetarism. The monetarists, led by Paul Volcker at the Federal Reserve Bank, tightened the availability of credit and forced unproductive firms to go out of business. In 18 months of 1981–82, the Reagan administration conducted an "industrial shakedown"—they pioneered the process that the IMF would export to the Third World, the Structural Adjustment Program.[38] The United States and sections of Europe became a "factory desert," as industrial units closed down and abandoned a workforce once disciplined and loyal, but now embittered.[39] Once the process weeded out the unproductive firms (at great human cost), "the Reagan administration, which had come to office on a programme of balancing the budget, launched what turned out to be the greatest experiment in Keynesianism in the history of the world. The supply-side program which accompanied monetarism in the US," Brenner continues, "highlighted by record tax cuts, did succeed in transferring enormous sums of money into the hands of capitalists and the rich from the pockets of almost everyone else."[40]

If unions claimed 35 percent of US workers in 1954, by the end of Reagan's tenure they could vouch for only 14 percent. As Reaganism pulled the rug from under the US worker, the strategy of business unionism followed by US unions meant that they offered immense concessions to corporations in the 1980s rather than act in antagonism to them. From Reagan's first election to the present, the bottom 60 percent of the US population saw their income drop, while only the top one percent (that same one percent), saw their income explode over 80 percent. In 1965, the wage gap between the highest and lowest paid workers was 44 to one, but by 2000, it stood at over 200 to one. The wage gap exploded not only because of the immense increase in CEO compensation, but also because of the stagnation of wages for the bulk of the population. In August 2002, the Commerce Department released figures that indicated that the wages of more than 100 million US workers had stagnated, and that as unemployment rises in a weak economy, "the bargaining power of the nation's wage earners has diminished." Reporting this development, the *New York Times* noted, "The stagnation in the nation's total wages and salaries, adjusted for inflation, affects 110 million workers, most of them below management rank. It results not only from meager raises, but also from cutbacks in hours, the disappearance of nearly 1.7 million jobs since March 2001, and the rise in the unemployment rate, which now stands at 5.9 percent."[41] Hours have been cut for workers in each workplace, but with many workers holding down two jobs, parents in two-parent middle-income families added more than twelve weeks or 600 hours of work per year between them between 1979 and 1998.[42]

Not only did wages stagnate, but unfair tax laws and the rigged stock market protected and increased the wealth of those on the top of the pyramid. In the 1980s, the top tax rate was 68 percent, but the revised tax law decreased this to 28 percent in 1988. While corporations in the early 1950s paid 33 cents of every dollar toward tax, today they pay less than ten cents. Monies that might have been taxed for socially useful work were used in a speculation binge that, in real estate, for example, raised rents to render homes unaffordable to much of the population. The speculation fever increased activity in the stock markets and allowed the one percent to gradually claim the saved income of the many into their coffers. Some of those untaxed monies that were supposed to enter the pockets of venture capitalists, find their way into productive enterprises, and trickle down into the pockets of the American worker, got diverted to the great havens of free enterprise, the tax-free Cayman Islands, for instance. In 1999, Microsoft CEO Bill Gates, Berkshire Hathaway CEO Warren Buffett, and ex-Microsoft executive Paul Allen enjoyed a combined wealth of $156 billion, an amount more than the Gross National Product of the poorest 43 nations combined. The wealth of the world's 475 billionaires ($1.7 trillion) is well above the gross wealth of the poorest half of humanity. Inequality within the US is also stark, with the richest one percent in possession of 40 percent of the nation's household wealth, while the entire bottom 95 percent could call on less than that share. In the Second Gilded Age, wealth trickles upwards as the rest of humanity takes its chances at the lottery, the casino, or the stock exchange. But even stocks, as we've seen, are rigged against the ordinary folk.

The last year of the Christian Millennium was not, however, good for the investor class, since the Dow Jones lost just above 6 percent of its value, while the S&P 500 lost just above 10 percent, and the Nasdaq composite index (mainly of technology stocks) fell by more than 39 percent. An investor class unused to the woes of capitalism turned immediately to the fourth chamber of the US government (after the executive, the legislature, and the judiciary): the Federal Reserve (the "central bank" of the US created in the aftermath of the Panic of 1907 to bail out the blunders of the robber barons and their ilk). Rather than admit to the contradictions of overproduction at the core of the system, the captains of finance and industry blamed bad state policy for their socioeconomic troubles. The managers of the Fed have, since the late 1970s, adopted the posture of "neutrality of money" (monetarism) and tended to use their power to set interest rates toward the management of inflation. The Fed, especially under the Ayn Randian Alan Greenspan, has labored to act according to the principles of the Phillip's Curve: economist Milton Friedman took a rather innocuous formula to argue that if the unemployment rate fell, then workers would have more strength at the bargaining table, and so prices would rise to create inflation; if the Federal Reserve worked to maintain a basic rate of unemployment, then those with wealth would be saved from an assault on the value of their saving by inflation. The canard of an "overheated" economy is used to reproach those who call for full employment, and the specter of inflation and a contracted stock market scare the US public into submission.[43] After all, we may not invest as individuals in the markets, but our pension money is wrapped up in money market accounts; we may not understand the complex neoclassical alchemy of inflation, but we know that prices have already started to inch up.

The stock market is, therefore, a poor indicator of what its analysts call the "fundamentals," the indices of production that are meant to guide the investments of the consumers (of course "analysts" have long since ceased to do any analysis, because they are now essentially sales persons for glamorized investments[44]). Far too many of the US government's indicators are unreliable, being based on spurious statistical analysis. Take the unemployment rate from the Bureau of Labor Statistics (BLS) that was (in September 2002) at 5.9 percent. The poll conducted by the BLS ignores all those workers discouraged from the job market as well as those who work only part-time. An analysis that includes these workers provides us with a rate of close to 9 percent. But even this rate does not fully grasp the underbelly of the US economy. Out of a population of 200 and 80 million, just over six million people languish in the judicial system and in the prison complex (with almost two million in prison and the rest on probation or parole).[45] At a rate of 690 per 100,000 the United States has the highest rate of incarceration in the world. Due to racist drug laws and a racist police force, the weight of incarceration falls on the shoulders of African Americans and Latinos. Almost a third of the young African American male population and one in eight young Latino males are in the web of the prison complex, and the rate of incarceration for women of color is on a dramatic increase.[46] We are at the point now when almost two million people, at a cost of $40 billion, sit behind bars. Their potential to work is uncounted, as they join those off the job rolls (including those who get disability payments) as the reserve army of labor. The desolate cannot be found in the lines for work, those whose heads come before the surveyors of the BLS. When there is even a marginal downturn in the US economy, the grief is exaggerated in those zones that are already in distress, such as among the working class and the working class of color. As Langston Hughes wrote in *The Big Sea*, "The depression brought everybody down a peg or two. And the Negro had but few pegs to fall."[47]

Fed Chairman Alan Greenspan's three statements on the Bush economic plan from 2001 to 2003 alert us to the class bias of the Fed in particular, but also public policy in general. In early 2001, Greenspan testified before Congress in favor of President Bush's enormous $1.34 trillion tax cut, arguing for supply-side stimulation to the economy. On September 12, 2002, Greenspan reassured the legislators that "to date, the economy appears to have withstood [the post-9/11 economic downturn], although the depressing effects still linger and continue to influence, in particular, the federal budget outlook." Then, following the tired, but still respectable, logic that once things are bad because of giveaways to the rich, suck more from the working class, Greenspan warned against "the built-in bias in favor of budget deficits." "History suggests that an abandonment of fiscal discipline will eventually push up interest rates, crowd out capital spending, lower productivity growth, and force harder choices on us in the future." In February 2003, Greenspan chided the administration's move to a more than $300 billion budget deficit, but he accepted the increase in military spending.

> The events of September 11 have placed demands on our budgetary resources that were unanticipated a few years ago. In addition, with defense outlays having fallen in recent years to their smallest share of GDP since before World War II, the restraint on overall spending from the downtrend in military outlays has surely run its course—and likely would have done so even without the tragedy of September 11.

While the media felt that his speech was critical of the Bush tax cuts,[48] Greenspan did not single out the tax cuts as much as worry about deficits because of both governmental programs (spending) and tax cuts (revenue): "We are all too aware that government spending programs and tax preferences can be easy to initiate or expand but extraordinarily difficult to trim or shut down once constituencies develop that have a stake in maintaining the status quo." Out of the verbiage, a few salient points emerged: the rich must get their tax breaks (even if not to the Bush extent), they are under no obligation to spend them on the productive capacity of the economy, and when the price of those tax cuts strikes the heart of the government's ability to function, the government must balance its budget and make the working class and working poor pay with fewer services. The logic laid out by Greenspan is the US version of neoliberalism and it is the framework that sets the terms for all discussions about governmental responsibility and the nature of social life in the US.

GROWTH OF A SWEATSHOP ECONOMY

> "All the executives agreed that 'zero training' [for workers] was the fast food industry's ideal, though it might never be attained."[49]

In 2001, the World Bank estimated that almost a quarter of the planet's industrial capacity declined in the previous decade. In the US, however, the industrial plant was regenerated by greater mechanization and by a streamlined production process.[50] However, the current industrial concerns do not hire people in large numbers to work on the assembly lines. Being largely automated, the plants require a much smaller workforce than older factories, and those workers who are on the job are now organized in scientific ways so that their expended energy provides the maximum output. Furthermore, surveillance on the factory floor ensures that labor purchased by capital for eight hours is committed to capital and not to leisure. In the 1990s, these new concerns raised equal parts of fear and hope at "jobless growth."[51]

High rates of productivity and low rates of employment in these firms missed the fact that those who once held solid blue collar jobs now find themselves in need of several jobs for survival. The debt trap for the American worker is a result not of poor management of desire and the checkbook, but of the global sweatshop economy.

The term "sweatshop" derives from the practice of "sweating," or the subcontracting of work either done in the supervised and regulated factory complex or else given to contractors. To save money, the factory would accept the cheapest contracts and leave the regulation of labor to the wiles of the contractor. The factories of these contractors came to be known as the "sweatshops," as a way to distinguish its almost pre-capitalist form of labor discipline from the discipline of the factory shop floor. In our day, the logic of the "sweatshop" has taken hold in most work-sites, whether in the classic field of textile production or in the zones of the New Economy (from computer hardware production to computer software design). In the early 1970s, as the economy took a nosedive, organized subcontracting in advanced capitalist countries produced new forms of labor organization, such as homework, outwork, and piecework.[52] Feminist economist Maria Mies calls these forms "housewifization," or, "labor that bears the characteristics of housework," or nonunion, unregulated, and isolated labor which is seen not as "labor" itself, but as simply "activity"; women largely enter the workforce in these zones (in *maquiladoras*, export-processing zones, sweatshops, outwork), but soon, men also get "housewifed."[53] These procedures enable small businesses to thrive at the interstices of monopoly firms; their survival is premised on mutual competition to sell their products to a few firms, which in economic theory is called a condition of monopsony. The competition amongst these small firms drives them to "renegotiate" their compact with their workforce; in order to cut costs, the firms drive wages down and cease to provide the sorts of benefits previously offered by capital as a concession to the concerted drive by workers from the 1880s. In the 1970s, what appeared at first hand to be feudal relics, reappeared as capitalist forms in the production process.[54]

The US General Accounting Office (GAO) defines a "sweatshop" as a work-site whose "employer violates more than one federal or state labor law governing minimum wage and overtime, child labor, industrial homework, occupational safety and health, workers compensation or industry regulation."[55] In 1996, the US Department of Labor reported that there were about 13,000 sweatshops in operation within the borders of the US, and that these employed about 300,000 people.[56] On June 1, 1996, Secretary of Labor Robert Reich offered the administration's view of the problem: "All of us must demand that the industry accept the moral responsibility for ending Third World conditions in the most prosperous nation on earth."

The state planned to eradicate sweatshops by investigation and by the enforcement of labor laws. These initiatives are limited for at least four reasons. First, the government takes an overly nationalist view of a shift in global relations of production. To insist that sweatshops be eradicated within the US has simply meant that firms move their production to offshore locations. Second, to target producers without any sense of the implication of the entire ensemble of retailers-wholesalers-producers in the process, or any policy that can strangle the determinant of cutthroat competition among the various producers, is disingenuous. Sweatshops exist to maximize profit for each of the enterprises along the chain and not just for the producers. Third, without a recognition that monopoly corporations, such as Wal-Mart, not only profit by sweatshops, but win customer satisfaction by their low prices (as a result of the sweatshop conditions of labor), the government will be unable to pursue the core of the crisis. Finally, it pins the blame for sweatshops on a few concerns without care that the labor process for the bulk of the workforce is now steeped in the logic of sweatshops—whether you work in a "no collar" high-tech firm or as a "pink collar" secretary.[57]

The workplace regime that dominated US and (to a lesser extent) European factories for much of the 20th Century goes by the name of Fordism. Here, large companies mechanized the workplace and set up a highly regulated and disciplined form of labor that is named Taylorism (the scientific management of the work-site, with managers eager to create the most efficient use of the human body at the desk or on the assembly line). At the same time, the workers earned decent salaries that enabled them to become consumers of the products that they produced on an increasingly sped-up assembly line. In the 1970s, Fordism moved from its base in the US and Europe into the periphery—into the heartland of Asia, Africa, and Latin America. "Fordism has shifted to the periphery," wrote the economic historian Robert Cox. "It is developing there alongside a revival of more archaic production methods—sweatshops—and putting out. Fordism has colonized some of the service industries, for example, fast foods, and also the production with standardized technology of consumer goods in Third World countries, destined both for domestic and world markets."[58]

What Cox describes has actually also occurred within the US, as its domestic economy is not immune from the tide of sweatshops. What Lipietz describes seems to be quite appropriate as a rendition of the type of labor regime in place *within* the United States these days. While many commentators concentrate on the garment industry when they write of sweatshop labor, the logic of sweatshop work can be found in various forms of assembly work (toys, fake jewelry, electronics, etc.) and in the Taylorist process of assembly installed in fast food outlets and other facilities that provide instant service (oil change, etc.). On the surface, the existence of these jobs for the multitude may lead us to believe that the US economy is itself in a condition of what accumulation theorist Alain Lipietz calls "peripheral Fordism,"[59] or a Fordism stripped of its high value sector and reduced to the service industry. Such an analysis would, of course, be incorrect because it would neglect the hoarded knowledge industries that are protected by the Trade-Related

International Property Rights regime, the array of agro-business and software concerns whose executive and engineering branches are high-value sectors of a generally low-wage industry (that is, for agricultural workers and for those who produce the actual computers). So, while the vast low-wage sector resembles the peripheral Fordism of the Third World, its workers live in an ocean of poverty that laps occasionally on the shores of the small islands of affluence.

Sweatshops in the Third World are, of course, a crucial part of the work of global corporations and the stabilization of the US dollar. The industrial sectors in many of these countries are in an extended process of mechanization and intensive accumulation as well as a gradual process of domestic market creation for consumer durables—these are the attributes of Fordism. Skilled manufacture and engineering do not dominate these industries, which are mostly assembly units for export to the overdeveloped states. The Third World imports electronics, heavy machinery, and many consumer goods that are produced in the overdeveloped states' skilled and mechanized sector (or else by subcontract, in China) and off the drafting board of their conceptual engineers. Sweatshops in the Third World operate along a different, if related, logic than their counterparts within the US and in Europe. The First World sweatshop is not under national compulsion to generate foreign exchange, mainly US dollars. Third World sweatshops are a crucial part of their nations' economic strategies to export goods in exchange for dollars to cover the import bills (dominated as they are by the import of such expensive items as oil, weaponry, technology, or consumer durables). First World sweatshops operate in a regime of mutual competition, where one such shop competes with another to produce cheaper goods to supply the calculated manipulations of the monopoly retail outfits (such as the Old Navy–Gap chain). In the Third World, the sweatshops negotiate at a national level with global corporations who move from state to state to bargain for less oversight of labor and environmental regulations and fewer tariffs. The main contradiction in this case is not only between one sweatshop and another, it is also between nations and global corporations. Sweatshops in the Third World are, of course, under compulsion to produce cheaper goods (mainly by reducing the cost of labor), principally because one nation's sweatshop will compete with another nation's sweatshop to win low-priced contracts whose merit is that they pay in dollars. For workers, these differences are not consequential: The workers in both cases comprise vulnerable populations, mostly women and children who come to these infernos to make a cruel subsistence. The question of "choice" is irrelevant in their lives, as they are structurally constrained to work in whatever jobs are available. Choice, the leitmotiv of individualism, is only an option for the privileged who are ensconced in conditions of relative surfeit; for the sweatshop workers the issue of choice is obfuscated by more pressing material conditions.

What are some of these conditions? The history of the US sweatshop begins with a tragedy, the Triangle Shirtwaist Factory fire of March 24, 1911, where workers perished in an inferno fueled by greed. The Triangle Shirtwaist Factory fire returned to the US working class once again in 1991 when a fire broke out in the Imperial Foods Chicken Processing Plant in Hamlet, North Carolina. The management locked the doors of the plant to prevent, in their opinion, theft of the chicken, so that when the hot-oil fryers (at 400 degrees) exploded, 25 workers died and 60 suffered horrible injuries. One worker reported, "I pluck ninety wings a minute. Sometimes I can't bend my wrist. Then when we get hurt, we can't bend our wrists, we can't get no medical care, and they fire us cause we crippled." Another, "I'm seven months pregnant. We stand in two inches of water with two five-minute bathroom breaks a day. Sometimes we can't hold our water and then our bowels break and then we faint."[60] Conessta Williams, another worker, reports, "The doors were kept locked and the plant had boarded-up windows so we couldn't steal the chicken. They never put up a fence or hired a security guard. But no one would want to steal that chicken. When you eat chicken, you don't know what you're eating." On the fateful day, in these terrible work conditions, the workers tried to break out of the plant, and one recalled, "It was like being locked in hell."[61]

Even if most of us do not work in such horrendous conditions, the formal aspects of the sweatshop economy drive our workplaces: unskilled work, deskilled labor, low wages, poor working conditions, and an intensified supervision regime to extract the maximum labor for the minimum expenditure.[62]

Those who live in relative deprivation, in the shadow of the American Dream, cannot be found easily. Their neighborhoods are often segregated by racism as much as by class inequality, or else by the urban disregard of the full-time rural dwellers (as opposed to those who go to the "country" for the weekend). Their existence is frequently denied, or else if they are acknowledged, it is only to be criticized for one or another personal failing of those who cannot make it in this country of opportunity. In 1962, socialist leader Michael Harrington published *The Other America*, a book that challenged a society eager to see itself as above the fray of history's contradictions. "The millions who are poor in the United States," he wrote, "tend to become increasingly invisible. Here is a great mass of people, yet it takes an effort of the intellect and will even to see them."[63] The impress of Harrington's book gave sustenance to the anti-poverty movement from below, but it also embarrassed President John F. Kennedy enough for him to call for an "unconditional war against poverty in America." In January 1964, Congress adopted the Economic Opportunities Act, but the measure fell far short of what was necessary. In essence, as sociologists Frances Fox Piven and Richard Cloward show us, the government's anti-poverty program provided relief to the poor not so much to overthrow poverty as to dull the anger of the impoverished.[64]

With poor health, tenuous shelter, and unreasonable access to transport, the US public still finds the means to survive. How is this possible? Unemployment is high, but the working class ekes out the means to a livelihood through the burgeoning illegal narcotics trade, working outside the tax system for cash, and other such sundry and creative means.[65] Since centuries of gender construction has placed the role of care in the hands of women, women of the contingent class struggle hard to keep families and people together.[66] From the 1970s, the buying power of workers has declined quite dramatically, so that even the corporate-dominated press had to acknowledge, "The share of worker's compensation has decreased to the lowest proportion since 1968." The reason for this decline is quite plain, since corporate profits "are taking an ever-rising share of national income," and "companies are boosting their profits more by squeezing labor costs to lift productivity."[67] An incredible 98 percent of the gain in total household income between 1980 and 2000 went to the richest fifth of the country![68] Those with legal employment, like their brethren without legal work, could not find their way out of the Other America: almost a third of all full-time workers in 1997 earned poverty-level wages, with African Americans and Latinos bearing the brunt more than white workers. The annual earnings of a minimum-wage full-time worker ($10,300) was still $2,500 less than the three-person family poverty line, and $6,000 below the line for a four-person family.[69] In 1999, a third of working women earned wages at or below the poverty level, significantly more than the share of men (almost 21 percent) at that level.[70] Those at and around the minimum wage typically work more than one full-time job, mainly in the service sector where advancement is relatively unknown. We are in the Purgatory of the Service Economy, where "temporary work" is the new euphemism for indentureship in the workforce. These women and men are often without union power, suffering under the burdens of the ideology of self-advancement, and with all the pressures of a collapsed infrastructure (shelter, transport, and medical care) for the poor.

The structural adjustment of the US created a sweatshop economy. Machines allowed each worker to be more productive. But the workers in the factory and the office also became more automated, as ergonomic modes of work and a more efficient use of the worker's time allowed firms to increase productivity quite dramatically. On the latter point, workers in fast-food restaurants, for instance, have to get ready for work before they can clock in (rather than clocking in and then using work time to put on their uniforms), they cannot do any personal things on the clock, and in many firms, workers have to clock out to take a bathroom break.[71] The better use of the workforce allowed firms to release a large number of surplus workers into the world of the unemployed, the underemployed, the contingent, and the two-job crew.

THE CONTINGENT CLASS

In 1991, before he joined the Clinton cabinet as secretary of labor, Robert Reich published his bestseller, *The Work of Nations*. In it Reich offered a view of the "three jobs of the future": routine production services, in-person services and symbolic-analytical services.[72] Factory jobs are emblematic of routine production services, but Reich also included any job that is "tedious and repetitive." About a quarter of the jobs in the US economy, in 1990, fit in this category. While the products of routine production can be sold worldwide, those of in-person service cannot be shipped elsewhere. Otherwise, that 30 percent of the US workforce that conducts in-person service has a workday as "tedious and repetitive" as routine production. Finally, symbolic-analytical services include "all the problem-solving, problem-identifying, and strategic brokering activities," whose services can be traded worldwide and whose work is not at all "tedious and repetitive." About a fifth of the US workforce in 1990 worked in this sector. The rest, about five percent, were employed as farmers, miners, and "other extractors of natural resources." Reich is concerned about the decline of wages in the first two sectors, and he is eager to turn all American workers into symbolic-analytical professionals, a task he admits is "daunting," but well worth it in the service of his "positive economic nationalism." In other words, we should strive to make the US population into the thinkers of the planet and let the rest of the world be our drones. The problem for the US workforce is not the sweatshop economy, but its own lack of useful skills.[73] Such is the proposal from the most liberal wing of the Democratic Party.

Most of those who work in the routine production and the in-person service sectors experience similar work patterns: they are frequently in temporary positions with no benefits, and while they may spend a lifetime in an occupation, they do not spend more than a few years at a particular firm. In 2000, the National Alliance for Fair Employment (NAFE) released a major study on such "contingent workers." Who are contingent workers? NAFE offered the following list:

- Part-timers: those who work less than full-time workers.
- On-call workers: those who are on an "as-needed" basis.
- Short-term hires: those who work on short projects or in peak seasons.
- Workfare workers: those who are on the "welfare to work" rolls.
- Temp workers: those who work for a temp agency like Manpower, Inc.
- Permatemp workers: those who work permanently for a firm, but with a renewed temporary contract.
- Day laborers: those who work on a "day-to-day" basis.
- Contract employees: those who work for companies that provide services (cleaning, security).
- Independent contractors: those who legally work for themselves.
- Leased workers: those who work for a leasing company (often called a "body shop").

- Prison labor: those who work within the penal system.
- Guest workers and immigrant workers: those who work in the US under short-term employment visas (H1B, H2A, H2B).

In NAFE's survey, three out of ten Americans worked in the contingent sector, but the most crucial number is that three out of five Americans either worked in this sector or knew someone who did. Those who know someone who works in the contingent sector also know the generally abhorrent nature of the working conditions, and would be loath to enter these jobs without compulsion. We also know that just short of a third of firms that "downsized" or fired their waged workers in the 1990s replaced them with contingent workers. As the NAFE survey noted:

> When employers expand contingent work as a staffing strategy, regular employees have cause to worry that they too may be replaced by cheaper contingent workers, and they hesitate before asking for raises or better working conditions. The result is a downward spiral in which permanent full-time workers are, in effect, made to compete with lower-paid workers in contingent jobs to see who will work for the lowest wages and the fewest benefits. In this way, the growth of contingent work is a significant reason for stagnant or falling wages during the current economic boom.[74]

Following from this analysis, I refer both to those who work in temporary jobs and those with full-time employment, but in fear of becoming temporary, as part of the contingent class. Both those with jobs and those without pressure each other and face a similar condition in the face of capital.

Data from 1995 shows us that the typical contingent worker is black, female, young, and enrolled in school. The highest use of contingent work is in the service sector as well as in the construction trade.[75] About ten percent of the contingent workers that year were teachers. In February 1995, the contingent workforce totaled between 2.7 and 6 million workers (depending upon whether the totals included those whose jobs were limited to one year by choice), but the government adds another 6.5 million because of workers who toil at multiple jobs and are therefore not counted in the Current Population

Survey as "contingent workers." Of the latter, the multiple-job holders, the most common characteristic is that they are young, mainly women.[76] While the literature is divided on the reasons for such an extensive turn to part-time work, the most compelling argument is that "the use of contingent work has arisen because of the decline in unionism, which permits firms to take advantage of the cost savings embodied in more flexible staffing arrangements."[77] While this is accurate, the statement fails to engage with the broad shifts in the economy, with the deterioration of manufacturing within the US, and with a general tendency toward making the productive process efficient for capital generation and not for social welfare.

How is the contingent class to survive in cities and small towns whose bureaucracies have made it impossible to build shantytowns, beg on the streets, and be fed by the charity of restaurants? Who will pay for the upkeep of this reserve army, this unemployed and shiftless population? Families can no longer absorb the costs, as more and more members of the household take up less and less lucrative jobs. Furthermore, decline in municipal expenditure has meant a lack of basic services, such as cheap transportation. This makes life onerous, if not impossible, since families must go vast distances to buy their necessities from chain supermarkets (where goods are reasonably inexpensive) or else fall prey to the small shopkeepers (who do not enjoy the supermarkets' economy of scale). Welfare, or state funded financial support, has slowly dried up as the government cuts social spending, but leaves intact, indeed increases, expenditure for the military, for subsidies to agro-businesses, and for tax breaks to corporations.[78] Who, then, is to feed, clothe, and shelter the contingent class? Let us take two basic needs, housing and healthcare, to put some flesh to the general complaint.

Housing

With the stock market in turbulence from the late 1990s, real estate markets absorbed much of the capital and produced a boom in property. While the link between the real estate market and rental property is not direct, there has been a correlative rise in rents across the country.[79] With high rents, landlords are very strict about how many people camp out in an apartment. Small motels and courageous families become the homes of those who once held steady jobs. In an unusually reflective article,

Time magazine reported on "the dearth of working class jobs that pay enough to support a life with even the bare necessities."[80] Stagnating wages and escalating real estate prices have raised the problem to "crisis proportions." A local journalist in Telluride, Colorado, pointed out that homelessness "brings instability and a surly work force. We can't expect nice worker attitudes when people come to work begging a shower." In the same town, a worker in a shop who sleeps in a sleeping bag during -40 degree Fahrenheit nights had a very different perspective: "The town doesn't realize that the people who do their dishes and clean up after them have to live someplace too."[81]

During the Clinton years, the Department of Housing and Urban Development admitted that ten million people spent some time on the streets or in overcrowded shelters, while 15 million homes and apartments (and 1.4 million hotel rooms) remained unoccupied (1999).[82] The implication is clear, that homeless people should be allowed to move into unpeopled homes, but Clintonian liberalism did not allow it to accept the full implications of its grief or to create a program of action to tackle the problem. When the Bush team took over, it revised the methodology for data collection, so that the Department of Health and Human Services reported in their overview document, "HHS Programs and Initiatives to Combat Homelessness," that the number of those without homes is about two or three million—seven to eight million less than the Clinton assessments of only two years previous. The HHS claimed that only 200,000 people are "chronically homeless." I am reminded of Ronald Reagan's statement on *Good Morning America* (January 31, 1984): "One problem that we've had, even in the best of times, is the people who are sleeping on the grates, the homeless who are homeless you might say, by choice." These rugged pioneers of free market America should, therefore, not be counted as the indigent because they exercise their *choice* to be in the outdoors. Incidentally, the US Conference of Mayors rejected this assessment. Its Task Force on Hunger and Homelessness reported an overwhelming increase in demand for shelter and food in 80 percent of the 27 cities surveyed in 2001.

> Lack of affordable housing leads the list of causes of homelessness identified by the city officials. Other causes cited, in order of frequency, include low paying jobs, substance abuse and the lack of needed services, mental

illness and the lack of needed services, domestic violence,
unemployment, poverty, prison release, and change and
cuts in public assistance programs.

In late 2002, New York City, the touchstone of homelessness in the
nation, reported an increase in the population that does not have a
permanent home. Almost 80,000 people sleep in the city shelters each
night, the highest number since 1991. With the emphasis on "law and
order" in the city, the police ruthlessly enforce the "public nuisance
laws," when those without a home must take refuge in whatever warmth
is available. The police report that their arrests of the homeless on these
charges increased by 300 percent between 2001 and 2002. Tony
Harrigan, executive director of the Center for Urban Community
Services, said in reference to the new faces that come to the shelters,
"Clearly something is happening out there."[83] Indeed.

Healthcare

In 1999, after the collapse of a nationwide attempt to remedy the
medical insurance program, the number of those within the US without
health insurance numbered 44.3 million.[84] The annual Current
Population Survey in 1998 and 1999 showed that those without health
insurance had two attributes in common: they were people of color
with relatively little access to education. Those who did not enjoy the
privileges of class and race, then, could not count on medical care even
in times of a general economic boom. The rate of women without
health insurance increased in the 1990s, bolstered by the cuts in welfare
supports and therefore the use of Medicaid (the government's
insurance program for the destitute). If the government decided not to
care for adults, and particularly for the health of mothers, it started a
meager program in 1997 called Children's Health Insurance Program
(CHIP) to cover eleven million children who lacked coverage. Without
the social capital to know about CHIP, with innumerable bureaucratic
roadblocks to the use of the program, and with the disregard for the
health of the family in total, the program has not succeeded in the
maintenance of the health of the population.[85] In 2000, 17 percent of
children of uninsured parents remained without coverage, compared
with 12 percent of all children. In late 2001, the American Medical
Association reported that the numbers of those without insurance would
rise dramatically in the decade to come.[86] Since an average of one in three

workers who lose their jobs lose health insurance, those 17 million who lost their jobs in 2001–2002 will add to the rolls of the uninsured. The 2001 figure for those uninsured in the US (under age 65) is 16 percent, but by this analysis the fraction may rise to 21 percent. Meanwhile, hospitals conduct corporate mergers, close "surplus" hospitals, and retrench medical facilities.

From the 1960s, the United States provided a safety net for those without income (such as welfare or Aid to Families with Dependent Children), but in 1996 the so-called Welfare Reform laws erased the state's liberalism. Now those who had found shelter in a social system moved from welfare to workfare, to a punitive strategy to make people work in menial jobs for low wages and remain trained elements of the unemployed reserve. As recipients of cash assistance these people did not pose the kind of disciplinary threat to an active labor movement that they will now pose, trained and desperate, to take any work whatsoever. It is often these people who now sit behind cash registers or clean corporate buildings at night, the sorts of service sector jobs that are the main engine for "job growth" in the US. As the government announces that it has helped husband more jobs, one can almost hear people at the nether end of the economy say, and several of those jobs are mine; it is not uncommon now to find people work at least two full-time jobs, to wear out their bodies and souls to pursue the American Dream, or at least survival. The reserve army of labor in the contemporary US is maintained at high levels of readiness in the prisons (where incarcerated workers toil for private corporations, such as the Corrections Corporation of America) and in the low-end service sector (either in desperation, as part of the workfare packet or else as legal and illegal immigrants unable to find better occupations). Capitalism, in its current US configuration maintains this reserve army through the coercive mechanisms of incarceration,[87] the fear of being illegal, and of being without dignity (as the state and media stigmatize welfare or cash assistance). The illiberal thrust against those within the safety net did not come from fiscal motives only, because (as New York City's Supportive Housing Network estimates) in 1998 the state spent $40,000 to incarcerate a person, whereas it would have to spend only $12,500 to provide that same person with affordable housing and other supportive services. The state's riposte against social services comes, therefore, as part of its class war against organized labor, to discipline workers away from any ambition to challenge the structure of the system.[88]

THEY MAKE THE BULL SEE RED

> I commend today's "street warriors" for standing up for what they believe in, and knowing that civic engagement is the American way. Let us all do our part to engage and create positive and progressive, social, economic, and environmental change. We need global justice or else "Workers of the World Unite!" will become more than just a hackneyed slogan; it'll become the only way to survive.
>
> —Representative Cynthia McKinney, Georgia, in the midst of the Battle of Seattle, 1999

To combat debt is not simply to demand its forgiveness, but principally to change the conditions that produce inequality. To fight inequality is not simply to bargain for higher wages, but principally to change the way power is held in our society, to fight to radically alter the institutions and attitudes that shape accumulation and dignity.

One of the most barren disputes that took place in the sheltered ranks of the US Left came from intellectuals such as sociologist Todd Gitlin and philosopher Richard Rorty. Annoyed by social and cultural assertions of what they termed the "cultural Left," Rorty called for the "reformist Left" to put forth a "People's Charter" of mainly economic reforms to "achieve our country" to live up to its constitutional ideals.[89] The intervention from such figures missed what is arguably the most dynamic achievement of the labor insurgency in recent years: the eruption of the social and the cultural into the world of labor unions to both disrupt the corporate culture of business unionism *and* to insist that the full world of the rank and file must be under the purview of the union movement. It is not enough for a union bureaucracy to bargain behind closed doors for a better contract (which means generally better wages, and perhaps protected seniority). The union must now work to liberate the workers in all aspects of their lives, and union actions must harness the collective energy of all the workers, not just those who are its paid members. Without the dynamism of the social movements, such as the anti-racist struggle, feminism, the gay and lesbian movement, the disability movement, the basic needs struggles, and the human rights campaigns, among others, the unions will slump back into the politically ineffective strategy of the bottom line. If unions do not take up the issues of the people, they will be unable to fight beyond the narrow confines of the workplace and they will not be able to fashion a program for widespread social change.

Let us look at a few examples of this strike of the social into business unionism, illustrations of the work that has energized workers to make sociocultural demands within the corridors of what was once the world's most retrogressive labor institution.

Free Mumia

Labor locals across the country supported the "Free Mumia" call in 1999, on behalf of the black militant on death row in Philadelphia, and, on April 24, 1999, International Longshore and Warehouse Union members closed down the ports of the western coast of the US for the day. As Larry Adams, president of Local 300 of the National Postal Mail Handlers Union put it, "Mumia is us. We are Mumia. Trade unions exist for the right to defend democratic rights of working class people, due process, fair treatment, freedom from police brutality—all of which is being denied Mumia in this effort at a legal lynching."[90]

Free Labor

Labor unions have, since the early 1990s, been concerned about the growth of penal labor, partly as a defensive strategy against its degradation of wages in general, but also because of its degradation of the working class. Failed legal attempts to end government contracts with correctional industries such as UNICOR are one indication, but another is the reminder that if US workers get too worked up about penal labor in China, they may forget what happens in the US (Sharon Cornu of the California Labor Federation noted, "Every politician who decries the use of prison labor in other countries [should] look at what's happening in California").[91]

Free Childcare

In 1994, Hotel Employees and Restaurant Employees (HERE) International Local 2 conducted a study among its 7,000 members who work in San Francisco's hotel industry.[92] One of the main priorities for the workers was childcare, and in contract negotiations the union forced the management to recognize that worker absenteeism was often related to a lack of childcare. After a struggle, the union won the Local 2/Hospitality Industry Child and Elder Care Plan—management paid 5 cents per worker into a fund managed by a joint worker/management committee. In 1996, management agreed to increase their contribution to 15 cents per worker. That provided benefits such as contributions toward childcare ($60–$100 per worker per month), newborn expenses ($125), youth programs, and summer camps, as well as a resource and referral service in multiple languages. "This is a terrific benefit," said Local 2 president Michael Casey. "The bottom line is respect for members. These benefits address workers' needs beyond health and welfare and working conditions. They address people's family needs."[93] Local 2 is not alone. Local 1000 of the California State Employees Association/SEIU has a Labor Management Child Care Committee to encourage the formation of a nonprofit foundation to provide childcare for its members. In April 1999, United Auto Workers pushed the Big Three automakers to create the Alliance for Children and Working Families, with a $6 million down payment.[94] Finally, AFSCME Council 6 organized childcare workers at the Minneapolis Community College Child Care Center as a first step toward the recognition of the importance of childcare to the labor movement. The workers at the center now have Civil Service classification, receive between $8.42 and $12 per hour, fully paid health, dental and life insurance, ten paid annual holidays, and paid vacation and sick time.

Free AIDS Care

HERE Local 2 in San Francisco negotiated the first AIDS disability benefit plan in the country for its workers. The benefit comes out of a health and welfare fund set up by the union, but with funds from the hotels, it pays $1,000 per month and covers expenses such as medical co-payments. There are also provisions for licensed home care, hospice, medical equipment, non-covered prescriptions and rent assistance. The extensive plan generated enthusiasm from the AIDS movement toward the labor union, so that when Local 2 began to organize Park 55 Hotel, AIDS activists came out in force. "We have a pretty extensive community support plan," reports Lisa Jaicks of Local 2.

> We go out with the workers and speak to local
> organizations about our campaign and how it fits in with
> our community struggles. We commit to joining other

people's events. We can't just expect people to show up for our events without us contributing to the larger struggle.[95]

Free Housing

In the 1920s and 1930s, the Union of Needletrades, Industrial and Textile Employees (UNITE) created housing cooperatives in New York City and offered apartments to workers at very reasonable rates. In 1934, the Full Fashion Hosiery Workers' Union built a housing development, the Carl Mackley Apartments, in Philadelphia, drawing on federal aid and union funds to do so. The 5.4 acre apartment complex was the first housing development of Roosevelt's New Deal and it offers an early example of the International Style of architecture. With 184 rental units in the property in four separate buildings, the complex provides a necessary space for low-income families to this day. The Mackley complex returned to the news in 1999, when the AFL-CIO's Housing Investment Trust spent $20 million of a $123 million spree to use pension funds toward the renovation of workers' housing. The AFL-CIO re-entered the fray after much good work had been (and continues to be) done by one of the United States's great social movements of the impoverished, the tenants' rights movement.[96] In 2002, this same trust (founded in 1965, but rather dormant until recently) started a $100 million home-ownership program for union families and municipal workers in Los Angeles. "The need is so great," said the trust's public finance director Carol Miriam Nixon. "Our unions are very strong in the city of LA [800,000 families in the LA area]. It's important that we show our union members we're willing to invest in the community."[97] As Stephen Coyle, the head of the trust wrote in late 1999:

> In 1995, more than a quarter of the 5.3 million households with what housing experts call worst case needs had earnings at least equivalent to that of a full-time worker at minimum wage. A household with worst case needs has a very low income, and either pays more than half of its income for rent or lives in severely substandard housing, and nonetheless receives no government housing assistance. There are nearly 10 million minimum wage workers in our country, and it takes 86 hours of work for a minimum wage worker to afford median rent. In some cities the number of hours jumps to more than 160.[98]

These examples offer a taste of the complex world of labor organizing. The rest of the chapter will trace four more examples, in greater depth. One of them is from the world of formal unions, the 1997 Teamsters strike against contract labor. The next example highlights the 1998 taxi workers strike in New York City, an example of immigrant worker formations that are chary of the AFL-CIO bureaucracy, but welcome unions. Then we visit with a workers' center of sorts, the Asian Immigrant Women Advocates (AIWA), where the purpose is not only to organize workers but also to generate massive community support via moral campaigns against corporate entities. Finally, we end with De-Bug, a collective of young workers who are eager to use various forms of expression to dog the bosses and to energize the classes. These four examples are varied, but they share one salient characteristic: They all reject the world of debt and envision something more powerful, something that comes to us in that banal word—freedom.

Strike Against the Temporary

Angry at the economy of the temporary, workers who dominated the United Parcel Service (UPS) and who were frustrated with the company's reliance upon outsourced workers, struck on August 4, 1997.[99] A new generation of workers took on the old accommodation of the craft unions under the leadership of a then rejuvenated International Brotherhood of Teamsters. By August 19, the union ended the strike with a clear verdict: the company conceded to each of the workers' demands. The victory was very significant, since it shows that "American workers can stand up to corporate greed," Teamsters President Ron Carey declared. "After fifteen years of taking it in the chin, working families are telling big corporations that we will fight for the American Dream. This is not just a Teamster victory—this is a victory for all working people." The US state's attack on the air traffic controllers' 1981 strike inaugurated the 15-year period mentioned by Carey. In 1997, the tide turned just a little bit.

UPS is the US's largest parcel transportation service with control over about 80 percent of the market. With a net worth of $21 billion and with posted profits of $1 billion in 1996, UPS is an important component of US infrastructure, although it is a private company (it is also not traded on the stock exchange). The Teamsters understood that their strike was not just for their own demands, but was a test case for the newly militant union movement. On March 11, Carey noted that the negotiations "will help determine whether our children and grandchildren can look forward to good, safe, full-time jobs with decent health care and pensions." The strike was significant not just for the issues, but also for a shift in the political climate and for the main agent in this shift, the rejuvenated trade union movement.

The Teamsters made four demands: higher wages and retirement payments, conversion of part-time to full-time jobs, enhanced job security, and finally, improved job safety. UPS, at that time, employed 308,030 people, of whom 43 percent were full-time (with an average wage of $19.95 per hour) and the rest were part-time (with an average wage of $11.07). Since 1993, of those hired by UPS, 83 percent had only part-time jobs at a starting salary of $8 per hour (unchanged since 1982). The turn to contract and part-time work in US enterprises has been steady since the 1970s, with most corporations opting to use employment and temporary work agencies to supply them with an endless list of those fired from full-time clerical, service, and, increasingly, manual labor positions. In this way, corporations have displaced many of their costs onto a society unable to handle a situation in which one in four children are born in poverty. Part-time, contingent work changed the character of the workplace and made it hard for unions to organize workers (nevertheless, in the late 1990s, the Teamsters included 84 percent of the part-time UPS workers).

The weakness of the workers enables corporations to cut back on health and safety standards and also use pension funds for their own purposes. On the first score, UPS refused to invest $55 per truck to fit rearview mirrors; due to this and other malfeasance, about one driver is killed per month. On the second point, workers contribute a significant sum of their wages toward a pension fund. Corporations hold these funds in trust and they use them in the organized usury of the stock market. The unions want to control these funds in order, perhaps, to use them in the people's interest rather than to both fuel the bubble at Wall Street and pay corporate executives enormous salaries with inflated stock options. If the unions controlled these funds and began banks for their workers, some wealth might go toward the creation of opportunities for the working class. The Teamsters, on August 19, won the gradual conversion of 20,000 part-time to full-time jobs, an increase in pensions controlled by the Teamsters, a limit to subcontract usage, an increase in wages, safety protection, and a new five-year contract. These gains were significant.

In 1981, Reagan's action against the air traffic controllers was the proof of the pudding that the state operates at the behest of capital. Reagan gave striking workers two weeks to return to work. When they did not, he fired 12,000 controllers without discharge allowance, right to pension, or right to seek public service. He levied huge fines on 72 union leaders, imprisoned five of them, and deprived the union of its representative status. Between 1979 and 1989, the hourly wages of 80 percent of the workers declined and the National Labor Relations Board (the arbitration body of the US government) began to rule in favor of management more than labor. Hit with deregulation of major sectors and with "downsizing," the workforce was unable to confront an aggressive and class-conscious management. Most strikes ended with a whimper; for example, in 1994, the Teamsters went on a one-day strike against UPS that won nothing. Stephen Roach, chief economist at the brokerage firm Morgan Stanley, noted at the start of the 1997 strike, "The pendulum could be shifting back." In other words, renewed labor militancy may transform US politics.

Since the Teamsters prepared the ground well for their strike, President Clinton was unable to intervene with ease. The instrument available to Clinton, the Taft-Hartley Act of 1947, did not make it easy for him to act (the president can only act if there is "significant damage" to the country by the strike).[100] Under pressure from the National Association of Manufacturers, the US Chamber of Commerce, and the National Retail Federation, and from the national media, Clinton was only able to apologize for this inaction. The US public supported the Teamsters' firm stand on the issues and their disregard for all talk of profits and market shares in the face of the future of their workers. When Steven Trossman of the Teamsters noted, "This strike is not going to be decided by the finances of the Teamsters. It will be decided on the issues," his sacrificial militancy was met with a rise in fellowship for the union (most polls found that support for the strike increased as it went along). On August 15, Ron Carey announced, "In my 40 years as a UPS driver and union leader, I have never seen so much public support for workers who are fighting corporate greed." Support for the union also came from the almost 40 percent of UPS employees outside the union; with 99 percent of the workers on strike, this support was unambiguous.

When the Teamsters appeared to run out of strike funds, the AFL-CIO provided $11 million per week for the strike fund. This was in stark contrast to the formerly opportunist and bureaucratic AFL-CIO whose leadership was called, in 1972, a bunch of "businessmen engaged in the business of unions." Even the right-wing sociologist Daniel Bell noted in 1970, "[M]any union leaders have become money-hungry, taking on the grossest features of business society." The leadership of the AFL-CIO from Samuel Gompers to Lane Kirkland followed a policy of "businesslike unionism," what we generally call class collaboration.[101] The renewed union pledged itself to frontal combat with corporations and its support for ongoing strike activity and the organization of workers was a notable illustration of its new policy. However, this strike and the AFL-CIO's new position did not imply an increase in class consciousness and organization; it was as yet a defensive challenge to capitalist aggression. The Teamsters enjoined UPS to hire more full-time workers, since part-time work "has negative consequences for the company's productivity."[102] There was still a tendency to appear businesslike and to argue for increased productivity rather than for the social good. Nevertheless, the strike sent a tremor through the heart of corporations and it warmed the working class and many of their allies.

The power of the 1997 strike held in July 2002, when UPS negotiated a relatively strong contract with the Teamsters. The workers won a 22 percent pay increase over six years and the company agreed to convert 10,000 nonunion jobs to full-time work with union membership. The new contract came despite the concessionary tone of the Teamsters' new leadership, especially from its new president, James P. Hoffa, son of the old Teamsters' mobbed-up boss.[103] Even with tepid leadership, the rank and file militancy held the line against a management not known for conceding to workers' demands.

Strike in the Yellow Four-Wheeled Sweatshop

If the Teamsters put the labor movement on notice about temporary work, militant immigrant workers transformed the *character* of the labor movement from the ground upward. In 1990, the Service Employees International Union (SEIU) Local 399's Justice for Janitors campaign run by mainly immigrant workers won a substantial victory after a vigorous struggle. Conventional labor wisdom suggested that immigrant workers are quiescent, but the composition of the militant Justice for Janitors put an end to that theory (the share of Latino workers in the service field rose from 28 percent in 1980 to 61 percent in 1990).

Eight years later, in New York City, almost all of the 24,000 taxi drivers went on a day-long strike against municipal regulations and the brokerage system. On May 13, 1998, New York City woke up to a historic strike.[104] On a call given by the New York Taxi Workers Alliance (NYTWA), 98 percent of the city's yellow cab drivers had struck work. Mayor Rudy Giuliani blamed the strike on a handful of reckless cab drivers and predicted an early end to the strike. But the strike held. One conservative estimate put the decline in street traffic at 75 percent. Subways and buses were crammed. The personal schedules of thousands of travelers descended into chaos. The NYTWA, an immigrant-led organization with two years of experience under its belt, had brought one of the world's biggest cities to a grinding halt.

The immediate cause of the strike was a set of 17 new rules that the Mayor's Taxi and Limousine Commission (TLC) had proposed for a "public hearing" and vote on May 28, part of Giuliani's "quality of life" program to restore "civility" to New York. The proposed rules included an increase in fines, some up to $1,000, for rude behavior, smoking, and speeding as well as an increase in pressure to suspend drivers' licenses (through a points system). This was the proverbial last straw for drivers who had been facing deteriorating working conditions for the past several years. Louis, a Haitian driver, explained patiently to a smug television reporter that the TLC's new rule packet was a sham, that none of the rules really dealt with safety, that all they intended was to extract more money off drivers and force them out of work. "This strike," he said deliberately, "is about economic conditions, about our working conditions, about our demand for dignity and justice."

Taxi driving has become a sweatshop on wheels. Taxi drivers are kept in a vise by a troika that enjoys the fruits of this $1.5 billion business: the garage owners, the brokers, and the TLC that regulates the taxi industry. Assisting them is the New York City police force, long famous for its acts of harassment against the mainly immigrant drivers. Beatings and routine citations for trivial infringements of traffic rules appear to be the norm in the drivers' lives. The industry is tightly controlled through the city's system of medallions that gives one the right to put a cab on the road. By strictly limiting their availability, the city has inflated the price of a medallion to between $260,000 and $300,000, far out of the range of individual drivers. A driver thus leases a medallion and car from a garage for an average of a little more than $100 per shift. Since drivers must pay for their own gas, they are $120 in the hole before they even start. On a good day, a driver may meter about $180–$200, leaving $60–$80 to take home. From this must be deducted costs that are invariably associated with spending twelve hours a day on the road—tickets, sick days, car breakdowns, and TLC fines. Since they are seen as "independent contractors," the drivers are not entitled to health benefits, vacation time, or retirement benefits. By contrast, the TLC reported earnings of $70 million in the last six months of 1996 alone. Forty million dollars of this came from fines, hack license renewal fees, and inspection fees—in other words, money out of the drivers' pockets. A small garage with control over ten to 15 medallions reports revenues of close to $100,000 a month—again, money out of the drivers' pockets.

In opposition to the "taxi terrorists" and the "lawless immigrants," Giuliani portrayed himself as a champion of the "concerned consumer" and the "responsible citizen." "There has been a constant bashing of the taxi driver by the media and the politicians," said Bhairavi Desai, staff organizer at NYTWA, "until the public feels that the taxi driver is a bad person who can be punished and punished." As per a TLC survey of 1992, 89 percent of NYC yellow cab drivers are recent immigrants, with nearly 50 percent of them South Asian (Bangladeshi, Indian, or Pakistani) followed by Haitians, immigrants from the ex-Soviet Union, Africans, white and black Americans, Arabs, and Latinos, in that order. Drivers are, in a sense, people without a home. While capital and commodities flow freely around the world, to the vast majority of the world's population—whether a Malaysian worker at Nike or a New York City taxi driver—the world is peculiarly circumscribed, as they spend longer and harder hours at work. Taxi drivers are working here because they have been driven out of their home economies, and while they are here a significant number of them lead a precarious life on the edge of deportation.

And they know that they cannot afford to leave—in the home country, elderly parents, indigent siblings, and children are dependent on the $200 that arrives by mail each month. They are suited therefore for a profession such as this, where all you need is a hack license, where there are no wages to report, no social security numbers, and no single employer. The garages and the TLC understand this vulnerability better than anybody else. In this context, NYTWA's successful organizing effort is remarkable: the popular wisdom that ethnically diverse, independent taxi drivers are isolated, without power, and beyond organization has been shattered.

In 1992, the South Asian drivers organized themselves into the Lease Drivers' Coalition (LDC) through the efforts of the late driver Saleem Osman and the sponsoring Committee Against Anti-Asian Violence (CAAAV). The next year, the South Asian drivers conducted a major demonstration against police brutality (partly organized by LDC). In 1997, LDC decided to leave CAAAV and the drivers and organizers re-established themselves as NYWTA in order to broaden their base to non–South Asians and to take full control of their own efforts. In 1998, the NYWTA had a base of 1,500 drivers. With a handful of volunteers and a shared office, the NYTWA seemed an unlikely foe for Giuliani. Yet Giuliani's new rules struck a nerve. Drivers took NYWTA flyers and made copies with their own resources, sometimes adding their own notes and drawings to the posters. One driver happily declared that he handed out 4,000 flyers in the week preceding the strike. The drivers also used CB radio to communicate about the strike. Organizers stood at the locations where drivers changed shifts, handing out flyers and talking to the drivers.

Opposition to Giuliani's rules created immediate solidarity, which held even as India and Pakistan locked into an escalating nuclear arms race that threatened to inflame nationalist passions. "The Pakistani and Indian drivers didn't blink. They kept going not for a moment allowing nationalisms to interfere with the organizing," Mathew reported. "And, unlike in the past, drivers from other communities [Haitians, West Africans, Iranians] have come forward to take on leadership positions." Mathew added, "We have found the most successful strategy in dealing with ethnicity and nationalism is to talk most explicitly about it, constantly reminding people that problems can come up."[105] In fact, the richness of national heritages actually worked in favor of the drivers. Bangladeshis brought skills honed in their liberation movement, Haitians imported their *métier* from the *Lavalas* struggle, and others drew from their experiences of resistance to tyranny in their home countries.

From the start, Giuliani threatened to call in the IRS and the INS. "I don't negotiate with people who want to close the city down," the mayor said. "Never have, never will." He signed an executive order that allowed vans and livery cabs that normally serve the outer boroughs to encroach upon the Manhattan taxi industry, effectively authorizing scabs. But no livery cabs entered Manhattan. Not only had the NYTWA call of May 13 united an ethnically diverse workforce of 24,000 workers, but also another 30,000 drivers from the outer boroughs extended their solidarity. Their message was clear—"We stand by our yellow cab brothers and sisters." On May 21, 80 percent of the cabbies supported a second strike in spite of the city's misinformation campaign. Seven days later, NYTWA held a rally in front of City Hall, a snub at Giuliani who forbade such an event. At both events, the garage owners, large medallion owners, and brokers organized as the Metropolitan Taxicab Board of Trade broke ranks and circulated a flyer calling off the strike. Small medallion owners were in a quandary. But the unity and morale of the ordinary drivers held. "We cannot back down," said Bhairavi Desai, "the stronger we get the harder [the city and owners] will fight." At the TLC hearing on May 28, drivers, owners, and industry experts testified that the new rules would destroy the industry. And yet at the end of the day, the TLC voted in favor of implementing 15 of the 17 new rules.

But sometimes the struggle is victory enough. That seemed to be the mood among taxi workers and their supporters in New York City. After two taxi strikes, the 24,000 taxi workers rode a buoyant tide despite the harsh response from City Hall and most of the media. Those who know labor politics in the city recognize that this has been one of the most significant events of the last three decades. In late May 1998, it appeared that a new day was dawning in New York City, with the New Directions slate at Local 100 at work on the leadership of the Transit Workers Union, with the homeless and the street vendors on board to combat Giuliani's draconian "quality of life" program, and, notably, as the city's construction workers closed down midtown Manhattan on June 30, 1998. Forty thousand construction workers organized by Local 79 proved for a day that the Laborer's International Union was not still steeped in its long history of corruption and business unionism (in 1996, ten former locals of the Laborer's Union in New York formed Local 79).

The jolt of radicalism from these immigrant workers pushed senior AFL-CIO organizers like Warren Mar to argue, "Basically we feel immigration laws should be broken. We should protect undocumented workers, we should harbor them, we should not cooperate with the INS." Mar understood that the labor movement had begun to rely upon the militancy of immigrant workers. If the movement did not put immigration issues front and center, it would fail to represent the hopes and desires of its militant base. AFL-CIO vice president Chavez-Thompson put Mar's strong words into institutional focus with her February 16, 2000, pronouncement that "the current system of immigration enforcement in the US is broken. If we are to have an immigration system that works, it must be orderly, responsible, and fair." The AFL-CIO called upon the government to restructure its immigration policy mainly to protect the rights of all workers and to hold employers accountable for the exploitation of immigrants. "Employers often knowingly hire workers who are undocumented," Chavez-Thompson noted, "and then when workers seek to improve working conditions employers use the law to fire or intimidate workers." Certainly, the net result of this policy is that the immigration law is used to discipline the workforce. "The law should criminalize employer behavior," the AFL-CIO noted, "not punish workers."[106]

In the immediate aftermath of 9/11, the unions seemed to go silent in their call for amnesty. Since the unions are made up of so many radical immigrant workers, the silence can only last a short time. When the US Supreme Court declared in *Hoffman Plastic Compounds v. National Labor Review Board (NLRB)* that undocumented workers do not have the right to back pay remedy if they are illegally fired, the General Vice President of HERE Local 11, Maria Elena Durazo, told the press on May 17, 2002, that the union "denounces the US Supreme Court decision." "It is very hypocritical," she continued, "for the US to take advantage of the hard work of millions of immigrant workers while at the same time trying to deny a basic worker right—the right to organize for a better life." The programmatic goals for HERE, she said, remained the same:

> 1. Complete and immediate citizenship for all immigrants who currently work in the US; 2. The right of immigrant workers to organize into unions as well as have complete labor rights; 3. Whistleblower protections; 4. Removing the power and responsibility of employers to enforce INS laws.

In August 2002, a coalition of unions, immigrants' rights groups, and religious organizations announced that in the spring of 2003, there would be a new freedom ride on behalf of immigrants within the US. "A freedom ride is a great idea to make our land live up to the ideal of equality of all," said Reverend James Lawson, a freedom rider from the 1960s. "Our business is not primarily in Afghanistan or the Middle East but to secure equality and justice here." The Reverend Lawson, a comrade of Martin Luther King, Jr., noted that the freedom rides of the 1960s showed the country the character of the oppression against blacks. "We have something of the same thing going on with the matter of immigrants," he said.[107] Finally, House minority leader Dick Gephardt declared in mid-2002 that he would fight to put a bill before Congress to give amnesty to undocumented workers.[108] With the rout of the Democrats in November 2002, such measures seem unlikely to come to pass.

The AIWA Affliction

Formed in 1983, Asian Immigrant Women Advocates (AIWA) is neither a community organization nor a trade union.[109] AIWA's founders, however, came from these two worlds: Young Shin and Elaine Kim from the Korean Community Center of the East Bay and Patricia Lee from HERE, Local 2 in San Francisco. AIWA is somewhat like the many workers' centers that provide services to immigrant workers from Long Island to Seattle. Yet, AIWA provides services to its many members: one of the first tasks of the organization was to teach "survival English" to the immigrant Korean workers at the newly organized Fairmont Hotel in San Francisco. Local 2 did not have anyone on its staff who could speak Korean, so AIWA came into the picture to provide this auxiliary function. AIWA is also more than this, because it functions as a strategy center for organizing among immigrant workers in the Bay Area. In many ways, then, AIWA is the hub of a social movement, one spoke in the wheel of Bay Area progressivism, and indeed an important cause of the upsurge of immigrant workers that has transformed the AFL-CIO. Its most famous campaign was the Garment Workers Justice Campaign (from 1992) that will get the most attention in this section.[110]

AIWA emerges in a political space pioneered by those immigrant women who fought against the sweatshops in San Francisco's

Chinatown, to form, in time, the Chinese Progressive Association, and those who, in the 1960s, struck at a Farah factory in El Paso, Texas, to form the vibrant organization, La Mujer Obrera. These two organizations and four others (New York City's Chinese Staff and Workers Association, Los Angeles's Korean Immigrant Workers Advocates, the Bay Area's Mujeres Unidas y Activas, and San Jose's Services, Immigrant Rights and Education Network or SIREN) joined together in late August of 2001 for an Asian and Latina immigrant workers' National Leadership Gathering. Cecilia Rodriquez of La Mujer Obrera told the gathering, "Immigrant women, in particular, bear the triple stigma of racism, sexism, and classism and have not had the opportunity to tell our stories." At the gathering, the groups told their stories of struggle and they underscored the importance of organization. One New York immigrant leader pointed out the importance of "raising awareness so [immigrant women] can help themselves and receive justice."[111]

In May 1993, twelve Chinese seamstresses from the Lucky Sewing Company in San Francisco came to the AIWA office on Eighth Street in Oakland. For their work during ten to twelve hour days over six or seven days a week from April 1991 to February 1992, the workers had been given a series of bad checks that totaled $15,000. "They were really upset," AIWA executive director Young Shin told the *Los Angeles Times*. "They felt cheated."[112] AIWA took up the cudgel, went to the owners of Lucky and found out that the firm had filed for bankruptcy. By law, the company should have sold its assets to pay back wages *first*. However, as with most sweatshops, the Lucky Sewing Company was a bare operation, with few assets whose real beneficiary was protected by the law through a simple move: it had no formal relationship with Lucky even thought it was the principal recipient of the factory's goods.[113] That firm was Jessica McClintock, Inc., and it had been the main beneficiary of the production relations at Lucky's for at least six years. As 200 people rallied before the headquarters of Jessica McClintock, Young Shin laid out the strategy for the campaign: "Jessica McClintock is one of the many clothing manufacturers who abdicated all responsibility for their workers' health, safety, and just compensation by using independent contractors."[114] Referring to a chart, Shin noted that for each $120 dress, $10 went to labor, $10 to material, and $10 to the contractors: the rest went to Jessica

McClintock who made $145 million that year. While Jessica McClintock complained that the attention was "unfair and totally unjustified" because it required its contractors to follow federal and state labor laws, Lora Jo Foo of the Asian Law Caucus argued, "Subcontractors really don't have a choice. Contract prices are set by manufacturers and it's a take it or leave it situation. When you look at the contract price, 90 times out of 100 that price will not guarantee even minimum wage, and it's not going to cover overtime."[115] Young Shin explains the strategy:

> We reached out to the subcontractors through this campaign. AIWA is more an ally rather than trying to crack down on them for the poor working conditions and wages. The connection we made with the contractors gave us more power, because they brought hard evidence of how much they get paid from the manufacturer and that they don't have any power at pricing the goods. We can really tell the consumers, Americans, the public, that manufacturers need to be responsible. We shouldn't be excusing the contractor and subcontractor who have made the profits in the past and didn't pay the women, but people need to be educated about the whole injustice of the economic structure.[116]

In 1992–93, AIWA inaugurated a host of innovative campaign techniques to humiliate Jessica McClintock and to put the idea of corporate accountability at the center of US culture. In October 1992, AIWA ran a full-page advertisement in many national papers, including the *New York Times,* with the heading "Let Them Eat Lace." "It's rags to riches for Jessica McClintock," the ad said, "but the women who sew in the sweatshops have still not been paid." McClintock responded on November 2 with her own broadside entitled, "I Will Not Tolerate Intimidation or a Blatant Shakedown!" Then, on December 2, AIWA came back with a piece called "Fantasy vs. Reality," that quoted from Eleanor Dugan, a former McClintock production supervisor, "I hope your efforts will be the wedge that starts people re-evaluating their basic assumptions, like Rosa Parks refusing to move to the back of the bus." In February, AIWA organized the "Jessie Have a Heart" Valentine's Day picket at her home in the exclusive Pacific Heights neighborhood of San Francisco. Support came in from across the country, as individuals and organizations sent money and conducted solidarity rallies at shopping malls and before McClintock offices. From the Southwest Network for Environmental and Economic Justice (Phoenix, Arizona) to the Division of Public Ministries of the American Baptist Churches, from the Social Justice Resource Center of Catholic Charities (Oakland) to Native Americans for a Clean Environment (Tahlequah, Oklahoma), from Direct Action for Rights and Equality (Providence, Rhode Island) to the National Organization for Women—the movement grew apace. In March, AIWA organized the "Shopping District Protest Tour" for allies and friends who had come to the Bay Area under the auspices of a Center for Third World Organizing (CTWO) convention for women organizers. Asian Pacifica Sisters picketed the McClintock Sutter Street boutique in May with the slogan, "We're queer, we're Asian, we're not going shopping!" In June, AIWA held a "We've Got the Unpaid/Wedding Day Blues" mock wedding ceremony/street theater at the McClintock boutique, and in July, students and youth created the "Summer Vacation Protest" from the boutique to a picnic at Baker's Beach.

As these innovative events unfolded across the country, people felt a sense of revulsion at corporate greed and at the wage slavery of capitalism. California state assembly member (and now member of the US House of Representatives) Barbara Lee attended a hearing at the Oakland Museum on May 1, 1993, heard the workers testify to the barbarism of the system and offer their recommendations, and then she said:

> My ancestors were brought here in chains from Africa as slaves. This country was built on the basis and on the use of slave labor. It's only been one hundred thirty years since African Americans have been emancipated from that horror of slavery and…we really haven't begun to recuperate from that devastating experience. We understand very well the plight that your struggle is about. I want to say to you that along with the recommendations that you have laid out here for me which I commit myself to, I'm also going to go back and talk to the NAACP and some of the African American organizations to ask them to embrace this struggle. I join you in your struggle. Thank you again for being so brave.

After the hearing, Young Shin said, "We are building national awareness of the situation of the seamstresses."[117] In 1996, the main corporations reached an agreement with the workers to pay back pay and to reform themselves. This was not perfection, but it was certainly a model for the campaigns of corporate accountability that are now legion across the labor movement. As Miriam Ching Yoon Louie points out in *Sweatshop Warriors:*

> Eventually, the International Ladies Garment Workers Union/UNITE, the National Labor Committee, and Global Exchange used what they observed of AIWA's campaign in their anti-corporate campaigns against Gap, Nike, and Guess, and in organizing students through Union Summer and United Students Against Sweatshops.

Drawing from the McClintock campaign energy, AIWA created the Youth Build Immigrant Power (YBIP) project in 1997 to organize many of the young people who walked the line on behalf of their mothers, aunts, sisters, and friends. In December 2000, the YBIP youth joined with the National Mobilization Against Sweatshops (NMASS—housed at the Chinese Staff and Workers Association in New York City) to conduct a "Girl"cott against DKNY's exploitative sweatshop conditions. NMASS held a rally in New York on December 17, to remind Donna Karan of DKNY that the $600 million gross profit from 2000 was made off the backs of the garment workers. YBIP, according to member Kam Sung, saw "that there were many similarities between what garment workers here in San Francisco faced and what the workers in New York City faced." Therefore, YBIP decided to hold a solidarity rally at the San Francisco Shopping Center. One hundred youth came to the rally, performed skits, chanted, and "demonstrated that youths have the power to make a change in the garment industry. United, we can fight the injustices brought onto our immigrant community by the big corporations."[118] Now with a summer youth internship, the YBIP program creates a long-term legacy and organizes the entire family rather than simply the worker.[119] Finally, when the labor movement failed to address issues of environmental and labor injustice in the sweatshops of Silicon Valley, where electronic assembly workers inhale toxic fumes, work long hours, and experience the injustice of a misogynist and anti-immigrant workplace, AIWA opened a branch office in San Jose in 1991 and, with the University of California, San Francisco, formed the Asian Immigrant Women Workers Clinic in 2001.

There is nothing automatically good about community or advocacy organizations like AIWA. They perform a role in the movement for justice that helps push the labor movement on several fronts and enjoins it to enter these areas on pain of extinction. However, there are moments when the labor movement enters the life of a community organization and enables it to be true to its own ideals. One such example was when the workers at the 24-year-old Asian Health Services in Oakland, California, went to Local 790 of SEIU and formed a union at the organization in May 1997. Local 790 has a long history of anti-racist activism, with its key role in the anti-apartheid struggle, and it now entered this unique zone to push a community organization forward. "We don't want to slip into a service model now that we have been organized," warned Ray Otake, a worker at the Asian Health Service and a member of the organizing committee for unionization.

> The workers here have seen how they could effect change and associate the union with the tools to organize, solve problems, and empower ourselves. We need to continue using the creative tactics we had during the campaign to orient new members with self-empowerment so our internal base will have an activist foundation.[120]

The De-Bug Virus

If AIWA mainly organized among the immigrant workers, what about the children of the immigrants, those who are now in their twenties and who are the main workforce in the software and hardware industries of Silicon Valley? At a 2001 gathering called by the AFL-CIO at the Paris Hotel in Las Vegas, organizer Raj Jayadev saw that the younger unionists spent a considerable amount of their time in the parking lot, rapping with each other, rather than in the ballroom hearing speeches from the leadership. One of these young folk told him that "the union newsletter goes from the mailbox to the trash can," because, as Jayadev notes, "young workers don't want to simply hear the union line—they want to create it. The younger generation does not like to receive messages passively. Just look at the explosion of youth-created media in recent years."[121] Of course, the older generations did not want to be given media either, and there is evidence of the way people told their own stories. Now, what is strikingly different is the access among young workers in the First World to technology that enables them to tell their own story in print or on the web.

A cursory search on the web, for example, leads us to any number of young worker created web 'zines and materials, and there are a slew of anarchist and other left-wing periodicals such as *Clamor* magazine available around the country that come from young workers and address the complex framework within which they work and organize. As Jayadev notes:

> Young working people are already organizing against the prison-industrial complex, environmental racism and racial profiling and hate crimes. These movements may have little to do with workplace issues, but they have everything to do with the labor movement. Regardless of the struggle, they are giving young people an experiential point of reference that confirm that collective action is a way to change oppressive realities. This is fundamentally what unionism is about.[122]

To introduce us to this new wave of unionism, I want to offer a profile of the author of these words, Raj Jayadev. While my story is about only one person, I hope that you can find in him an example of the many active young people whose multiple labors have not only restarted a Left dynamic in the US, but they have done so around the Labor movement. There are also people just a little older than Jayadev, such as Amy Dean who is now almost 40 and is the head of the AFL-CIO's Silicon Valley office, who are also playing a crucial role in the struggle to kick-start a progressive dynamic in the country. "The labor movement was strongest when we were the moral voice in the community," Dean says. "That's when people were attracted to us, wanted to be part of us, wanted to be mobilized into action with us."[123] Dean is right about the moral voice part of it, but Jayadev would perhaps insist that the voice should be fashioned by the workers, not simply given to them from above so that people get "attracted to us." This story is also not just about Jayadev, but also about the collective he founded with others called De-Bug. "Debug" is the word computer specialists use to describe the process of finding a malfunction and fixing it. This De-Bug is the name of a collective of young workers, writers, and artists who are organizing to improve Silicon Valley. The story is about De-Bug as much as Jayadev.

I'm sitting with Raj Jayadev in a café off Valencia in San Francisco. "In San Francisco you can't spit and not hit an activist on the head," he tells me. And Raj is one of those activists, shaved head, earrings, young, dynamic, full of intellectual and moral energy, a veteran of the anti-WTO blowout in Seattle. I force his biography out of him. Activists like Raj are not happy to talk about themselves, always eager to talk about the struggles at hand. He tells me that his family comes from Karnataka, India. That they came to California to make it, but like most South Asians, uncovered the trials of life in the US. Raj went to UCLA angry at the world, but unsure how to direct that anger. "I didn't know what it was that I was so pissed about." Being in Los Angeles clarified things about race, color, and class. "I started to get involved in the movement down there, with labor," he says. Thanks to UCLA's liberal interest in workers' rights, Raj got course credit for his shenanigans with the working class of Los Angeles. Hard work with virtuoso labor organizations like Los Angeles Manufacturing Action Project (LAMAP), under the direction of Peter Olney, allowed Raj to get "out of the UCLA bubble." LAMAP's idea was to organize industry-wide and be culturally particular.[124] Every immigrant community will not join the labor movement in the same way, so the labor organizers need to be cognizant of the differences between workers.

Raj was radicalized by other youth of color and by this innovative labor organization. He got a grant to travel to India and was moved by the experience. "It was a whole different thing," Raj said. "I didn't even know Indians when I was growing up. To step on the bus and not be the only Indian brother on the bus, to look like everyone else on the bus, that was something I didn't even know I missed. Until the second I stepped on that bus." The idea of the *bundh*, the total strike, blew his mind, and introduced him to that side of India so rarely talked about in Indian America.

Raj moved back to the Valley, to live with his family and to organize workers. He went to work at Hewlett-Packard on the assembly line and to see if justice can be served in this heart of the new America where 13 billionaires make their homes (combined wealth of $45 billion), with several hundred more residents worth $25 million or more. "There's no place else like Silicon Valley in the world," says Morgan White (a Menlo Park investment counselor). "You've got the biggest wealth creation machine man has ever seen."

Workers at all levels of the industry come from among immigrants, whether from Latin America (mainly Mexico), Vietnam, the Philippines, India, Ethiopia, or Somalia. Seventy percent of the high-tech manufacturing workers in the Valley are people of color. Elizabeth Gonzalez, a 24-year-old native of Santa Clara, California, a former assembly worker at Pemstar and now an undergraduate at Evergreen State College, wrote:

> Recent immigrants were [in the factory] because it was one of the few jobs they could get with their limited English. A lot of them wanted to take courses in school to become certified technicians and get higher pay. They played the weekly lottery and said every time, "If I win tonight, you won't see me tomorrow."[125]

But of course they are there the next day and the next. If the workers are divided by language, they are united by their conditions. "You know how to communicate around certain issues," Raj says of his interaction with the workers. "A universal language develops, particular words or phrases like 'overtime pay' or gestures like coughing (an indication of common respiratory problems)." The conditions bring these disparate workers together, something as deep as the links forged by a common diet or dress. Divided by language, but united by their conditions, these workers make our computers and other electronic goods. But these 258,000 workers in Silicon Valley (a third of the workforce) make only between six and eight dollars per hour. Many of these workers live in homeless shelters or else ride the bus all night. Women, who keep the clean industry clean, come into buildings at night and feel threatened by sexual violence. Marina Vargas, a 26-year-old migrant from Mexico City, works as a janitor at Semina Corporation, a major PC board maker in the Valley. She reports, "My boss likes the women to ask him 'Como estas papito? Y como te va? (How are you, Daddy? How's it going?). I don't say this, so he treats me differently. He doesn't work the women who say this as hard."[126]

Software workers don't necessarily enjoy better work conditions. Many young workers who are US nationals go into the dot.com world with enthusiasm and find themselves within "a volunteer low wage army." Here is cultural critic Andrew Ross's description of the software workers in New York's Silicon Alley:

> Deeply caffeinated 85-hour work weeks without overtime pay are a way of life for Webshop workers on flexible contracts, who invest a massive share of sweat equity in the mostly futile hope that their stock options will pay off. Even the lowliest employee feels like an entrepreneurial investor as a result. In most cases, the stock options turn into pink slips when the company goes belly-up, or, in some cases, employees are fired before their stock options are due to mature.

In Seattle, another home of software starving artists, the workers created WashTech, an affiliate of the Communication Workers of America (CWA). The goal of WashTech is to struggle with the problem of temporary work within the industry—a sign that labor is aware of the shifts in the economy. The concept of "flexibility" and management's creative use of technology has recreated the work structure in certain fields. The challenge for unions is how to craft militancy in the age of "flexibility," and that is just what the CWA, among others, is up to.

Most of the immigrants who work in the software end of things are here on H1B visas, an entry document that compels the worker to be obsequious to the management (who holds the right to fire the worker, and, therefore, deport the worker without recourse) and to be without the right to organize in a union. Labor contractors who bring the H1B workers to the US are known as "body-shoppers" and many of them charge up to 70 percent of the worker's wage as a commission.[127] Seventy-five percent of the workers are from India, many of them brought by Indian firms such as Tata Consultancy Services. Until 9/11, the rate of complaints about labor violations from H1B workers to the Department of Labor was on the rise: from a steady 50 complaints a year, the number jumped to over 100 in 2001. If the situation is bad for the pool of H1B workers, their spouses who come on H4 visas are even worse off. "If an H1 divorces an H4," says Sandhya Puranic who works on cases of domestic violence, "she is immediately considered deportable." New York City's Sakhi for South Asian Women reported 150 cases of H4 abuse in six months of 2000.[128]

The exports of the high-tech industry have doubled to about $40 billion from 1991 to 1998. Vinita Gupta of Digital Link Corp. says, "We were immigrants because we were risk takers. We left our safe land behind and came to this place looking for something bigger and better." Indian entrepreneurs make it, Ms. Gupta implies, because of the hard work of the migrants. Obviously the entrepreneurs work hard and are dynamic, but this is hardly the reason why the firms make such thumping profits. A 1999 study by the Public Policy Institute of California notes that the migrants do well because of "ethnic resources." [129] They mean professional and social networks that make possible exchange of information and that help access to capital. But the other "ethnic resource" is the exploitation of migrants; many of who are disciplined in much the same way as New York Chinatown's restaurateurs discipline their workers. We are Asian. This is a white country. Do not protest. Work hard to make Asians successful.

The anti-union dynamic of Silicon Valley runs along the same grain of the distorted nationalism of the Silicon Valley entrepreneurs. In the nation, 2.3 million workers toil in the high-tech manufacturing industry, the largest number of workers in any one sector. Yet, only 27 percent of these workers are in unions (in steel the number is 56.2 percent). Raj tells me that Bob Noyce, founder of Intel, wrote that to remain "non-union is essential for survival. If we had work rules that unionized companies have," Noyce wrote in 1984, "we'd all go out of business." Profits accrue from the toil of the workers. And can you imagine in our Alice in Wonderland world, we think that computers beget computers, that ideas make profits. We also believe that computers are a clean industry, that they are sleek and not environmentally as ghastly as the smokestack industry. Someone should tell this to the family of Rodrigo Cruz, who died of grievous brain damage at work in the Valley.[130]

There are enormous barriers to overcome, such as the weight of being the international labor aristocracy and of being part of the "American exceptionalist" universe (where, the theory runs, socialism is not possible because of the close relationship between workers and their overlords). The US Census of 2000 shows that the foreign born now account for almost a tenth of the population, and among the working class this is a higher figure. Such a fact leads us to anticipate a revolt against American exceptionalism, since many of these workers only come to the US after being displaced in their homelands by the will of US imperialism. The lie of the capitalist core is already unmasked in their previous lives, since many of them have deep connections with the workers overseas. The workers of the world enjoy a fragile unity; the point is to strengthen it.

1   Harold Meyerson, "A Second Chance: The New AFL-CIO and the
     Prospective Revival of American Labor," *Not Your Father's Union
     Movement: Inside the AFL-CIO*, Ed. Jo-Ann Mort, London: Verso, 1998.
2   Fred Garboury, "Kirkland dumped from AFL-CIO office," *People's
     Weekly World*, August 4, 1995.
3   Ruth Milkman and Kent Wong, "Organizing the Wicked City: The 1992
     Southern California Drywall Strike," *Organizing Immigrants. The Challenge
     for Unions in Contemporary California*, Ed. Ruth Milkman, Ithaca: Cornell
     University Press, 2000.
4   The AFL-CIO, however, still bears vestiges of protectionism in its policy
     claims (as well as a tendency to believe in the inevitability of the market).
     It fights against sweatshops in Mexico, but it is not clear if this is toward
     the growth of union and worker power there or to end wage competition
     between the Mexican and US worker (or indeed to fight for socialism).
     The main AFL-CIO agency against sweatshops is UNITE (the garment
     workers union), but this union does little to combat sweatshops within
     the US that are frequently union shops, mainly to prevent job loss: the
     logic of job preservation is a relic of business unionism and it often
     curtails the movement. To be wary of these changes is healthy because
     Sweeney's own account of US labor history suggests that the 1950s was
     the heyday of the movement, when in fact that decade set the stage for
     the racist business unionism of the Cold War era. A clear indication of
     the protectionism in the AFL-CIO is in its anti-China campaign. Kent
     Wong and Elaine Bernard's "Labor's Mistaken Anti-China Campaign"
     offers the arguments against the AFL-CIO anti-China position, while
     Mark Levinson and Thea Lee's "Why Labor Made the Right Decision"
     defends the AFL-CIO. Both articles appeared in *New Labor Forum*, no. 7,
     Fall/Winter 2000.
5   Ross Levine, "Stock Markets: A Spur to Economic Growth," *Finance &
     Development*, vol. 33, no. 1, March 1996, p. 7.
6   There is a long-standing debate over whether the stock market
     contributes to genuine economic growth and whether there are socially
     better ways to raise funds for economic activity. In a survey of twelve
     papers presented to a World Bank conference on "Stock Markets,
     Corporate Finance and Economic Growth," Ross Levine notes that
     while banks do provide a crucial service, stock markets do provide some
     value as well. "Stock markets offer opportunities primarily for trading
     risk and boosting liquidity; in contrast, banks focus on establishing
     long-term relationships with firms because they seek to acquire
     information about projects and managers and enhance corporate
     control." Levine, "Stock Markets," pp. 9–10.
7   Doug Henwood, author of the most useful summary of the world of
     stocks, points out that in the nineteenth Century, the stock market became

an instrument to settle matters around the ownership of the productive capacity of the nation, recently bought up by monopoly firms from the hard working people of Main Street. "Late 19th Century promoters," he writes, "also thought of the market as a way to ease the burden on small producers who were being displaced or enveloped by corporatization: modest stock holdings were a compensation for the loss of real capital ownership." Henwood, *Wall Street: How It Works and For Whom*, London: Verso Books, 1997, p. 14.

8   The logic of economic populism expounded in our time has been thoroughly upended by Thomas Frank, *One Market Under God: Extreme Capitalism, Market Populism and the End of Economic Democracy*, New York: Doubleday, 2000.

9   Gretchen Morgenson, "Another Slap at Democracy on Wall St.," *New York Times*, September 15, 2002.

10   "What the firms were really dispensing," writes Morgenson, "was free money." Morgenson, "Another Slap at Democracy on Wall Street." For this and more I am indebted to Gretchen Morgenson's column "Market Watch" in the *New York Times*.

11   This data and analysis is from Lawrence Mishel, Jared Bernstein, and Heather Boushey, *The State of Working America 2002/2003*, Washington: Economic Policy Institute and Ithaca: Cornell University Press, 2003.

12   "Recent Changes in US Family Finances: Results from the 1998 Survey of Consumer Finances," *Federal Reserve Bulletin*, January 2000, p. 22.

13   "Recent Changes," pp. 23–24.

14   "Recent Changes," pp. 20–21 (Table 11).

15   The racism in the home loan market continues. In California, one seven-year study shows us that while the number of home loans to nonwhites increased, African Americans continued to have an enormously hard time securing the capital to build their personal equity. California Reinvestment Committee, *Who Really Gets Home Loans? Year Seven*, San Francisco: CRC, 2000.

16   "Recent Changes," p. 26.

17   Henwood, *Wall Street*, p. 65.

18   Since 1980, individual bankruptcies have skyrocketed, from about 1,500 in 1980 to close to 7,000 in 2000, and personal debt as a percentage of personal income has gone up enormously in the same period, from about 70 percent to over 110 percent. Much of the access to credit can be via rapacious credit cards that charge enormously high interest rates. Karen Alexander, "Minefields Abound in Attempts to Reduce Debt," *New York Times*, September 22, 2002.

19   Vijay Prashad, "Another America," *Frontline*, vol. 16, issue 23, November 6–19, 1999.

20   On September 24, 2002, the US Census Bureau announced that the number of people below the poverty line is now 32.9 million—about

11.7 percent. How do we get to 33 percent? For its poverty line threshold, the government takes the figure of $18,104 (for a family of four) and $14,128 (for a family of three). This is far too low. Living wage campaigns across the country take a standard that is about 200 percent of the poverty line, so that would make it about $36,208 (for a family of four) and $28,256 (for a family of three). Almost a third of the population, then, lives below the livable wage poverty line.

21 Molly Ivins, "Hoping to Make 2 Americas into 1," *Abilene Reporter-News*, June 26, 1997.

22 For an extensive treatment of the structural problem of corporate imperialism, see my *Fat Cats*.

23 Geoffrey Colvin, "The Great CEO Pay Heist," *Fortune*, June 25, 2001.

24 David Leonhart, "Options Math: Why So Much to So Few?" *New York Times*, February 16, 2003.

25 Geraldine Fabrikant, "GE Expenses for Ex-Chief Cited in Filing," *New York Times*, September 6, 2002.

26 Andrew Ross Sorkin, "Tyco Details Lavish Lives of Executives," *New York Times*, September 18, 2002 and James B. Stewart, "Spend! Spend! Spend! Where did Tyco's Money Go?" *New Yorker*, February, 17 and 24, 2003.

27 Rakesh Khurana, *Searching for a Corporate Savior: The Irrational Quest for Charismatic CEOs*, Princeton: Princeton University Press, 2002.

28 Kevin Chauvin and Catherine Shenoy, "Stock Price Decreases Prior to Executive Stock Options Grants," *Journal of Corporate Finance*, no. 7, 2001 and Joseph Blasi, Douglas Kruse, and Aaron Bernstein, *In the Company of Owners: The Truth About Stock Options (And Why Every Employee Should Have Them)*, New York: Basic Books, 2003.

29 For an excellent overview of CEO compensation, see Scott Klinger, *The Bigger They Come, the Harder They Fall: High CEO Pay and the Effect on Long-Term Stock Prices*, Boston: United for a Fair Economy, 2001.

30 David Leonhardt and Geraldine Fabrikant, "Many Chiefs Are Retaining Extra Benefits in Retirement," *New York Times*, September 11, 2002.

31 Jeffrey H. Birnbaum, "Washington Power 25: Fat and Happy in DC," *Fortune*, May 28, 2001. The list is available on-line at "The Power 25: Top Lobbying Groups," www.fortune.com/lists/power25.index.html.

32 Ken Silverstein, *Washington on $10 Million a Day: How Lobbyists Plunder the Nation*, Monroe: Common Courage, 1998, p. 4.

33 Thorsten Veblen, *The Theory of the Leisure Class*, Harmondsworth: Penguin, 1979, chapter 4.

34 W. Elliot Brownlee, *Federal Taxation in America: A Short History*, Washington: Woodrow Wilson Center Press and New York: Cambridge University Press, 1996. It is important to note that when the tax reappeared in 1910, it was pushed by the monopolies essentially to garner sufficient funds to set up a central bank that would work for the

interests of the monopoly firms. The history of the 16th Amendment is one that is studied by all.

35   *Apex Hosiery v. Leader*, 310 US 469 (1940).

36   The Edith Wharton quote is from chapter 8 of her *Touchstone*, New York: Scribner, 1900; the Populist Party statement is known as the Omaha Platform and it can be found in *A Populist Reader: Selections from the Works of American Populist Leaders*, Ed. George Tindall, New York: Harper & Row, 1966, pp. 90–96.

37   Reagan made this great statement on April 15, 1982 before the students at St. Peter's Catholic Elementary School in Geneva, Illinois. The entire conversation can be accessed at www.reagan.utexas.edu/resource/speeches /1982/41582b.htm.

38   Robert Brenner, "The Economics of Global Turbulence: A Special Report on the World Economy, 1950–98," *New Left Review*, no. 229, May/June 1998, p. 182. The argument regarding the United States is elaborated in his *The Boom and the Bubble: The US in the World Economy*, London: Verso, 2002. I am indebted to Lisa Armstrong (Women's Studies at Smith College) for a decade-long tuition on this theme. Oliver Stone's *Wall Street* (1987) is the cinematic commentary on the culture of the adjustment, while Tom Wolfe's *Bonfire of the Vanities* (1987) offers us the prose of the counterrevolution of property.

39   The idea of the "factory desert" is from Marco Revelli, *Lavorare in FIAT*, Milan: Garzanti, 1989.

40   Brenner, "The Economics of Global Turbulence," p. 182.

41   Louis Uchitelle, "Stagnant Wages Pose Added Risks to Weak Economy," *New York Times*, August 11, 2002.

42   Lawrence Mishel, Jared Bernstein, and John Schmitt, *The State of Working America, 2000/2001*, Ithaca: Cornell University Press and Economic Policy Institute, 2001, p. 98.

43   Gretchen Morgenson, "Missing the Mark in 2000: Stocks Look for a Steadying Hand Ahead," *New York Times*, January 2, 2001.

44   Gretchen Morgenson, "How Did So Many Get It So Wrong? As they do little but shout 'buy,' analysts often send investors astray," *New York Times*, December 31, 2000.

45   Allen J. Beck, *Prisoners in 1999*, Washington, DC: Bureau of Justice Statistics, August 2000.

46   Marc Mauer and Tracy Huling, *Young Black Americans and the Criminal Justice System: Five Years Later*, Washington, DC: The Sentencing Project, October 1995.

47   Langston Hughes, *The Big Sea*, New York: Hill and Wang, 1963, p. 247.

48   For example, John Berry, "Greenspan: Restore Fiscal Discipline to Balance Budget," *Washington Post*, February 11, 2003.

49   Eric Schlosser, *Fast Food Nation: The Dark Side of the All-American Meal*, New York: Perennial, 2002, p. 72.

50   World Bank, *Global Economic Prospects and the Developing Countries 2001*, Washington, DC: World Bank Group, 2001. Apart from the United States, the only other country to record ceaseless industrial growth was, of course, the People's Republic of China.

51   Early indications of the "post-industrial" and "jobless growth" condition of our present comes to us from Alain Touraine, *The Post Industrial Society*, New York: Random House, 1971. Jeremy Rifkin believes that "jobless growth" means that the workers will now have more leisure as technological shifts will allow for greater productivity and less time on the job. *The End of Work: The Decline of the Global Labor Force and the Dawn of the Post-Market Era*, New York: Putnam, 1995. Stanley Aronowitz and William DeFazio argue that technological improvements do not increase leisure, rather they intensify exploitation and cast off a vast number of people outside the workforce: *The Jobless Future: Sci-Tech and the Dogma of Work*, Minneapolis: University of Minnesota Press, 1994. Aronowitz and DeFazio argue that we should fight for a shorter work week in order to create the leisure future that Rifkin suggests is our present.

52   Michael Piore argues that the "sweatshop" is defined by low fixed costs and the mode of labor organization. "The Economics of the Sweatshop," *No Sweat: Fashion, Free Trade, and the Rights of Garment Workers*, Ed. Andrew Ross, London: Verso, 1997.

53   Maria Mies, et. al., *Women: The Last Colony*, New Delhi: Kali, 1988, p. 10 and Mies, *Patriarchy and Accumulation on a World Scale: Women in the International Division of Labour*, London: Zed Books, 1999.

54   Philip Corrigan, "Feudal Relics or Capitalist Monuments? Notes on the Sociology of Unfree Labour," *Sociology*, vol. 11, 1977.

55   Cited in Andrew Ross, *No Sweat*, p. 12. I have omitted agricultural work from this précis on the sweatshop. The GAO accepts that the field is as much a sweatshop as the factory: GAO, *Child Labor in Agriculture: Characteristics and Legality of Work*, Washington, DC: GAO, 1998 (GAO/HEHS-98-112R).

56   For an excellent ethnographic look at sweatshops in the US, see Gregory Scott, "Sewing with Dignity: Class Struggle and Ethnic Conflict in the Los Angeles Garment Industry," Santa Barbara: University of California, Santa Barbara, Department of Sociology, Ph. D., 1998.

57   Andrew Ross, *No-Collar: The Humane Workplace and Its Hidden Costs. Behind the Myth of the New Office Utopia*, New York: Basic Books, 2003, and Louise Kapp Howe, *Pink Collar Workers: Inside the World of Women's Work*, New York: Putnam, 1977.

58   Robert W. Cox, *Production, Power and World Order: Social Forces in the Making of History*, New York: Columbia University Press, 1987, p. 344.

59   Alain Lipietz, *Mirages and Miracles: The Crisis of Global Fordism*, London: Verso, 1987, pp. 78–79.

60   Jesse Jackson, "You Do Not Stand Alone," speech in New York City, July 14, 1992.

61   These quotes are from Robert Cotter and Maureen Costello's documentary, *Hamlet: The Untold Tragedy*, screened at Harvard University. For more information, contact 02 Productions, PO Box 16651, Chapel Hill, NC 27514.

62   An early analysis of this condition is in Harry Braverman, *Labor and Monopoly Capitalism: The Degradation of Work in the Twentieth Century*, New York: Monthly Review Press, 1974. For an update, with a sense of how even the most computerized workplaces are part of the sweatshop economy, see Barbara Garson, *The Electronic Sweatshop: How Computers are Transforming the Office of the Future into the Factory of the Past*, New York: Penguin Books, 1988.

63   Michael Harrington, *The Other America*, New York: MacMillan, 1962, p. 191.

64   Francis Fox Piven and Richard A. Cloward, *Poor People's Movements. Why They Succeed, How They Fail*, New York: Vintage, 1979, pp. 267–70.

65   For a shocking look at the poverty wages earned by most of the workers in a narcotics gang, see Steven D. Levitt and Sudhir Venkatesh, "An Economic Analysis of a Drug-Selling Gang's Finances," *The Quarterly Journal of Economics*, August 2000, pp. 755–89.

66   On the economics of care, I recommend Nancy Folbre, *The Invisible Heart: Economics and Family Values*, New York: The New Press, 2001, and (from a more philosophical standpoint) Elizabeth V. Spelman, *Repair: The Impulse to Restore in a Fragile World*, Boston: Beacon Press, 2002.

67   *Business Week*, August 25, 1997.

68   For more data, see "Wealth News," *Left Business Observer*, no. 94, May 5, 2000, p. 3 and p. 5.

69   Woodrow Ginsburg, *Income and Inequality: 8 Years of Prosperity, Millions Left Behind*, Washington, DC: Americans for Democratic Action, January 1999.

70   Jared Mishel, Lawrence Bernstein, and John Schmitt, *The State of Working America, 2000/2001*, Chapter 2, and Marlene Kim, "Women Paid Low Wages," *Monthly Labor Review*, vol. 123, no. 9, September 2000.

71   Barbara Ehrenreich's book, *Nickle and Dimed*, is the best current ethnography of the war over time and space in the service workplace, but for details, see Schlosser, *Fast Food Nation*, pp. 59–88.

72   Robert B. Reich, *The Work of Nations*, New York: Vintage, 1992, p. 174. All citations in this paragraph come from this book.

73   The AFL-CIO divided the workforce into four categories: core, skilled workforce; skilled peripheral workforce; unskilled core workforce; and unskilled peripheral workforce. Skilled workers include professionals, technicians, and skilled craftspersons that have either full-time jobs with benefits (core workers) or else they work as consultants, freelancers, temporary employees, agency employees, or contingent workers. The latter do not have a stable workplace, but they have a stable occupation (the occupation will now be the focus of union activity rather than the shop floor). Unskilled work includes the occupations that have now been rendered deskilled, such as restaurant workers, hotel workers, nursing aides, and garment workers. "These unskilled workers are completely vulnerable to what has become an integral part of the anti-union campaign: the permanent replacement threat." AFL-CIO, *Union Survival Strategies for the Twenty-First Century*, Washington, DC: AFL-CIO, 1996.

74 National Alliance for Fair Employment, *Contingent Workers Fight for Fairness*, Boston: NAFE, 2000, pp. 11–12.

75 Anna E. Polivka, "A Profile of Contingent Workers," *Monthly Labor Review*, October 1996.

76 "A Different Look at Part-Time Employment," *Issues in Labor Statistics*, Department of Labor, Bureau of Labor Statistics, April 1996, and Jackie Chu, Sonya Smallets, and Jill Braunstein, *The Economic Impact of Contingent Work on Women and Their Families*, Washington, DC: Institute for Women's Policy Research, 1995.

77 Polivka, "A Profile," p. 19, summarizes Lonnie Goldstein and Eileen Applebaum's, "What Was Driving the 1982–1988 Boom in Temporary Employment," *American Journal of Economics and Sociology*, October 1992, p. 473.

78 In the current process of stabilization, there are predominantly three components: Structural Adjustment Programs in the Third World and in Eastern Europe, technological developments of "smart weapons," and downsizing in businesses in the overdeveloped world. For the purposes of this short book, I am not going to conduct an analysis of the first two components of US stabilization since there is much good work on that found elsewhere. I have covered some of this ground in *Fat Cats and Running Dogs*.

79 David Talbot, "Sky-High Hub Rents Change Face of City," *Boston Herald*, January 3, 1999; David Benda, "City's Supply of Affordable Housing is Drying Up," *Redding Record Searchlight*, December 11, 2000; Hisham Aidi, "A 'Second Renaissance' in Harlem?" *Africana.Com*, December 18, 2000; Brian J. Rogal, "Real Estate Boom Threatens Affordable Housing Options," *Chicago Reporter*, November/December 2000.

80 Gregory Jaynes, "Down and Out in Telluride," *Time*, September 5, 1994, pp. 60–61.

81 Ibid.

82   US Department of Housing and Urban Development, *Homelessness: Programs and the People They Serve. Findings of the National Survey of Homeless Assistance Providers and Clients*, Washington, DC: HUD, December 1999.

83   Leslie Kaufman and Kevin Flynn, "New York's Homeless, Back Out in the Open," *New York Times*, October 13, 2002.

84   Robert J. Mills (US Census Bureau), "Current Population Reports: Health Insurance Coverage (1999)," Washington, DC: US Commerce Department, September 2000.

85   When George Bush was governor of Texas, he fought to reduce the number of children eligible for the CHIP program. The Bush people found that when low-income or unemployed parents brought their children to register for CHIP many found that they did not make enough money to sign up for the program, but that they could qualify for Medicaid. "When Bush realized the legislators weren't going to deny 200,000 kids health insurance, his office began to fight for separate applications for CHIP and Medicaid. In other words, if CHIP applicants qualified for Medicaid, they would have to make an appointment at a Medicaid office and fill out another application. And that application is difficult and complicated, requiring applicants to prove they have less than $2,000 in total assets. 'All the studies show that 66 percent never return,' [State Representative Austin] Maxey said." Molly Ivins and Lou Dubose, *Shrub: The Short but Happy Political Life of George W. Bush*, New York: Vintage, 2000, p. 95.

86   Amy Snow Landa, "Uninsured Ranks Are Predicted to Jump," *AMA News*, December 10, 2001.

87   Christian Parenti, *Lockdown America: Police and Prisons in the Age of Crisis*, London: Verso, 1999, pp. 238–42.

88   During periods of stagnation the reserve army of labor, Marx noted, "weighs down the active army of workers; during the periods of overproduction and feverish activity, it puts a curb on their pretensions." The "despotism of capital" is revealed as the demand/supply equation shows that "capital acts on both sides at once," not on one side with labor on the other. "*Les dés sont pipés*," Marx wrote, the dice is loaded. Karl Marx, *Capital. Volume I*, London: Penguin, 1976, pp. 792–93.

89   Richard Rorty, *Achieving Our Country: Leftist Thought in Twentieth Century America*, Cambridge: Harvard University Press, 1998, and Todd Gitlin, *The Twilight of Common Dreams: Why America is Wracked by Culture Wars*, New York: Metropolitan Books, 1995.

90   Dave Roediger, "Mumia Time or Sweeney Time," *New Politics*, vol. VII, no. 4, Winter 2000, pp. 11–15.

91   Cynthia Young, "Punishing Labor: Why Labor Should Oppose the Prison Industrial Complex," *New Labor Forum*, no. 7, Fall/Winter 2000, p. 49.

92 For background on Local 2, a feisty union, see Mariam J. Wells, "Immigration and Unionization in the San Francisco Hotel Industry," *Organizing Immigrants.*

93 Lea Grundy and Netsy Firestein, "Bargaining for Families," *New Labor Forum*, no. 2, Spring 1998, pp. 22–23.

94 Laureen Lazarovici, "How Can I Take Care of My Family and Do My Job? Strategies for creating a family friendly workplace," *America@Work*, February 2000.

95 While the volume does not delve into the role of Local 2, I strongly recommend Kitty Krupat and Patrick McCreery's edited book, *Out At Work: Building a Gay-Labor Alliance*, Minneapolis: University of Minnesota, 2001.

96 For the California story, see Allan Heskin's *Tenants and the American Dream: Ideology and the Tenant Movement*, New York: Praeger, 1983.

97 Jocelyn Y. Stewart, "Union unveils $100 million plan to help workers buy homes," *Los Angeles Times*, July 19, 2002.

98 Stephen Coyle, *Out of Reach*, Washington: National Low Income Housing Coalition, September 1999, "Preface."

99 For an overview of the struggle, written by two Teamsters, see Matt Witt and Rand Wilson, "Part-Time America Won't Work: The Teamsters' Fight for Good Jobs at UPS," *Not Your Father's Union Movement: Inside the AFL-CIO*, Ed. Jo-Ann Mort, London: Verso, 1998.

100 Bush II did use the Taft-Hartley Act in October 2002 to break the lockout by port owners in their dispute with the Longshoremen.

101 Paul Buhle, *Taking Care of Business: Samuel Gompers, George Meany, Lane Kirkland and the Tragedy of American Labor*, New York: Monthly Review Press, 1999.

102 "Half a Job is Not Enough," Teamsters' handout, June 1997, also analyzed in Witt and Wilson, "Part-Time America," *Not Your Father's Union Movement*, pp. 183-185.

103 Indeed, this was predicted by Thaddeus Russell, "'Restore Teamster Power: Militancy, Democracy and the IBT," *New Labor Forum*, no. 4, Spring/Summer 1999: "The evidence presented here indicates that even an 'empty suit' like Junior, facing a restive membership and unrelenting opposition, would have no choice but to take on UPS with the full force of the union's power," p. 120. Russell, in his longer account, makes too much of the powerful leader and dismisses the importance of rank and file militancy, of union democracy. He also minimizes the role of the new energy in the 1997 strike, arguing that it was really a victory for the long-dead Hoffa Senior. This is not viable. Thaddeus Russell, *Out of the Jungle: Jimmy Hoffa and the Remaking of the American Working Class*, New York: Random House, 2001.

104 My analysis is significantly weaker than the major study by Biju Mathew, *Taxi! Cabs and Capitalism in New York City*, New York: Verso, 2003. When

I first wrote of the strike for *ColorLines* and *Frontline,* Biju Mathew guided me into the material with patience and generosity. Parts of this section appeared in the final chapter of my *Karma of Brown Folk,* Minneapolis: University of Minnesota Press, 2000.

105 At the other end of the country, Margaret Zamudio, in a superb dissertation, found much the same thing among the immigrant Latino workers at the Kajima Corporation (Japan) owned New Otani Hotel in Los Angeles. As immigrant labor and nonresident capital battled it out in the streets of LA before a public routinely afraid of both, the conversations about ethnicity did not allow it to become the xenophobic subtext in the struggle. Margaret Zamudio, "Organizing the New Otani Hotel in Los Angeles: The Role of Ethnicity, Race and Citizenship in Class Formation," Los Angeles: University of California, LA, Ph. D., 1996.

106 Much of this draws from my article "The Hunt for Mexicans," *Frontline,* June 23, 2000, but for details on immigrant organizing, see Hector Figueroa, "Back to the Forefront: Union Organization of Immigrant Workers in the Nineties," *Not Your Father's Union Movement,* and Rachel Sherman and Kim Voss, "Organize or Die: Labor's New Tactics and Immigrant Workers," *Organizing Immigrants.*

107 Duncan Campbell, "New Freedom Ride for America's Illegal Workers," *Guardian,* August 12, 2002.

108 "Gephardt Is Preparing a Measure to Legalize Illegal Immigrants," *New York Times,* July 23, 2002.

109 For an excellent overview, see Gary Delgado, "How the Empress Gets Her Clothes: Asian Immigrant Women Fight Fashion Designer Jessica McClintock," *Beyond Identity Politics: Emerging Social Justice Movements in Communities of Color,* Ed. John Anner, Boston: South End Press, 1996.

110 Like many community organizations, AIWA produced a newsletter (*AIWA News*), it pursued a sophisticated media strategy (and therefore got into the local and national news), and one of its pioneer workers and program associates, Miriam Ching Yoon Louie, wrote an excellent book that placed AIWA on the map of feminist immigrant organizations. See Miriam Ching Yoon Louie, *Sweatshop Warriors: Immigrant Women Workers Take on the Global Factory,* Cambridge: South End Press, 2001, and her earlier paper that provides the political economy of the sweatshop, "Immigrant Asian Women in Bay Area Garment Sweatshops: 'After Sewing, Laundry, Cleaning and Cooking, I Have No Breath Left to Sing,'" *Amerasia Journal,* vol. 18, no. 1, 1992. In a brief history of the 1996-founded United Students Against Sweatshops, AIWA appears as a pioneer in the anti-sweatshop struggle, alongside groups like New York City's Chinese Staff and Workers Association, Texas's La Mujer Obrera, and New York City's National Labor Committee. Liza Featherstone (and USSA), *Students Against Sweatshops*, London: Verso, 2002, p. 8.

111 "Asian and Latina Immigrant Women Come Together," *AIWA News*, vol. 17, no. 2, December 2001, p. 3.

112 Sarah Henry, "Labor and Lace: Can an Upstart Women's Group Press a new Wrinkle into the Rag Trade Wars?" *Los Angeles Times Magazine*, August 1, 1993, p. 22.

113 AIWA did not pioneer this approach, because anti-sweatshop campaigns in LA had already gone after the manufacturers, as was the case in the campaign against En Chante/Su Enterprises/Addison Fashions in 1990. See Sonni Efron, "Targets Get Bigger in Sweatshop War," *Los Angeles Times*, February 5, 1990 and the analysis by Harry Bernstein, "Sweatshops a Complex Problem," *Los Angeles Times*, July 10, 1990. The legislature sent Governor Pete Wilson a bill to make manufacturers liable for the infractions of subcontractors, but Wilson refused to sign it into law. "A Fair and Square Deal," *Los Angeles Times*, February 21, 1992.

114 Kelly Gust, "No Frills Given," *Oakland Tribune*, October 14, 1992.

115 Gust, "No Frills Given." This problem is general across the industry, as shown in an investigation by Susan Headden, "Made in the USA," *US News and World Report*, November 22, 1993, pp. 54–55 and by Sarah Henry, "Labor and Lace."

116 *We Are the Ones*, p. 49.

117 Brenda Payton, "Meek No More," *Oakland Tribune*, May 6, 1993.

118 Kam Sung, "AIWA's Youth Lead the 'Girl'cott Against DKNY," *AIWA News*, vol. 17, no. 1, May 2001, pp. 4–5.

119 For a description of the 2001 program, "Another Successful Summer Youth Internship at AIWA," *AIWA News*, vol. 17, no. 2, December 2001.

120 Nancy Snyder, "Organizing Among Friends: Asian Health Services Unionizes," *Third Force*, vol. 5, no. 4, September/October 1997, pp. 28–29.

121 Raj Jayadev, "Learning to Listen—Unions Must Tap Power of Today's Young Workers," *Pacific News Service*, December 16, 2001.

122 Jayadev, "Learning to Listen."

123 Steven Greenhouse, "The Most Innovative Figure in Silicon Valley? Maybe This Labor Organizer," *New York Times*, November 14, 1999.

124 Héctor Delgado, "The Los Angeles Manufacturing Action Project: An Opportunity Squandered," *Organizing Immigrants*.

125 Elizabeth Gonzalez, "Mindless Monotony," *De-Bug*, February 2001.

126 Marina Vargas, "Cleaning the Clean Industry," *De-Bug*, February 2001.

127 Sarah Lubman, "Middlemen Thriving in Lucrative Industry While Foreign Workers Complain of Abuse," *San Jose Mercury News*, November 19, 2000.

128 Lakshmi Chaudhry, "Immigrant Wives of Silicon Alley Seek Protection from Battering," *Village Voice*, October 2000, pp. 4–10.

129 *The Silicon Valley Reader: Localizing the Effects of the Global Economy*, Edited by Raj Jayadev and Lisa Juachon. Available from JustAct: justact@justact.org or 415-431-4204.

130 For more information on the environmental costs of computers, visit the Silicon Valley Toxics Coalition's website at www.svtc.org.

PRISON

"See in the ghetto the sun it barely shines
But so many nags in jail and the welfare lines
And all my life I thought Bill Clinton ran the country
Until I found out Bill Gates had all the money."

—Mystikal, "Ghetto Child," *Unpredictable*, 1997

"A political event is reduced to a criminal event in order to
affirm the absolute invulnerability of the existing order."

—Angela Y. Davis[1]

On November 13, 1993, President Bill Clinton stood at the pulpit of the Church of God in Christ in Memphis, Tennessee, where Martin Luther King, Jr. gave his final address. After he thanked the largely black congregation for their support in the 1992 elections, Clinton touted his economic policy initiatives and his attempt to bring African Americans into the administration. King, said Clinton, would be proud of the developments since his death in 1968. But there was one thing that would rankle him if he were here. Speaking in his voice, Clinton told his audience:

> But he would say, I did not live and die to see the American
> family destroyed. I did not live and die to see 13-year-old
> boys get automatic weapons and gun down 9-year-olds just
> for the kick of it. I did not live and die to see young people
> destroy their own lives with drugs and then build fortunes
> destroying the lives of others. That is not what I came here
> to do. I fought for freedom, he would say, but not for the
> freedom of people to kill each other with reckless abandon;
> not for the freedom of children to have children and the
> fathers of the children walk away from them and abandon

them as if they don't amount to anything. I fought for people to have the right to work, but not to have whole communities and people abandoned. This is not what I lived and died for. My fellow Americans, he would say, I fought to stop white people from being so filled with hate that they would wreak violence on black people. I did not fight for the right of black people to murder other black people with reckless abandon.

The problem in the US, Clinton emphasized, is not the dynamic of corporate power, nor the racism and sexism that defrauds millions of people from social and political power, nor yet the enormous sums of public money that support an international military that does the bidding of global corporations. The problem, for Clinton, is the collapse of the black family and the consequent "black on black" violence. Clinton put these words in King's mouth. On April 4, 1967, exactly one year before he was assassinated, King stood before a congregation at the Riverside Church in New York City to offer his own analysis of the futility of life among the black working class:

As I have walked among the desperate, rejected, and angry young men, I have told them that Molotov cocktails and rifles would not solve their problems. I have tried to offer them my deepest compassion while maintaining my conviction that social change comes most meaningfully through non-violent action. But, they asked, what about Vietnam? They asked if our own nation wasn't using massive doses of violence to solve its problems to bring about changes it wanted. Their question hit home, and I knew that I could never again raise my voice against the violence of the oppressed in the ghettos without having first spoken clearly to the greatest purveyor of violence in the world today—my government.[2]

Furthermore, King said, "Our only hope today lies in our ability to recapture the revolutionary spirit and go out into a sometimes hostile world declaring eternal hostility to poverty, racism, and militarism." This was the context of King's call for an "economic bill of rights" and for a "poor people's march" to Washington, DC, in the summer of 1968.

Bill Clinton's ventriloquism of King transformed the civil rights leader into another neoconservative who believed that the problems of racism are lodged not in the structures of economics and political power, but in the imputed family dysfunction of blacks themselves. When King read Daniel P. Moynihan's influential report on the black family (1965), he did not unequivocally condemn it as many of his aides suggested. Rather, King felt that the report provided "dangers and opportunities." King had already written of the trials of life in the working-class black neighborhoods in language that can only be called depressing: "The shattering blows on the Negro family have made it fragile, deprived and often psychopathic. Nothing is so much needed as a secure family life for a people to pull themselves out of poverty and backwardness." King saw that the report provided the opportunity to garner cash for his program of renewal, for housing loans and health care, for jobs and parks, for recreation and reproduction. The danger, he felt, was that "problems will be attributed to innate Negro weakness and used to justify, neglect, and rationalize oppression."[3] King's optimism was unwarranted.

Ten days after his appearance at the Memphis church, Clinton stood in a school playground in east Los Angeles to address a mainly Latino audience. If he forced words into King's mouth at Memphis, here he did the same with Cesar Chavez. "Think how horrified he would be, God rest his soul, if he were here today and could pick up the paper and read about the two-year-old child being killed [in a shootout between gangs]," said Clinton. Chavez, he continued, "was a devotee of non-violence and self-sacrifice, not violence and self-indulgence." Drawing from this legacy, Clinton told the Latino leadership, "We are doing everything we can to try to give you the tools you need to try to make your community safer. But we have to make up our minds that we will no longer tolerate children killing children; children having guns and being better armed than police officers; neighborhoods unsafe. We can do better."[4] As he did with King, Clinton distorted the heritage of Chavez, who told writer Peter Matthiessen, on August 9, 1968, "The real problem we have in America is whether or not we are becoming a police state. And if we do, the Negroes will get it first."[5]

The danger King and Chavez warned us about came to pass on November 19, 1993, when the US Senate passed the Violent Crime Control and Law Enforcement Act (the "Crime Bill") at the initiative of President Clinton and the Democratic Party. The act, formally signed in 1994, created a $30.2 billion Crime Trust Fund to support the measures that filled up this long piece of legislation. Not one item in the

Crime Bill came from King's agenda. Everything was about law and order, about the mechanisms that the police use "to justify, neglect, and rationalize oppression." The provisions of the Bill are straightforward:

- More Police: $8.8 billion for 100,000 more officers to hit the streets and $1.2 billion for 4,000 new Border Patrol officers to hit the border.
- More Prisons: $7.9 billion for the states to build more prisons and an additional $1.8 billion for the incarceration of "criminal aliens." These "criminal aliens," or a subsection of them called "suspected alien terrorists," could, by the Bill's provisions, be tried with "secret evidence."
- More Prisoners: Longer sentences for those arrested for drug possession and sale, and less opportunity for parole. The Bill allowed children under 14 to be tried in court as adults and, as such, block up the prisons.
- More Capital Punishment: The number of federal death penalty offenses increased from two to 60.

The press told us that the bill responded to the needs of the American people. However, in February 1993, only four percent of those surveyed by *Time* magazine said "crime" was a primary concern. By January 1994, after the hoopla over the Crime Bill hit the newsstands in August 1993, the numbers jumped to 19 percent. Even as criminal acts either decreased or leveled off, the moral panic engendered by the Crime Bill made "the criminal" the new enemy of the US "individual" and it was this "criminal" who became the replacement of the "communist" as the Cold War ended in 1991. The deliberations around "crime" and the Crime Bill allowed the US public to believe that "crime" is a major problem and that they must support the extensions of the law and order apparatus, even if this means that everyday life becomes regimented by military order. As the bull market continued its ascent, and as inequality spiraled upwards, the US government, who subscribes to neoliberal principles, had a proposal to deal with the unrest and anger of the poor: jail them, or else, by the application of racist standards, allow blacks to bear the brunt of the malevolent public policy while the white workers find some comfort in their "freedom."

THE RACISM OF "CRIME"

In the fall of 1994, as the Crime Bill came into operation, a white woman named Susan Smith went to the police in Union, South Carolina, and told them that a black carjacker stopped her at an intersection, brandished a gun, threw her out of her car, and sped off with her children. The country was transfixed. People across the country prayed for the Smiths and many people came around to the wisdom of the Crime Bill. Beverly Russell, a leader in the local Republican Party and the Christian Coalition, as well as the lost children's step-grandfather, asked the nation to join the Smiths in their prayers. Then, a few months later, as the police interrogated Smith about inconsistencies in her story, she confessed to the murder of her children and to the fabrication.

"What we see here," wrote award-winning columnist Robert Scheer, "is the other side of the Norman Rockwell painting that was always there."[6] It turned out that Susan Smith's father committed suicide during a messy divorce, that Beverly Russell married her mother when she was 13, that Russell began to sexually harass her when she was 15, that she attempted suicide at 17 because of this, that Russell repeatedly raped her after her marriage to David Smith, that she had an abortion during the marriage, that her marriage to David Smith was not pleasant and that she had started an affair with Tom Findlay and found her children to be a hindrance in her life. No one talked about dysfunction here, only of the tragic circumstances of this white woman's life.

That she had initially blamed a black man for the crime reminded people of Charles Stuart, a prominent white Bostonian who shot his wife, then blamed a black man for the crime. The Boston police, well-known for their racism,[7] locked down the Roxbury area of South Boston, harassed scores of black men, until finally, thinking that the police would eventually get him, Charles Stuart jumped to his death off the Tobin Bridge.[8] In both cases, the public initially accepted as normal that a black man would randomly kill whites or else rob them with excessive violence. Black men are dangerous, was the message, particularly when they are young. Before Stuart's suicide, the police found a scapegoat for the murder. During their dragnet, the Boston police intimidated and harmed a 63-year-old woman, scoured her apartment, and then arrested her son, Willie Bennett, as the perpetrator. A month later, Stuart picked Bennett out of a lineup and all things seemed to move toward a conviction and then an execution. Until Stuart killed himself, that is, and then Bennett was released to a South Boston torn up by the racism of the entire affair. That the killers here were a white woman and a white man did not do much to change the basic framework within which crime is seen in the country.

At the same time as these murders, the country experienced a spate of school shootings. The first such in recent times took place in Olivehurst, California, on May 1, 1992, when Eric Huston, age 20, entered his former high school, killed four people, and wounded ten more as a riposte for a bad grade. Less than a year later, on January 18, 1993, Scott Pennington, age 18, took a gun into his English class at East Carter High School in Grayson, Kentucky, shot his teacher, Deanna McDavid in the head, and then shot the school's janitor, Marvin Hicks. Shocked by the rise of incidents such as these, in 1994, the US Congress passed the Safe and Drug-Free Schools and Communities Act. Three years later, as these shootings continued, the National Center for Educational Statistics reported that schools had sent them notices of almost 200,000 incidents of violence (including 4,000 cases of rape or sexual assault). There are no geographical areas more prone to frenzy, since 75 percent of US schools reported at least one incident.

The most spectacular case took place on April 20, 1999, at Littleton, Colorado. Two teenagers walked through their school, shot 13 people, planted bombs across the campus and then, when it looked like the game was up, took their own lives. The horror was so great that President Clinton took time out from directing the NATO bombardment of Yugoslavia to tell the public, "We must do more to reach out to our children and teach them to express their anger and resolve their conflicts with words, not weapons." Littleton (population 35,000) sits at the outskirts of Denver and houses mainly white college-degree holders who hold steady jobs (many at a Lockheed Martin plant that builds rockets and satellites for telecommunication as well as space exploration). With no obvious psychological problems, the boys had turned to neo-Nazism, built a vast arsenal of weapons (thanks to easy gun laws: in Colorado there are no requirements that guns be licensed or registered and there are no age restrictions for the possession of rifles or shotguns), and took action on Adolf Hitler's birthday to celebrate the Nazi heritage.

Despite this splurge of violence, the image of the petty criminal remained the black man. Indeed, that image helped elect a president.

In 1988, most polls showed that Vice President George H. Bush (Republican) would not defeat Massachusetts governor Michael Dukakis (Democrat) in the election. Then, following the lead of the ruthless political consultant Lee Atwater (a friend of George W. Bush), Bush the Elder released an advertisement about Willy Horton. Horton, it turned out, was a black man who had been released from a Massachusetts jail for a furlough under a humanitarian program started by Dukakis, and while on leave, he murdered another person. Using a picture of Horton, Bush the Elder promised that he would not allow criminals to roam the streets. The specter of the black criminal haunted the campaign, drew support for Bush the Elder from white fear, and won him the election.

The international bad guy, the one who conducts spectacular acts of terror, is not the black man, but the Muslim. When a bomb exploded outside the Federal building in Oklahoma City in 1995, prominent commentators spoke glibly about the perpetrators being one of the global Arab/Muslim gangs. On CBS, commentator Connie Chung summarized the views of a State Department official, "This has Middle East written all over it," and the *New York Times* offered an editorial view, "Whatever we are doing to destroy Mideast terrorism has not been working."[9] When the actual killer turned out to be a white man (Timothy McVeigh), it did little to change the view that acts of terror are done by Muslim hands. Bush the Younger, after 9/11, drives the specter of the Muslim Terrorist to obscure the political landscape as the establishment passes one bill after another in its own interest.[10]

The international Muslim terrorist and the domestic black criminal stand as alibis for revanchism.

Race free criminals (read white) are free the from extra detection or from the pious fulminations of the political class. For example, take the case of white-collar criminals, who defraud millions of people, rob their wages, and send them into the cold without pensions and social security—why not classify them as criminals and let them do hard? "How is it that someone is more likely to go to jail for robbing a liquor store than for defrauding the equivalent of the population of a mid-sized city?" asks journalist Kurt Eichenwald. "The answer goes to the nature of business fraud and the demanding standards of evidence in the criminal justice system. It is not enough to prove there are victims, or that some people got rich from others' suffering. Rules of evidence require the proof of several elements of the crime—some of which can look a lot like standard industry practice."[11] That's one point. The other is that white-collar crime is abstract, it is not like rape or murder, and the suicides and depression it leaves in its wake do not come with a murder weapon replete with fingerprints.[12] This is *white crime,* clean and untouchable.

Clinton began to sell the Crime Bill in August 1993, one year after the streets of Los Angeles exploded in a rebellion against police brutality and exploitation. On May 1, 1992, Bush the Elder went on national television to condemn the rebellion, at the same time as he revealed the establishment's defensiveness about injustice:

> What we saw last night and the night before in Los Angeles
> is not about civil rights. It's not about the great cause of
> equality that all Americans must uphold. It's not a message
> of protest. It's been the brutality of mob, pure and simple.
> And let me assure you, I will use whatever force is necessary
> to restore order.

Bush the Elder's logic after LA '92 resembled the logic of Bush the Younger after 9/11: both rendered their adversaries as Evil, and therefore outside the bounds of explicability and political engagement. Those who rose in LA and looted the shops may have used tactics that are not socially productive, but they did have a political grievance that required attention. Similarly, the 19 terrorists who turned civil aircrafts into cruise missiles conducted an unforgivable and heinous act, but they did come from social forces in West Asia opposed to the US military presence in Saudi Arabia and the US government's support of various undemocratic governments in the region (Saudi, but also Egypt).[13] In the aftermath of LA, Bush the Elder felt that the criminal riffraff had to be put in their place. His verdict repeated the findings of the Kerner Commission on the Watts riot in Los Angeles in 1965. Certainly, Bush the Elder was in line with his old comrade in arms, Ronald Reagan, who told the press in 1968, "Nationwide experience has shown that prompt dealing with disturbances leads to peace, that hesitation, vacillation, and appeasement leads to greater disorder."[14] "Prompt dealing," in the lexicon of the Right, means repression, or as right-wing ideologue William S. Buckley wrote in 1970:

> What is needed these days, properly understood, is very
> solid doses of repression: not in the spirit of vindictiveness,
> but in the spirit of teaching those who wonder, that the
> United States is very serious about surviving the current
> doubts about itself, and about the worthwhileness of its
> essential institutions.[15]

In 1992, the black community was not as organized as it was in
1965 to defend itself from state racism and from the amnesia of US
liberalism (In March 1968, the National Advisory Commission on Civil
Disorders tendered its report on the uprisings of the decade, and it
offered an indictment that covers this general sense of amnesia: "What
white Americans have never fully understood— but what the Negro
can never forget—is that white society is deeply implicated in the
ghetto. White institutions created it, white institutions maintain it, and
white society condones it.")[16] In 1992, in the midst of a recession and
an attempt at stabilization of capital, black America was the target of
political rivalry: who can be tougher on (black) criminals, the
Republicans or the Democrats? When the Republican Party released its
"Contract With America" in mid-1994, it did so in order to determine
the legislative agenda. One of the items in the Contract was a direct
response to the Crime Bill and it was aptly named: "Taking Back Our
Streets Act." The proposal was aimed to assert the dominant classes'
full ownership and control of more than the streets through a further
extension of the police and the system of incarceration. In order to
keep "dangerous criminals off the streets," the proposed act asked that
parole be denied, that the death penalty be made more "effective," and
that the police be securely funded. There was no effective legislative
opposition to the targeting of "criminals" and "immigrants" as *the*
reasons for the enduring recession and restructuring of capital. As the
agents of capitalism attempted to stabilize a floundering economy by
downsizing, the general population recklessly sought any promise of
action that offered hope of immediate relief (Government tax relief, aid
for business, etc.) or the prospect of jobs (on the police force,
replacement of immigrant workers).

There is no special criminal propensity among black males, so why
does the state arrest, sentence, and incarcerate so many black men?
Poverty by itself is no explanation for the attack on black youth,
because the white poor do not face such oppression from the police.

There is no substitute for an analysis of the systematic racism that gnaws at the dignity of the working class, of all colors: the working class of color become the special target of the state, and as more youth of color are arrested, the white working class can find, again, that the one thing that holds it apart from utter failure is that the cells on the skin keep them out of the cells of the state. A look at two separate moments in the recent history of racism and incarceration will help us see how racism structures social life so as to regulate discontent.

Racial Profiling

The police system disproportionately conducts surveillance on young black youth, tailgating them until they do something, anything, that gets them into the system. In 1988, California pioneered racial profiling with its Street Terrorism Enforcement and Prevention (STEP) Act (California Penal Code, Section 186.22), where a "criminal street gang" appeared as, "Any ongoing organization, association, or group of three or more persons, whether formal or informal, having as one of its primary activities the commission of one or more of the crimes listed below, having a common name or common identifying symbol, and whose members individually or collectively engage in or have engaged in a pattern of criminal gang activity." The vagueness of STEP provided the police with immense discretion, and the war against youth of color became so endemic in the state that it should bear the burden of responsibility for the uprising in LA in 1992. Chicago followed California with its June 17, 1992, Gang Congregation Ordinance that read, "Whenever a police officer observes a person whom he reasonably believes to be a criminal street gang member loitering in any public place with one or more other persons, he shall order all such persons to disperse and remove themselves from the area. Any person who does not promptly obey such an order is in violation of this order," and can therefore face arrest. After several legal challenges, the US Supreme Court heard the case in late 1998, and then declared on June 10 of the next year that the "gang loitering" ordinance was unconstitutional on due process grounds. While that case (*Chicago v. Morales*, 97-1121) returned the ordinance to the city, Chicago responded with another ordinance that applies not to the entire city, but to certain "hot spots," the residential zones of the black and Latino working class.[17] In late 1993, after *Chicago v. Morales*, the

Denver police department admitted that they kept lists of "suspected gang members," that only a small percentage of those on the list of 6,500 could be considered "hard-core gang members" and that most of them had not been arrested. In a town with only a five percent black population, the list included 3,691 black males between the ages of 12 and 24, that is about two-thirds of every black males in that age bracket that live in Denver. Latinos, who make up 12 percent of the population of the city, take up a third of the list, while whites, who cover 80 percent of the city's population, accounted for less than seven percent of the list.[18] In Providence, Rhode Island, the police have "a public relations problem in minority neighborhoods. Many people of color don't trust the police, and describe them as thugs in uniform who target minority males for harassment, pulling over their cars or stopping them on the street unnecessarily."[19]

By the early 1990s, this policy was known as "racial profiling." The history of official prejudice, of course, is not recent, because the legacy of the plantation society remained within US officialdom long after enslavement became illegal and after Jim Crow began to be dismantled. In recent times, the courts heard about the prevalence of police racism in two landmark cases, the first being *Papachristou v. City of Jackson* (405 US 156) in 1972, where a Florida police officer followed a vagrancy law to arrest two black men for "nightwalking." The court found the law unconstitutional. Then, in 1983, the Supreme Court declared in *Kolender v. Lawson* (461 US 352) that the police couldn't stop a person to ask them for "credible and reliable" identification without cause. The police stopped the plaintiff, a black man, 15 times in one night while he walked through a white neighborhood. No white man or woman had been stopped following the same rule. After sustained pressure for almost two decades, President Clinton, in mid-1999, admitted that "racial profiling" occurs across the country:

> We cannot tolerate officers who cross the line and abuse their position by mistreating law-abiding individuals or who bring their own racial bias to the job. No person should be subject to excessive force, and no person should be targeted by law enforcement because of the color of his or her skin. Stopping or searching individuals on the basis of race is not effective law enforcement policy, and is not consistent with our democratic ideals, especially our

commitment to equal protection under the law for all persons. It is neither legitimate nor defensible as a strategy for public protection. It is simply wrong.[20]

The Clinton Memorandum forthrightly condemned "racial profiling," even as its policy initiatives remained mainly at the level of data collection.[21] Without the data it is hard to make a case for oppression, so this was a marked step forward. A few days later, the American Civil Liberties Union (ACLU) published a report that established quite effectively the routine racism of the nation's police.[22] A year later, the US Government's Office of Civil Rights corroborated the ACLU's report with a scathing indictment of police practice.[23] Despite the conclusive evidence of the problem, the White House did nothing. The entry of the Republicans into the White House ended the official dithering over profiling...by shelving the problem. Bush the Younger's own "Memorandum for the Attorney General on Racial Profiling," released on February 28, 2001, retreated to the Clinton position, but without the open condemnation of the practice.[24]

The Presidential decrees did not do more than officially admit to the racism of the police forces across the country. That itself is significant.

The War on Drugs

In 1968, as the world despaired over the US bombardment of Vietnam and Cambodia, President Richard Nixon declared war on drugs. "Within the last decade," he told Congress, "the abuse of drugs has grown from essentially a local police problem into a serious national threat to the personal health and safety of millions of Americans.... A national awareness of the gravity of the situation is needed: a new urgency and concerted national policy are needed at the federal level to begin to cope with this growing menace to the general welfare of the United States."[25] Raising the problem of drugs to a "national threat" produced a national panic not over drugs, but over the imputed criminality of drug users. If Nixon could not get his entire package of anti-drug legislation passed, he set the ball rolling for future administrations to lock the US government into a state of warfare with its own people.

These are not strong words. In 1980, the number of people under the supervision of the correctional system totaled 1,842,100. In 2001, the number leapt to 6,592,800. In the same period the number of prisoners went from 503,586 to 1,962, 220.[26] The US now leads across the globe in per capita incarceration. With nearly two million people behind bars and an additional five million under the surveillance of the criminal justice system, the US far surpasses the rates of incarceration elsewhere. In 1994, the rate was 569 per 100,000 people—40 times the rate in South Africa and 15 times the rate in Japan. Since then, the difference has only increased. In the 1960s, the imprisoned population was but an eighth of its current size. Most of those who study the numbers argue that the explosion took place because of the war on drugs, with more than half the federal inmates now in jail specifically for drug offenses, and with a fifth of state prisoners hauled in for drug crimes as well.[27] In 1983, just short of nine percent of those in jail came in for the offense of drug possession; in ten years, more than a quarter of those in jail were drug offenders. By early 1992, three quarters of the new inmates since 1987 were in for drug offenses. With the total number of those in jail on the rise, the role of drugs certainly helped inflate the incarcerated population.

The data on prisoners shows the significance of race to any discussion on incarceration. The black population in the US is just below 12 percent of the total population. Yet, 45 percent of those arrested and 50 percent of those who do jail time are black. So blacks are vastly overrepresented in the nation's correctional system. Most studies show that only 13 percent of drug users are black, yet 35 percent of those who are arrested for drug possession are black and almost three quarters of those who do jail time for drug possession are black. Furthermore, 90 percent of those whose assets are seized because of drug possession (following the policy of "asset forfeiture") are people of color.[28] One in every 25 males in the US is under the direct supervision of the prison industrial complex; for African American males, the percentage is one in every three. The figures for incarcerated black males are remarkable: 23 percent of all black males between the ages of 20 and 29 are in jail and there are more black men in jail than in college.[29] Native Americans are ten times more likely than whites to be imprisoned. Latinos constitute the fastest growing group behind bars.

Why is this so? In 1973, New York state pioneered the use of mandatory sentences for those caught with drugs, including a 15-year term for possession of drugs for personal use. The most insidious part of mandatory minimum sentences is that they operate in a racist fashion. The 1986 Anti-Drug Abuse Act mandates that anyone with a first-time possession of five grams of crack must spend five years in jail, but if the same weight of cocaine is found on a person, then the sentence is probation. One would have to carry 100 times more cocaine (that is, 500 grams), and show intent to distribute the drug, to earn five years in the tank. The average crack mandatory minimum sentence is 52 percent higher than the average cocaine mandatory minimum sentence. This is plainly discriminatory, but it is perhaps not the root cause of the vast amount of blacks in the penal system for drug possession. After all, while 85 percent of those who are sentenced for crack possession are black, 80 percent of those who are sentenced for cocaine possession are also black.

In its war on drugs, the police and the public seem to have it that the average domestic drug dealer is black. By the same token, the international drug dealer is seen as Latin American, generally Colombian. There is no room in this stereotype for the white drug dealer, as well as the Wall Street banks and others who finance the shipments.[30] In 1997, then drug czar Barry McCaffrey cited a 1995 survey of much significance to our argument. The survey, published in the *Journal of Alcohol and Drug Education*, showed that 95 percent of those asked about a drug user pictured the person as black.[31] Since the police, as various studies argue, are motivated by much the same sort of logic as those who responded to the survey, then it is apparent that the war on drugs is really a war against people of color. In 1989, in New York City, for instance, 92 percent of those arrested in drug busts were either black or Latino, even as 80 percent of drug users were white. Of those arrested for drugs, only seven percent were white.[32] Racism, then, must play an extraordinary role in the formation of the prison population.

At least this is what Judge Lyle E. Strom of the United States Court of Appeals for the Eighth Circuit thought in 1993. Faced with the case of four black defendants in a drug possession case, the Judge declined the 30-year mandatory minimum and sentenced them to 20 years each. To justify his departure from the legislated minimum, Judge Strom wrote that blacks convicted in crack cases "are being treated unfairly in receiving substantially longer sentences than Caucasian males who traditionally deal in powdered cocaine."[33] Even the Bureau of Justice Statistics, the agency that keeps the data and from whom most of the data in this chapter comes, expressed its own guarded fear of racist discrimination in a modest "discussion paper" from as early as 1993.[34]

As the nation has come to accept the systematic forms of racism, such as racial profiling and the injudicious war on drugs, and as the forces of justice moved forward to gain this admission from the state, the courts had already undermined the use of data on systematic racism in the criminal justice system. The immediate background of the disavowal came with discussions of the death penalty. A cursory look at the data on the death penalty shows the disproportionate executions of people of color. David Baldus, Charles Pulaski, and George Woodworth looked at the data on murder cases and on death row in Georgia from 1973–1978, around the famous 1976 *Gregg v. Georgia* (428 US 153) case in which the Supreme Court approved Georgia's capital punishment statute, but asked that it be administered with checks and with fairness. Baldus, Pulaski, and Woodworth found, in contrast, that blacks who killed whites overwhelmingly received the death penalty, and that racism did operate across the spectrum in the various jury decisions.[35] Speaking at the American Bar Association in 1990, the late justice Thurgood Marshall said, "When in *Gregg v. Georgia* the Supreme Court gave its seal of approval to capital punishment, this endorsement was premised on the promise that capital punishment would be administered with fairness and justice. Instead, the promise has become a cruel and empty mockery. We cannot let it continue."[36] A host of studies from across the country came to the same decision, and Jeffrey Pokorak and his co-researchers from St. Mary's University Law School (Texas) showed that one of the reasons for this is that the key decision-makers in the judicial system are almost exclusively white men, and in states with the death penalty, almost 98 percent of the district attorneys are white.[37] In the context of the battle to save former Black Panther Mumia Abu Jamal's life, Baldus and Woodworth returned with a study that showed that in Philadelphia (where Jamal is on death row), the odds of receiving a death sentence are almost four times as high if the defendant is black.[38] Based on these studies (but mainly the 1980s studies by Baldus and his colleagues), Warren McCleskey filed a defense against the death penalty in Georgia. McCleskey had been found guilty of murdering a police officer, and the jury, with eleven whites and one black, sentenced him to death. McCleskey's defense against the death penalty came at the next stage when he argued (based on Baldus) that the penalty is exercised in a discriminatory manner in Georgia and that his Eighth and Fourteenth Amendment rights had been violated. The Supreme Court (in *McCleskey v. Kemp*, 481 US 279), in 1987, held that the defendant had to prove that he or she had been *personally* discriminated against during the course of prosecution.[39] To "merely" demonstrate a pattern of racist disparity over a period of time is now not seen as sufficient proof of bias. In his powerful dissent, the liberal justice William Brennan wrote, "Defendants challenging their death sentences thus far never have had to prove that impermissible considerations have actually infected sentencing decisions. We have required instead that they establish that the system under which they were sentenced posed a significant risk of such an occurrence." On September 25, 1991, the state of Georgia executed Warren McCleskey. The name *McCleskey* now refers to both the recognition by the state that racism exists in the criminal justice system *and* the refusal of the state to allow it to enter the clemency of the mandarins.[40]

THE ECONOMICS OF INCARCERATION

In the late 1980s, while in graduate school, a friend said to me that the only stable jobs in these times of insecurity within the US seemed to be security guard, repo man, and correctional officer. The first person protects the property of the rich, the second makes sure that the poor only have what they can earn, and the third takes care of anyone from among the poor who doesn't follow the rules. While many studies of late argue that the incarceration boom is about the political control of the poor, or else of irrational racism, I want to argue that these are only partial explanations. Incarceration, in these neoliberal times, is an economic solution to the problem of the contingent class as well as to the problem of widespread dissatisfaction with the emergent social contract (the Republican's Contract With America, for example, that makes sure the rich keep theirs, and the poor have none).

Once the Crime Bill allowed the treasury to write checks across the country for its many programs, new penitentiaries began to litter the landscape of the American countryside and within the precincts of several major cities. With $80 billion already in the hands of law enforcement before the Crime Bill, the addition of another $30.2 billion made the punishment industry one of the centerpieces of the federal stimulus for economic growth (what is otherwise called Keynesianism). With the demise of the Soviet Union, the population had come to expect a peace dividend, a diversion of funds from the military-industrial complex to the creation of socioeconomic equity. That was not to be, because, as community activist Libero Della Piana wrote, the "merchants of death" have produced a "new war budget—this time for police and prisons."[41] "Our society," he writes, "is reaching the point where there are only two classes of citizens: those in prisons and the police." If this is an exaggeration from the Left, perhaps we might consider an exaggeration from the mainstream, this time from Morris Thigpen, director of the National Institute of Corrections: "People joke [that] we seem to be heading toward the day when you're either going to be in prison or working in some sort of way with corrections."[42]

What is remarkable about the explosion of the correctional sector is that it occurred in a period when both the violent crime and the property crime rates dropped steadily. As far as murder is concerned, government data shows us that murder by someone known to the victim (an "intimate murder") accounts for about 45 percent of all murders, while murder by a stranger covers 15 percent, and a full 40 percent are murders with no established relationship between the killer and the victim. This is significant because it points to the prevalence of "domestic violence" (or, more correctly, violence against women—the greatest killer of US women) rather than of the random murders associated with the drug trade. Almost 35 percent of those who commit violent crimes do so under the influence of alcohol, whereas the percentage of those who are on drugs is negligible. Finally, from 1976 to 1988, the number of black men murdered fell by 74 percent, and so did the numbers of murdered black women: so much for the epidemic of "black on black" violence.

Given this context of a general decrease in criminality, why do we see a boom in the prison industry and in the correctional system in general? As the US economy's productive sector reorganized in the 1970s and 1980s, the working class was forced to radically readjust its position. Workers in manufacturing had previously earned a decent union wage with benefits, and white workers gained immeasurably from their racist access to federal credit to buy homes and other assets in the 1950s and early 1960s (before the Equal Rights Act).[43] With the formal victories of the Civil Rights Act, black workers and other workers of color, fought to get jobs in the protected sector *just as imperialist globalization devastated the very sectors that promised them freedom.* First, the big plants began to close down in the shakedown of the Reagan-era Structural Adjustment of the US. Second, workers of color thronged into union jobs at the many municipalities and state administrations (and then, into American Federation of State, County, and Municipal Employees (AFSCME)), but at this very time, the government began to shrink social services and cut back on these jobs. As the Civil Rights struggle won freedom in the horizon of the state, that institution suffered from the blows of imperialist globalization and cut the dreams of the millions off at the get-go.

As the industrial devastation proceeded apace, those without employment either turned to "contingent" work or else to the government for social welfare. The latter grew in name in the 1960s with the Great Society Programs, but it was always a small check for each household. Precious funds, but never anything to be too excited about, so that even those eligible for welfare worked off the books to supplement their household income. Everyone from the class that began to go to jail had some form of contingent job or another. Contract labor, piece work (including housework, childcare, as well as manufacturing outwork) and temporary labor are not new forms of labor, but they are increasingly becoming the paradigm for the US workforce. F. W. Taylor and Henry Ford would not recognize today's economy which relies less on factory discipline than on the discipline of starvation: contractors or jobbers offer a hard-pressed population work under unenviable conditions and the employers rely upon the desperation of their "outworkers" to produce the quotas. Quality healthcare, vacation time, etc., are the responsibility of the worker: the employer takes the best products, rejects the bad ones, and does not hire the worker during lean times or if the worker is ill.

In 1994, the Bureau of Labor Statistics reported that temporary agencies accounted for 15 percent of the new jobs created in 1993, and 26 percent of the new jobs created in 1992. In 1989, temporary agencies accounted for less than three percent of the new jobs. Reporting these figures, the *New York Times* explained, "In the recession, many employers, here and elsewhere, tried to keep their costs low by increasing their use of part-timers and temporaries, who work only during busy periods and usually get no benefits."[44] College graduates are confronted with a job market in which they are forced to work for short periods doing data entry, conducting market surveys, going door-to-door selling products, or driving trucks (the number of truck drivers with college degrees had increased from 99,000 in 1983 to 166,000 in 1990).[45] A generation of temporary workers is now moving into the workforce. Thirty million Americans, or 25 percent of the workforce, are employed in such conditions and they cost 40 percent less than full-time permanent employees. "The mushrooming service sector," Richard Barnet argued, "turned out to be vulnerable to the same fierce competition that has shriveled factory payrolls in the United States and caused real wages in manufacturing to drop nine percent since 1975. Indeed, there are by and large more low-wage jobs today in the service sector than in manufacturing."[46] These are terrible jobs, and more and more people from among the jail-going class hold them.

The class of the contingent generally enters the vice economy not for malevolent reasons, but typically to supplement a major decline in household income. Boston University's leading economist, Glenn Loury, on the other hand, argued, "The responsibility for the behavior of black youngsters lies squarely on the shoulders of the black community itself."[47] The only structural feature worthy of analysis, according to this view, is the lack of community values that push individuals to make bad choices, whereas one is asked to abjure other structural features such as the economic and political dynamics that might constrain the will of the "community" in general. Many studies show that urban blacks evince a desire not just to hold a job, but for worthwhile work and education, for a meaningful life. Significant numbers of those who are in poverty, further, are transients between meaningless jobs. There is widespread recognition in the literature of the distress and disaffection among urban (that is, working class) blacks and of their desires and struggles to fashion a destiny.[48] Even Bill Clinton's advisor on race, now Harvard professor William Wilson, argued in a popular book from 1996:

> A neighborhood in which people are poor but employed is different from a neighborhood in which people are poor and jobless. Many of today's problems in the inner-city ghetto neighborhoods—crime, family dissolution, welfare, low levels of social organization, and so on—are fundamentally a consequence of the disappearance of work.[49]

His advisee, President Clinton, did not pay much heed to this argument.

If the class of the contingent must be left outside the ken of work, there is a high chance that they will demand collective power or your individual wallet. Both political rebellion and individual criminality become a problem of the social order created by the dominant classes. As political scientist and co-founder of the Black Radical Congress Manning Marable argues, "Prisons have become the method for keeping hundreds of thousands of potentially rebellious, dissatisfied, and alienated black youth off the streets."[50] The US government will continue the process of controlling disgruntled and politically angry populations by the threat of prison and by the politics of "realism" that moves dissatisfied Americans to discourage an analysis of their situation and to immediately lay the blame for their ills on immigrants, on the poor, and on people of color.

As more people go to jail each year, jail becomes the storehouse of the redundant working population as well as its soup kitchen. The state prefers to provide social services to the unemployed if they submit themselves to total surveillance: the jail is the ultimate place for such debasement. As the contingent class grew in the early 1990s, the government slashed its social security net (welfare) and opted to deal with the indigent via prisons. The state did not stop spending funds, it simply redirected its social welfare money toward incarceration. Instead of priming the economic pump by cash disbursements to the working class (demand-side growth generation), the government preferred to offer the taxes it collects toward its own state enterprises (prisons, etc.) or else to private businesses who either run prisons or else work in the construction and maintenance of them (supply-side growth generation). Here is Angela Davis, former political prisoner, professor at the University of California–Santa Cruz, and founder of Critical Resistance (a group committed to the abolition of prisons):

> Imprisonment has become the response of first resort to far too many of the social problems that burden people who are ensconced in poverty. These problems often are veiled by being conveniently grouped together under the category "crime" and by the automatic attribution of criminal behavior to people of color. Homelessness, unemployment, drug addiction, mental illness, and illiteracy are only a few of the problems that disappear from public

> view when the human beings contending with them are
> relegated to cages.... Colored bodies constitute the main
> human raw material in this vast experiment to disappear the
> major social problems of our time. Once the aura of magic
> is stripped away from the imprisonment solution, what is
> revealed is racism, class bias, and the parasitic seduction of
> capitalist profit.[51]

In 1993, the state spent more on Aid to Families with Dependent Children (AFDC) than on corrections, but by 1996 (on the other side of the Crime Bill) the priority was reversed. The government added more than $8 billion to corrections in this period, while it slashed AFDC by almost $2 billion. Gregory Winter, who works at the Hamilton Family Center in San Francisco, notes, "When funds are siphoned away from social programs to prisons, communities are drawn inexorably toward incarceration." Furthermore if incarceration trumps social security at the same pace, "the criminal justice system will become the government's primary interface with poor communities, particularly those of color. Prisons will replace public entitlements, subsidized housing, and perhaps even the schools as the principal place where poor people converge."[52]

In 1995, according to surveys of prisoners done by the Department of Corrections, almost half of the state inmates had been unemployed when arrested, and the rest reported incomes of under $10,000. Part of the contingent class, these men and women are being swept up from their neighborhoods to do hard time, and then, because of high recidivism rates, many return to jail over and over again. Two of the best kept secrets of the recent wave of incarceration are the entry of large numbers of women and children into the correctional system, whereas previously the jails had been mainly filled with men.

By the mid-1990s, the number of women in jail totaled 138,000, an increase of 432 percent over the population of incarcerated women in 1985. Women currently enter jail at a rate faster than men, most come to jail because of nonviolent crimes, and the main crime that sends women to jail is possession or sale of illegal narcotics. Black women are eight times more likely than white women to be in jail, and Latino women are four times as likely as white women. Of the women in jail in 1999, over 2,000 came to jail pregnant and about 1,300 babies saw their first light inside prison walls. Furthermore, 200,000 children under the age of 18 watched their mothers go to jail (80,000 of the women in jail are parents, many single parents). In 1999, the Bureau of Justice Statistics revealed that over 700,000 prisoners were parents of almost 1.5 million children under the age of 18. Twenty-two percent of all minor children with a parent in jail were under five years old. Less than half of the fathers lived with their children before their arrest, while close to two-thirds of mothers raised their children before their incarceration. What happens to those children once the mothers are in the pen? Amnesty International, from whose report I derive much of this data, introduces us to Minnie Caldwell, age 75, who is in charge of her two grandchildren, Latisha, age 18, and Anthony, age 10, because her daughter, Elizabeth, age 36, is in an Alabama state prison for theft. With money tight to start with, women like Minnie Caldwell take on additional work, sometimes making food for sale or else going back into the contingent workforce. Sixty percent of the million children live with their grandmothers, and the financial and the psychological strain on the elderly needs no amplification.[53] If there is no grandparent available, the children enter the foster care system, and 90 percent of the children in this service have parents behind bars or in and out of jail.[54] Foster care, by all accounts, is an underfunded and mismanaged program that is itself a gateway to petty crime.

Which brings us to the other big secret: the close to 700,000 juveniles in correctional facilities, such as detention centers, training schools, ranches, camps, and farms. Half of the boys (average age of entry is 16) who enter the juvenile correctional network come for first offenses of drug possession or else for property crimes. Only a fifth of the boys committed serious, violent crimes. Among boys, blacks (56 percent) and Latinos (21 percent) predominate. Of girls, only half are of color, most are younger (average age of entry is 15) and they commit fewer violent crimes and more violations of court orders, among other bureaucratic offenses.[55] According to law professor Barry Feld, "The daily reality of juveniles confined in many 'treatment' facilities is one of violence, predatory behavior, and punitive incarceration."[56] For the kids who are not in jail, the working class neighborhoods that they live in have become a vast prison. We've already encountered the ordinances against gangs, but we should also bear in mind the curfews in place (in 1997, the number of cities that reported a curfew at night, and some during the day as well, amounted to almost 300, according to the US Conference of Mayors).[57]

The devastation wrought by imperialist globalization (when firms fled the US for cheaper labor) and by Reagan's response to that via the structural adjustment policies of the 1980s that further weakened the dignity among the working class, produced significant effects: the war on the poor and the contingent, the attempt to discipline this population, turned many into "criminals" and resulted in the destruction of family (however constructed) and of the semblance of civic community engendered by the poor.

From the side of the white working class and of the forgotten rural towns, prisons come as a saving grace. As less workers find permanent, well-paid jobs with benefits, the US working class (mainly white, but not exclusively so) is pleased to find work of any kind: building prisons is not a bad idea and working in a prison is better than starvation. This section of the workforce tends to invite extremist racists and sadists, many of whom create an atmosphere of violence that tends to whittle away the judgment of their peers. Here are some examples from a Human Rights Watch document (2001):[58]

- In July 1999, four guards at the Florida State Prison beat Frank Valdez to death. The guards beat Valdez with such brutality that his ribs broke and boot marks remained on his body. The guards claimed Valdez injured himself, but in February 2001, the state indicted them on murder charges.
- In June 2001, the state acquitted eight prison guards at California's Corcoran State Prison who had been charged with staging gladiator-style fights among inmates. In November 1999, the state acquitted four other guards for setting up the rape of an inmate by another very violent prisoner.
- From December 1999, the following events took place in women's prisons: the state indicted eleven former guards and a prison official on charges of sexually assaulting or harassing 16 female prisoners at a county jail operated by a private corrections company; a jury convicted a New Mexico jail guard on federal civil rights charges stemming from the sexual assault of a prisoner; the state sentenced a New York guard to three years of probation after he pleaded guilty to sodomy of two female prisoners; the state

sentenced an Ohio jail officer to a four-year term for sexually assaulting three female prisoners.

• In South Dakota, the state faced a class action suit that charged the prisons with widespread physical abuse against juvenile girls detained at the State Training School. The suit charged that guards routinely shackled youths in spread-eagled fashion after cutting off their clothes, sprayed them with pepper spray while naked, and placed them in isolation for 23 hours each day.

Finally, if we look at the major study of the Indiana correctional system conducted by Kelsey Kaufman, we get a sense of the presence of white supremacy within the ranks of the correctional officers. Kaufman details the growth of a group known as the Brotherhood in the Putnamville Correctional Facility (once known as the Indiana State Farm). This group began a process of sexual intimidation, physical assault, and drug trafficking against that half of the inmates who are black and Latino. Kaufman cites Department of Corrections investigations that verify incidents that were "racially motivated and very demeaning" and that took place "almost on a daily basis." White and black staff at Putnamville reported that the Brotherhood members among the correctional officers referred to the few black employees on the premises as "lazy niggers," "coons," and "goat farmers," that the Brotherhood staff routinely spat in the faces of black inmates as they handed them food, that the guards said that the inmates should be deported back to Africa, that one officer paraded about in a KKK-style hood (a feature noted in Connecticut, Florida, Maine, Massachusetts, and Wyoming), that swastikas and confederate flags decorate the officers' lockers (as in Rhode Island, for instance), and that racist tattoos and gang-style symbols of the radical Right are commonplace on the bodies of the officers.[59]

If this seems farfetched, and it might to some, I recommend a reading of the Department of Justice's "Good Ol' Boy Roundup" (March 1996), which is specifically about a July 1995 gathering in southeastern Tennessee of Bureau of Alcohol, Tobacco, and Firearms personnel and other justice employees (including correctional officers). This was the sixteenth roundup of justice employees and it took a report in the conservative *Washington Times* to force an official investigation of the event. When the Bureau concluded its study, it took pains to show that this was not a government-sponsored event, that others also attended, that it was not formally a "Klan rally" and that "alcohol, no doubt contributed to the recurrence of such incidents." The "incidents" are as follows:

- Racist signs such as "Nigger check point" and "Any niggers in that car" as well as caricatures of blacks inside a circle with a red slash across the image. These signs had been posted by local police officers.
- Checking cars to see that no blacks came to the Roundup.
- Racist skits as part of the Redneck of the Year Contest in which a man in blackface was traded for a dog, and then the man pretended to have oral sex on another man dressed in a Klan outfit. In another skit, a police officer went onto the stage with a watermelon and a black doll. He proceeded to beat the doll after telling the audience, "You have to kill the seed when it is young."
- Racist confrontations between white and black law enforcement officers. Two black officers came to the Roundup in 1995 and got into a fight with four white officers, backed up by the gathering. After the incident, someone painted "Whites Only" outside the toilet.
- The paraphernalia of white supremacy laced the camp, from Confederate flags to t-shirts with images of blacks being violently subdued at their car alongside slogans like "Boyz in the Hood." Richard Hayward of (former Klan head) David Duke's National Association for the Advancement of White People was a regular and he brought white supremacist literature that was given out to the officers.

But, as the adage goes, people do not live by bread alone. People live on freedom, on love, on solidarity, on bread too: those basic needs, however, seem to have lost their sanctity as the US government moved further towards an illiberalism whose inevitable outcome is a polarization of the population—racist prison guards and the passive beneficiaries of their brutality on one side, and the largely working class and of-color prison population and their contingent class on the other.

As the jail becomes a war zone with one side armed and the other disarmed, all talk of rehabilitation has disappeared. On January 18, 1989, Justice Harry Blackmun of the US Supreme Court affirmed the right of the legislature to hold sentencing guidelines. In his opinion for the majority in *Mistretta v. United States,* Justice Blackmun wrote, "Rehabilitation as a sound penological theory came to be questioned and, in any event, was regarded by some as an unattainable goal for most cases." Furthermore, Justice Blackmun cited a 1984 Senate report that called the prevailing penal philosophy an "'outmoded rehabilitation model' for federal criminal sentencing, and recognized that the efforts of the criminal justice system to achieve rehabilitation of offenders had failed." In agreement, the majority on the court defined the new penal philosophy as follows: "It rejects imprisonment as a means of promoting rehabilitation, and it states that punishment should serve retributive, educational, deterrent, and incapacitative goals." Prisoners' rights activists Eve Goldberg and Linda Evans are on point with their following characterization of rehabilitation:

> As "criminals" become scapegoats for our floundering economy and our deteriorating social structure, even the guise of rehabilitation is quickly disappearing from our penal philosophy. After all: rehabilitate for what? To go back into an economy which has no jobs? To go back into a community which has no hope? As education and other prison programs are cut back, or in most cases eliminated altogether, prisons are becoming vast, over-crowded, holding tanks. Or worse: factories behind bars.[60]

In jail, the prisoners are not reduced to monitored consumers. On the contrary, some of the inmates work in what are called correctional industries, where they often work hard to produce goods for the private sector, where they are fed and kept with taxpayer funds, and where they can earn slave wages for their efforts. Capitalism was founded on plantation slavery. We have now come full circle to a form of slavery which goes on at the fringes of American public life: penal slavery. People of color in jails now man the correctional industries and produce the few products that bear the bittersweet label, "Made in America." "Made in Prison" would be more appropriate.

THE BUSINESS OF JAILS

In 1992, when Clinton came to office, Westview Press in Boulder, Colorado, published Harry Wu's *Laogai: The Chinese Gulag.*[61] Wu, who was nominated for the Nobel Peace Prize a decade later, was a fellow at the Hoover Institute (located at Stanford University) and the famous spokesperson against the "forced labor prisons" in the People's Republic of China (PRC). In his book, Wu argues that while the government accepts that about 1.35 million prisoners work in *laogai* or prison camps, he holds that 20 million do so. By comparing the *laogai* to the gulag, and sitting before innumerable Congressional committees to denounce China, Wu made sure to paint a portrait of the Chinese regime as especially cruel to its people. What is freedom for Wu? In the *Washington Post*, he wrote, "Until private ownership is allowed on a wide scale, genuine liberalization—representative government, free markets, and individual rights—will remain elusive in China."[62]

In a more recent book by authors not known for their sympathy for the PRC, they show that the *laogai* population is fewer than two million (in a country of over a billion), with political prisoners being a negligible percentage of the total. Having established the exaggerations of Wu, the authors point out quite correctly, "It is not the size of the *laogai* that is outrageous, but what goes on within its worst prisons." An analysis of the Huise Uranium Camp shows us how the 2,000 prisoners work amidst an annual mortality rate of between ten and 20 percent, how coal miners in the camps suffer from black lung disease. Furthermore, the authors inform us that not only are there forced labor camps in China, there is also re-education through labor (*laojiao*) camps to interrogate political opponents and hold them in indefinite detention.[63] The material in the book shows us that the *laogai* are organized as autonomous units. The prisoners at these camps produce goods to make the camps self-sufficient. They raise livestock and grow crops for the market and for consumption, as well as to produce commodities for export (most of the *laogai* goods that come to the US are raw materials).

Each year the US Congress revisits discussion on its relationship with China. The format for this discussion is the Most Favored Nation (MFN) ratification, which is automatic for most countries except China. In 1980, the US Congress passed the Jackson-Vanik Act that prevents regular reauthorization of trade privileges due to emigration restrictions from China. But with US-China trade now over $60 billion per year, there is an enormous incentive to its passage. To ensure that the MFN status is not altered, lobbyists for major US multinational firms camp out in Washington, DC, and donate over $20 million to the Republicans and the Democrats. The Business Coalition for US-China Trade includes over 800 members, including trade associations (the Business Roundtable, the National Association for Manufacturers, and the Chamber of Commerce) and large firms (Boeing, IBM, Motorola, Ford, General Motors, ConAgra, Nike, and Eastman Chemical). US business has now come to rely upon the cheaper labor cost in China as well as its vast purchase of high technology goods. In the 1990s, for instance, Boeing sold one in ten of its planes to the Chinese.

Just as China has become indispensable for the US-based global corporations, the US politicians have used "China" as a weapon to strengthen their own dubious populist credentials. The Right, represented by most of the Republican Party and by the fringe elements of the by now almost defunct Reform Party (led by Patrick Buchanan), is joined by sections of the labor movement (such as the Hoffa leadership of the Teamsters and by the United Food and Commercial Workers Union) in its denunciation of the Chinese. Not only is China accused of stealing jobs due to its low wages, but also it is censured for human rights abuses, particularly in the *laogai*. The Democratic Party (under Clinton and Gore), but also sections of the Republican Party (under Bush the Younger), cannot turn their back on the Chinese markets and labor. Politicians of the neoliberal variety are vulnerable to the charge of being hypocritical on human rights and unconcerned about the woes of the US worker. Because of this bind, the neoliberals seek symbolic ways to attack China just as they want to continue to do business with China.

The *laogai* became that symbol. In October 1995, Wu spoke to the AFL-CIO convention in New York and told the workers' representatives that China's *laogai* system costs US workers their jobs, but it also "continues to destroy millions of people and create fear in billions more." Greg Denier of the United Food and Commercial Workers Union said, after Wu visited the UFCW convention, "We know that eight to ten million people are in the Chinese prison system and forced to produce items for sale overseas. We also have confirmed through import records that Wal-Mart produces goods from the Chinese People's Liberation Army."[64] Then, on June 8, 1999, John Sweeney sat before a congressional subcommittee on trade to alert them that "China repeatedly and flagrantly violates internationally recognized core labor standards, by denying Chinese workers freedom of association and the right to organize and bargain collectively, as well as by the abuse of prison labor." Before a mass rally on April 12, 2000, called "No Blank Check for China," Sweeney rallied the troops: "Meanwhile, our workers are forced to compete with prison labor and sweatshop workers making as little as 13 cents an hour. And while we are losing hundreds of thousands of jobs, China is setting new records for violations of human rights and polluting the environment." Not to be outdone, Senator Paul Wellstone of Minnesota told the Senate on September 12, 2000:

> Year after year, we are importing products made with forced prison labor from China. This amendment is in no way an exercise in China-bashing. We are merely insisting that China stop treating the bilateral trade agreements it has signed with us concerning prison labor exports as mere "scraps of paper." What does my amendment ask for? It asks simply that [permanent normal trade relations] be denied until President Clinton can certify that China is honoring agreements it has repeatedly violated in the past, signed agreements it has violated now. We already have these trade agreements with China, and they've not abided by them. We say in this amendment "We call on you to live up to your agreements before we automatically extend [permanent normal trade relations]." What is unreasonable about that?

On September 19, 2000, despite these pious declarations, Congress voted to approve a bill that enabled the US to avoid its annual review of China's human rights record, and to tie human rights to trade. For the labor movement, the *laogai* represented a competition for US workers, rather than an opportunity to forge connections with Chinese workers against the misery of corporate globalization. For the Right (including much of the Democratic Party), the main story remained symbolic. They fulminated against the PRC for its role in Tibet, for the *laogai*, for espionage (the Wen Ho Lee case[65]), and for campaign finance shenanigans (via Johnny Huang) at the same time as they voted to clear the decks for US-based global corporate deals with China. Representative Christopher Cox, the California Republican, led the charge against Wen Ho Lee, set himself up as a defender of Chinese Christians, and touted his credentials as an anti–Red China Hand. Yet, right through these campaigns, Cox fought within Congress to ensure speedy passage for pro-corporate legislation regarding China. When debate erupted over the Most Favored Nation status in 1999, Cox told the business press that he feared that more regulations would mean less profits for US-based firms with little impact on "national security." "The lion's share of stuff," meaning free entry of corporations into China, "should be fast-tracked," meaning, come without Congressional oversight, he told the press.[66]

Any alert person will know that the *laogai* is a red herring, because not only did it enable people like Cox to talk about liberty as they feted the most illiberal corporate figures on the planet, but it also allowed Sweeney to cloak US labor's protectionism behind talk of human rights, just as it allowed Buchanan to revive the Yellow Peril as a populist issue. The *laogai* also allowed the explosion of US prisons to disappear from the agenda from 1994 to 2000. In a formal sense, the *laogai* did the work of the Central American and Mexican *maquiladora* in the fight over NAFTA; in 1992, Texas Representative Henry Gonzalez, for example, wrote to the commissioner of US customs to complain about imported goods made by Mexican "slave labor."

> There has never been any possibility that United States laborers could compete with prison labor and still receive a viable living wage, and now it appears that our workers are going to have a choice—compete with serf labor in the *maquiladoras* or compete with slave labor from the [Mexican] prisons.[67]

Without a doubt the conditions in Mexican jails and *maquiladoras* are beyond defense, but the tendency of Gonzalez (and even significant sections of the US labor movement) was to turn the problem into a wage war between workers in different states rather than a united struggle against global corporations whose entire ethos is governed by the deterioration of the worker's wage. In the 1990s, all talk of prison labor was of China and of Mexico and not of prisons and forced labor within the American gulag.

In a very stimulating book on the general imprisonment of the US population, sociologist Christian Parenti asks if the prison boom of the 1990s provided an economic stimulus? Will the prison boom, in other words, create prosperity in localities? After assessing the growth of the prison industry in several areas, Parenti notes:

> It is safe to say that incarceration is a small-scale form of Keynesian, public-works-style stimulus. The gulag provides opportunities for localized growth but it does not and will not assume the mantle of de facto industrial policy, because it cannot and will not replace the economic role of military and aerospace spending.[68]

It is well to be careful about the claims made by the prison expansionists, but on the other hand, prisons *are* big business and, like football stadiums, they have allowed large corporations and the government to go on building sprees at the expense of towns and cities. So, while the prison complex does not benefit the bulk of the citizenry, it certainly is a boom for business and for bureaucracy. Both eat high on the prison hog, find ways to spend taxes other than to create a population able to challenge power, and hold down the contingent classes in these pens when they do get into disorganized forms of social rebellion.

The next section of this chapter will assess the boom in prison construction, the growth of prison labor, and the emergence of a class of deportable aliens who are held in new prisons, many of them owned and run by private corporations.

We Build Prisons To Life

As the Crime Bill dropped large amounts of cash into the prison markets, construction and design firms flocked to depressed parts of the country to "revive" the local economy and to make a decent profit in the margin. In 1995, expenditure on prison construction increased by $926 million, while outlay for university construction dropped by $954 million. Each year in the early 1990s, the various levels of the government spent almost $7 billion in taxpayer funds to build prisons. The $9 billion sum from the Crime Bill earmarked for prison construction was the down payment on funds that then came from state governments and elsewhere. The state simply raised the money from its nominally progressive taxation schemes, but really regressive taxation with the rich taking shelter in the offices of their tax lawyers.

That money then went to large construction and design firms that produced substandard buildings for vast profits, boosted by development subsidies, tax breaks, and cheap financing. By the mid-1990s, the annual funds spent by the state for prison construction and costs increased to $17 billion (1995–1996).[69] *Design-Build*, a construction trade magazine, estimates that in the 1990s, the government built 3,300 prisons at a cost of $27 billion, with another 268 prisons on the design boards at a cost of $2.4 billion.[70]

Two of the construction firms that earned many of the contracts in the 1990s come from the powerhouses of international business. The largest German construction firm, with its paws all over Europe, is Hochtief AG, and its US subsidiary, Turner Construction, is knee-deep in prison construction, with annual revenues at $6.3 billion. The second firm, Kellogg, Brown & Root, is another major player in prison design and construction and it is owned by Halliburton, the $13.3 billion energy and construction conglomerate lately run by Vice President Dick Cheney.[71] These two firms are joined by a host of smaller contractors who build the public and private prisons with taxpayer funds. Alongside them sit the major banks, such as Goldman Sachs, Smith Barney, Shearson, and Merrill Lynch—all of whom underwrite prison construction projects with lucrative bond issues.[72] Private prison firms or the state bureaus take out bonds to finance the large projects, and sell them to these banks, who in turn sell them to investors—the profits here for the banks range from $2 billion to $3 billion per year. Add to these players the small time manufacturers (for example, those who create sprinkler systems that ensure the inmates cannot hang themselves) and the medical firms (for example, those who provide medical care for inmates[73])—and you can imagine the type of market opportunities for businesses who know that the pipeline of prisoners means demand for their products will simply not flag.

To facilitate the building spree, Eli Gage began to publish *Correctional Building News* in 1994. Gage recognized that this growth industry needed its own trade journal, so he jumped into the breech to produce, according to writer Eric Schlosser, "the *Variety* of the prison world."[74] The magazine carries advertisements for the major construction and design firms as well as for such products as electrified fences and better techniques to handle juvenile rebellion. Since the late 1980s, the magazine of the American Correctional Association,

Corrections Today, has seen a 300 percent explosion in its advertisements. Products as diverse as handcuffs, chewing tobacco, and dandruff shampoo are advertised to attract prison administrators. Furthermore, prisons (both state and private run) offer contracts to telephone companies and the big firms (AT&T, Sprint, and the now defunct MCI) charge inmates at least six times the normal rate for a long-distance call. Profits here for the million- to billion- dollar players.

Meanwhile, new outfits have emerged to train correctional officers, many of them in the private sphere. As the Census Bureau reported in 1994, the recruitment and instruction of correctional officers is "the fastest growing function out of everything that government does."[75]

While private corporations make their real money as the ancillary to the public prison industry, they have also re-entered the prison management business. In the mid-1980s, private firms entered the business of running INS detention centers—with the Corrections Corporation of America (CCA) being the pioneer in 1986. In the past 15 years, private firms like CCA could only take control of five percent of the entire prison market, but there are expectations that the trend will continue. However, the two biggest firms that entered the business, CCA and Wackenhut Corrections Corp., are not in the best economic shape. CCA had revenues of $310.3 million in 2001, but its net income was a loss of $730.8 million, while Wackenhut made $535.6 million with a net income of $17 million.[76] These are not impressive figures, yet it needs to be underscored that CCA's capitalization is still almost $4 billion, and it remains a steady draw for investors at the New York Stock Exchange. They see a future in prisons.

In 2001, Good Jobs First published a report that revealed the extent of governmental assistance to these private prisons. Three-quarters of the 60 private prisons studied by Good Jobs First's Philip Mattera and Mafruza Khan received some form of governmental subsidy.[77] Tax-free bonds worth $628 million, low-cost construction financing, property tax abatements, infrastructure subsidies (water, sewer, utility hookups for free), state corporate income tax subsidies—these are some of the means used by the private prison firms, mainly CCA (almost 80 percent of its prisons received state subsidies) and Wackenhut (almost 70 percent of its prisons received state subsidies). These "jail breaks" allowed CCA, Wackenhut and the other prison profiteers to take few "free market" risks as they entered the business. Even this cash was no guarantee of profits.

In 1991, before the current prison blitz, Pricor joined up with the N-Group to convince six Texas counties to float a bond issue worth $74 billion to build prisons that Pricor would manage. The Graham brothers, who run the N-Group, spread money around among local elected officials and scored $2.2 million in cash for their labors. No prisoners came to the prisons, but the Grahams made a good deal of it until a West Texas grand jury indicted them, Pricor, and their underwriter, the already blemished Drexel Burnham Lambert. Gilbert Walker, of Pricor, joined up with David Arnspiger, a Drexel employee, to try to do the same sort of deal in Florida in 1992.[78] The problem for a series of rural prisons before the 1993 Crime Bill was that the profiteers did the deals, but the prisoners did not come.[79] The energetic construction spree of these firms from 1986 till 1993 overextended many of them financially, and with flatness of demand (that is, the rise of the prison population), the firms could not recoup their investments. According to journalist Ken Silverstein:

> Industry experts say a 90–95 percent capacity rate is needed to guarantee the hefty rates of return needed to lure investors. Prudential Securities issued a wildly bullish report on CCA a few years ago [before 1997] but cautioned, "It takes time to bring inmate population levels up to where they cover costs. Low occupancy is a drag on profits."[80]

The Crime Bill suddenly enabled them to fill the pens, reach out to Wall Street for investment, and also to a government eager to dole out cash to prison profiteers rather than to either rehabilitation programs or as cash disbursements to the working class.

Jenni Gainsborough of the ACLU's National Prison Project questions the sanity of letting the prison system get under the rod of the profit incentive: "There is a basic philosophical problem when you begin turning over administration of prisons to people who have an interest in keeping people locked up."[81] Alex Friedmann, a prisoner who was once in a CCA prison, informs us that 70 percent of prison-related expenses come from the costs of staff, "and this is where CCA really saves, beginning with sub-par starting salaries."[82] Going over various studies of life inside the CCA empire, sociologist Parenti calls them a "private hell," telling us how the guards are poorly paid, badly trained, and quick to violence, and that this is the cause of the high rate of prison riots at private jails.[83] Alex Friedmann captures the heart of the problem and has the last word of this section:

> The issue isn't privatizing prisons, but rather privatizing prisoners. Inmates, traditionally the responsibility of state and federal governments, increasingly are being contracted out to the lowest bidder. Convicts have become commodities. Certainly offenders should be punished for committing crimes, but should private companies and their stockholders profit from such punishment? Private prisons would be great if the primary purpose of the criminal justice system was to warehouse inmates without providing them with meaningful opportunities for rehabilitation. Private prison companies have no incentive to invest in such opportunities, especially when they profit from more crime, more punishment, more prisons.[84]

Back on the Chain Gang

Prison labor, we hear from Harry Wu and others, takes place in the Third World. But for some significant noises on the Left, there is otherwise a generous silence about prison labor in the American gulag. We all know that license plates are made in jail, but there is a tendency to think that this is just a good way for prisoners to whittle away their long days. There is little nationwide discussion about the prisoners who "do data entry for Chevron, make telephone reservations for TWA, raise hogs, shovel manure, make circuit boards, limousines, waterbeds, and lingerie for Victoria's Secret";[85] and more, infirmary beds, razor wire, flags, furniture, drapes, janitorial chemicals, garments, and decals; and then, conduct auto maintenance and bodywork, refinish furniture, do laundry, work in print shops, and then, go out into the world in work crews to offer their general labor for hire. The list of companies that hire prison labor includes American Airlines, Boeing, Compaq, Dell, Eddie Bauer, Hewlett-Packard, Honeywell, IBM, J.C. Penny, McDonalds, Microsoft, Motorola, Nordstrom, Pierre Cardin, Revlon, Sony, Texas Instruments, and Toys "R" Us. The top dogs of the corporate world are well represented behind the walls of Uncle Sam's pens.

In 1994, by accident, I ran into a pamphlet from Rhode Island Correctional Industries (RICI). "We provide an opportunity for inmates to practice and improve existing skills and work habits that are valuable in securing the retraining employment upon release," said the pamphlet entitled *Fifteen Secrets of Saving*. The pamphlet had been sent to state and municipal programs in the state, as well as to nonprofit organizations, because all three types of agencies could avail themselves of the cheap labor from RICI. Started over two decades ago, RICI enables the state to forgo training schemes for laid off (or downsized) workers, because it claims to do the work of retraining for that part of the contingent class now incarcerated, who, if they are released, anyway face a tough time being hired by a private sector that is chary of prison records. In jail, however, RICI offers the nonprofits and the state sector "quality workmanship" on furniture, "professional service" on construction, and "highly skilled technicians" for automobile repair. "The quality standards" for garment production, RICI claims, "can match any privately operating sewing shop on the outside." Because of the low costs and the high standards, the industry urges state agencies, municipalities, and nonprofit agencies to "Make Correctional Industries Your FIRST CHOICE."

One of the services offered by RICI was a work crew of minimum-security inmates for painting, litter cleanup, grounds maintenance, interior cleaning (including rug shampooing and floor stripping). "We are constantly called upon to handle unusual, labor intensive projects such as cleaning beaches or removing snow," the pamphlet explained. I called the office and inquired about the service.[86] I need a crew of ten, I said, for a day. The day runs for six hours, I was told, and it will cost me $350. I asked how much the inmates earned, but I could not get the cent figure. The inmates certainly do not get minimum wage ($4.25). For 60 hours of work, the employer would have to pay $255 at minimum wage (without benefits). That would leave $95 for the supervising correctional officer, the transport of the inmates, and for their lunch. Without lunch and transportation, the correctional officer makes under $16 per hour. That is well below the officers' wage structure, which leads us to assume that the inmates make subminimum wages.

Of course there is no need to speculate. On November 1, 1993, the Supreme Court ruled that inmates did not have the right to minimum wage.[87] Three hundred inmates who worked for the prison industries program sued the state of Arizona for work done between 1986 and

1988 under the Federal Fair Labor Standards Act (FLSA). They were paid between 40 and 80 cents per hour for their work with Arizona Correctional Industries. Further, Arizona law requires all wages earned by inmates above 50 cents an hour to be used for victim restitution, repayment to the state for room and board, and support payments to children or other dependents. Therefore, the prisoners effectively earn 50 cents per hour. This is so across the United States. After an earlier dismissal of the inmates' case, the Ninth US Circuit Court of Appeals reinstated the lawsuits after they found an "employer relationship" between the inmates and the state prison. The inmates' attorney argued that the subminimum wage structure produced unfair competition "that is harmful to private sector businesses." By "private sector," the attorneys surely meant the business enterprises run on small capital funds that must compete with other small concerns, rather than the large global corporations whose economies of scale dwarf the correctional industries, and whose taste for low wages leads them to travel overseas as much as to the local state farm. The state's attorney argued that the inmates who work for private businesses (such as those who make reservations for Best Western hotels) are paid at least the minimum wage (which they do not receive, since they can only effectively earn 50 cents per hour); those who work for other prison industries are not entitled to minimum wage. Of course, the state's attorney did not answer the charge of unfair business, since the correctional industries provided goods and services at a lower cost than the private sector who are obliged to pay minimum wage. The court agreed with the state that "prisoners working on a program structured by the prison" are not entitled to minimum wage.[88] The inmates, in the words of the Arizona Correctional Industries, work not for economic reasons, but to be better prepared to re-enter society once they leave prison. With the rates of incarceration on the rise, however, it seems as if there are to be more and more forced labor camps, which will attempt to produce cheap goods and services for state and nonprofit agencies. Besides, given the reticence of society to "take back" released prisoners, the rates of reincarceration force us to see the prison population as relatively permanent.

Through the Hawes-Cooper Act (1929) and the Ashurst-Summers Act (1940), the US government made it a felony to transport prison-made goods across state lines. While not a ban on prison labor, these laws restricted and regulated the use of prisoners for corporate profit. Nevertheless, bucking an international trend, President Roosevelt signed an order in 1934 to create the Federal Prison Industries (or UNICOR) to operate around Washington, DC, as an autonomous agency. In 1947, when the world's powers put together the General Agreement on Trade and Tariffs, they allowed states to erect barriers to "free trade" in certain exceptional circumstances (article XX)—to protect public morals, human, animal, or plant life, health, national treasures, exhaustible natural resources, and finally (in section "e"), "relating to the products of prison labor." The disgust at the use of convicts for profits came from the broad social democratic dynamic that overthrew Nazi racism, colonial barbarism, and the general disregard for human dignity that found its institutional champion at the UN and in the International Declaration of Human Rights (1948). Article 10.3 of the Declaration's Covenant on Civil and Political Rights (finally agreed upon in 1966 and ratified in 1976) states, "The penitentiary system shall comprise treatment of prisoners the essential aim of which shall be their reformation and social rehabilitation." If the post-war penal philosophy said that bibliotherapy would heal prisoners, the 1970s inaugurated a belief that work was the salve needed to straighten out and reform criminals. Criminology provided a scientific basis for the emerging system of penal slavery: work, not for remuneration, but for therapy. In 1979, the US Congress passed the Federal Prison Industries Enhancement (PIE) Act that allowed private firms to enter "joint ventures" with the state prisons, as well as opening the door to prison labor in general.[89]

Big corporations entered the prison labor trade, but not to an enormous extent. Sociologist Parenti and American Studies professor Cynthia Young are both clear that the prison labor situation should not be exaggerated. Parenti shows that less than five percent of inmates work in the prison industries, that the rate of increase of prison workers is not near the rate of increase in inmates, and therefore, "prison labor is a sideshow." Young, drawing from Parenti's work, argues, "The reasons for the increasing use of prison labor are, in fact, primarily ideological—not economic."[90] While this is so in terms of the prison system in general, it does not obviate the fact that for the businesses that enter the prisons, "prison labor is like a pot of gold."[91]

Prison labor profits private firms that enter the pens to take advantage of cheap labor, but the state-run enterprises, even with cheap wages, cannot seem to stay afloat without state subsidies. California's Prison Industry Authority (PIA), for example, pays its workforce under a dollar with no benefits, pays the Department of Corrections almost nothing for warehouse space, pays no taxes, does not have to advertise because its customers are other state agencies that are mandated to buy its products, sets its own prices, and yet it has lost money for at least a third of its existence.[92] The prison-made goods do, however, enable the state, municipal, and nonprofit sectors to gain access to goods for relatively low costs with labor that is disciplined by guards who are paid for by the state. The PIA does not make money because it absorbs all kinds of costs that are not passed on to the customer—so the solvency of the PIA is not at issue, rather, the generally low cost of goods that enable the state to pass by small business for prison business. Furthermore, as Cynthia Young puts it:

> Rather than generate huge windfalls for states or the federal government, prison labor has the potential to enrich private corporations, benefiting states only in so far as corporations remain in-state. The relatively low startup costs and paltry wages paid by corporations make prison labor a cost-effective alternative to relocating their factories to Mexico, the Caribbean, Southeast Asia, or the Pacific Rim.[93]

At least two social classes stand to lose from prison labor. The inmates are part of a captive workforce with no rights, only duties to capital, and they cannot bargain for higher wages or for most of the basic contractual arrangements. There are, of course, some prisoners' unions, such as the Missouri Prisoners Labor Union (MPLU), legally chartered by the state of Missouri on August 3, 1998 and now with a membership of over 500 prisoners. On July 1, 2000, the MPLU initiated an international boycott of the products made by Colgate Palmolive because the company did not back MPLU's demand that the state of Missouri establish a minimum wage for all Missouri workers, abolish forced labor, and condemn executions. In a letter to Colgate, which hires Missouri prisoners, the MPLU noted:

> We realize that your company didn't put us in prison. This is a matter of Colgate-Palmolive reaping immense profits for our incarceration and as the largest single consumer

block you have a social obligation to us. The situation I am outlining is the same argument organized labor has used to oppose sweatshop labor employed by Kathy Lee Gifford, Nike, etc. I would also like to add that we are not asking for anything from society except that we be treated in a fair manner as defined by the United States Constitution and numerous legal cases. We are not advocating for a cushy life style but simply a fair days pay for a fair days work and a safe, non-abusive work environment.[94]

Apart from a few instances such as this, the prison workers are by and large unable to make demands and this situation shows us that the correctional industries are the highest stage of capitalist extraction within a formally democratic framework.

Those who do not realize they are losers in this setup are the small business owners, those whose shops exist on the whim of banks, and whose margins are thin enough that a few cents here and there on wages make an enormous difference on the contracts they can offer. These people, the small business people and their class, pay a lion's share of US taxes. These taxes subsidize the expanding penal workforce who now produce the same sorts of goods that small businesses produce. The prison goods are cheaper, even if they are of inferior quality, and they have a captive market in the state, municipalities, and nonprofit organizations. These middling classes hurl their invective at criminals, but they have not yet organized against their economic competitors, the UNICORs and others who undersell them with their jail breaks.

Prison labor may not be the most efficient form of labor, but it is certainly not contradictory to the dynamic of capitalism. It might even be its most efficient and yet underutilized form. From 1972 to 1992, the number of prison inmates working in correctional industries increased by 300 percent, from 169,000 to 523,000. The prison industrial complex now hires more people than any Fortune 500 company with the exception of General Motors.[95] This does not mean that the prisons are fated to become the main industries in the US, but they are certainly a significant part of the economy, even if they seem to be only a "sideshow."

Detention

If the prison construction and management business went into a brief slump in 2000 and 2001, the events of 9/11 have made the prison CEOs jubilant. "The federal business is the best business for us," Cornell Company's Steve Logan told his prison CEO colleagues, and the fallout from 9/11 is "increasing the level of business."[96] In 1986, the CCA was formed to handle immigrant detainees, as they awaited deportation proceedings, and the other main private prison profiteer, Wackenhut, also began its career with immigration detention centers. They branched out to other correctional sites, but with a decline in demand there, and after 9/11 with a boom in immigrant detention centers, the private prison firms have returned to the basics. As the *Village Voice*'s Alisa Solomon notes, "The only incarcerated populations sustaining reliable growth now are INS detainees and federal prisoners, many of them noncitizens." The Federal Bureau of Prisons, in September 2001, issued directives to contractors to build prisons to meet its "criminal alien requirements (CAR)," a new category that harbingers a future for the prison industry.

Setting aside the unknown number (perhaps several thousand) of those picked up by the FBI since 9/11 and shielded from public view, the number of those who pass through the INS detention centers each year comes to about 150,000, with about 20,000 in residence at one time. According to a 2002 study by the Bureau of Justice Statistics, the number of alien detainees who serve a prison sentence increased by ninefold between 1985 and 2000. This increase is more than twice the rate of increase of the entire federal prison population.[97] Of those who served an INS-related prison sentence, more than half had Mexican citizenship, seven percent had US citizenship (but had violated INS regulations—such as sale of papers to a noncitizen), three percent had Chinese citizenship, and the rest were evenly spread among the planet's population. Before the state's drive to register, incarcerate, and deport Muslims, it went after migrants with HIV-AIDS. These survivors in the system could not even challenge their situation because they were not arrested. Awaiting deportation as "administrative detainees," these migrants could not challenge the system's lack of medical care. How can they claim "cruel and unusual punishment" when they are only being held, not punished?[98] The parallel with the post-9/11 detainees is very strong. The *Village Voice*'s Alisa Solomon has brought the stories of many of those who seek asylum, but live for intolerable amounts of time in jail: people like Uganda's Emmy Kutesa and Yudaya Nanyonga, Nigeria's Osabeda Egoibe, Ghana's Adelaide Abankwah, Congo's Lilian Loukakou, Togo's Fauziya Kassindja, Barbados's Kenneth Durant, Ethiopia's Lulseged Dhine, and so many others.[99] Thanks to the efforts of Desis Rising Up and Moving (DRUM) in New York City, we have the stories of Ahmed Raza, a migrant worker from Pakistan and now a 9/11 detainee in Passaic County Jail, of Mohammed Akram (a convenience store owner also at Passaic as a 9/11 detainee), and so many others.[100] These people provide the human face to the underground expansion of state power, and of prison profiteering. As Egoibe told Solomon, "A person cannot be in confinement like this and feel that he is safe. But I did come to America because I thought it was a place I could find safety."

What accounts for this explosion, prior to 9/11? Marika Latras and John Scalia, of the Bureau of Justice Statistics, note:

> A major portion of this growth was attributable to changes in federal sentencing law that increased the likelihood of a convicted immigration felony offender receiving a prison sentence—from 57 percent in 1985 to 91 percent in 2000—in lieu of some lesser sanction. The growth was also the result of increased sentences and time actually served, which increased from about 4 months in 1985 to 21 months in 2000.[101]

The numbers arrested after 9/11 may grow, but they are a small fraction of those who are held by the INS for deportation, for crimes they committed, or else until their asylum applications are processed. In 1999, long before the USA Patriot Act, the INS anticipated that it would need jail cells for almost 30,000 detainees. Richard Wackenhut, head of Wackenhut Corp. reported:

> We are very optimistic about our continued growth in view of our current backlog of 8,260 correctional facility beds under development. Federal and other agencies are expected to issue additional requests for proposals on additional prison privatization projects for over 20,000 additional beds in the coming year.[102]

The US government has now appointed a Detention Trustee (the first appointee to this post is Craig Unger, a former Bureau of Prisons procurement officer), who has a budget of $615 million to contract for beds for the expansion.

To hold these "criminal aliens," the INS operates nine Service Processing Centers (SPCs) in Puerto Rico, New York, California, Texas, Arizona, and Florida. The newest INS SPC is located in Buffalo, NY, where there are not only 300 INS beds, but also 150 for use by the US Marshals Service (FBI). In addition, the INS contracts for seven other facilities, in Colorado, Texas, Washington, New Jersey, New York, and California, in addition to use of Bureau of Prisons sites in Louisiana and Arizona. To run these sites, the INS spends over $600 million per year. Stunningly, the Federal Bureau of Prisons guaranteed CCA a 95 percent occupancy rate for its prisons—that is, the government will pay CCA for 95 percent of its bed capacity regardless of how many inmates are held in the jail. This is akin to the power purchasing agreements that Enron insisted upon in its pioneering shakedown of the world.[103]

Conditions in these INS detention centers are atrocious. The tale of the detention center in Elizabeth, New Jersey is sufficient as an illustration of the broad structural violence experienced by INS detainees, asylum seekers, and others caught in the INS dragnet. Esmor Correctional Services Corporation began its correctional career in "halfway houses" for the homeless in New York City, but in 1989, as the city cut back on social welfare, Esmor "turned to the next emerging housing program: prisons."[104] In 1993, Esmor won a $54 million contract to run the immigrant detention center in Elizabeth, New Jersey. Their bid was $20 million less than their closest competitor, so that the upshot of their bid was that they failed to provide the inmates with anything like humane occupancy when the jail opened on August 3, 1994. About six months after the holding area was up and running, the INS ordered a review and investigation of the facility; the seventy-two page report showed that "detainees were subjected to harassment, verbal abuse, and other degrading actions perpetuated by Esmor guards." Such treatment "was part of a systematic methodology designed to control the general detainee population and to intimidate and discipline obstreperous detainees through use of corporal punishment." The violence formed part of "an atmosphere of penny-pinching in the jail [as] poorly paid, ill-trained guards physically and verbally abused detainees, shackling them with leg irons, roughing them up and waking them without reason in the night."[105]

On the night of June 18, 1995, after the INS reviewed the jail, but before they published the interim report, some INS detainees at the Esmor facility took control of the jail. The Esmor guards fled and the local police sent in a SWAT team that viciously retook the jail.[106] The police brought the "ringleaders," about 20 men, to Union County Jail, in Elizabeth, who were, according to Human Rights Watch, "beaten, held naked, made to crawl on their hands and knees through a gauntlet of jail officers, and forced to chant, 'America is Number One.' One Indian detainee claimed that between beatings, correctional officers used pliers to pinch the skin on his genitals and squeeze his tongue."[107] Esmor's share price fell from 20 dollars to seven dollars in the aftermath of the riot. The INS shut down the facility, but in 1997, reopened it under the management of CCA.

Little has changed. In July 1998, guards at the Jackson County Correctional Facility in Florida used electric batons to shock detainees, torturing them into submission. When the matter was brought before the INS, the INS assistant deputy for detention and deportation at the Miami office told the media, "We cannot dictate to the county or the state of Florida what standards they should have in their facilities. They're another government agency. We have to rely on their integrity."[108] The US signed the 1994 Convention Against Torture and Other Cruel, Inhuman, or Degrading Treatment or Punishment, whose second article notes, "no exceptional circumstance whatsoever, whether a state of war or a threat of war, internal political instability or any other public emergency, may be invoked as a justification of torture." What happened in the Jackson Correctional facility, what happens at the Guantánamo Bay Camp X-Ray or elsewhere is a violation of that Convention and yet, the bureaucracy is able to make the case for interagency trust!

JONESING FOR FREEDOM

Between Broadway and the Bowery in Manhattan you'll find Great Jones Street, home to dope addicts who lived there in the 1970s. Folklore from the street tells us that these addicts started to talk of their addiction as the "jones," and the verb form, "jonesing," referred to being high or craving dope. So here we are, after this excursus in the world of corrections, jonesing for freedom, the greatest drug of them all.

The history of US liberalism is torn by a contradiction that it cannot overcome: it pledges to promote equality, but it also pledges to a system founded on mechanisms of social control that are authoritarian. The conservatives resolve this contradiction simply: they believe that the goal of equity is precisely what creates inequality and forces a benevolent US state to act illiberally. People are inherently and forever unequal (based on race or culture or some version in between),[109] therefore to try to make equity forces the state to be authoritarian. Get rid of the equity programs, they argue, and let "individuals" fight it out. A corporation, however, is treated as an "individual," albeit with a lot of accumulated power and capital. Real, living people are matched against this foe, but since they are increasingly outside unions and other organizations, they must struggle without power and without capital. The deck is stacked overwhelmingly on the side of global corporations.

Despite their obvious corporate partisanship, US conservatives pose as the true champions of equality and freedom. The process of equality, in the conservative argument, is now "privatized" or made the responsibility of each citizen. The government, in this scenario, must withdraw from the goal of producing equity and must actively pursue the role of executioner and jailer. The contradictions of American liberalism are now simplified: there is inequality because people don't try hard enough (therefore former House Speaker Newt Gingrich's statements about closing down the "Department of Happiness").[110] The inflection of US conservatism is deeply racist. The "people" who do not try hard enough for conservatives are urban blacks: the stereotypes of the welfare queen and the drug pusher are emblematic. Here US liberalism's practices are articulated *openly* as legitimate practices by US conservatism: the convergence between Republicans and Democrats on this issue is remarkable.

If the mainstream politicians fail us on the prison score, there are others who are eager to confront the prison-first mentality. The movement against prisons is not new, having antecedents in Frederick Douglass's campaign against the "convict lease system" in the 19th Century.[111] To make matters simple, I'm going to create a few analytical distinctions within the anti-prison section of the movement.

Political Prisoners

Even as the government denies that it holds political prisoners, the history of US imprisonment shows otherwise from Henry David Thoreau (imprisoned for refusal to support the war against Mexico) to the mass incarceration of the leadership of the Communist Party (in the 1950s) as well as the Black Panther Party for Self-Defense (BPP) in the 1960s. The state adopted various tactics against the BPP, whether assassination (of Fred Hampton, Mark Clark, Bunchy Carter, John Huggins, and others), or fraudulent arrests (Angela Davis, Dhoruba bin Wahaad and the New York 21, Huey Newton, Assata Shakur, Mutulu Shakur, Geronimo Pratt, and others).

What is a political prisoner? Susan Rosenberg, a political prisoner herself, writes in the *Journal of Prisoners on Prisons*:

> There are over 150 political prisoners in US prisons. We are in almost every federal prison in the country and spread throughout different State prison systems. I define a political prisoner as someone whose beliefs or actions have put them into direct conflict with the US government, or someone who has been targeted by the government because of his/her beliefs and actions. While this is a somewhat generic description, it complies with international legal definitions. The other grouping of people who are in prison who are political are the prisoners of war from the Puerto Rican and New Afrikan/African American liberation movements. These are individuals who make that claim under international law in pursuit of the recognition of their national liberation struggles for self-determination. The political prisoners and POW's in the US who have struggled for human rights and social liberation—people who come from movements that range from the anti-imperialist left to the Native American struggle for sovereignty—have all been treated by the government as political dissidents, but have been denied the dignity of recognition as political prisoners. Rather, we have been criminalized or wrongly defined as "terrorists." We have been repressed to the maximum.[112]

The most famous political prisoner in this period was George Jackson, whose book *Soledad Brother* informed the progressive community about the condition within the jails as well as about the political war the state conducted against the poor. In his posthumously published book, *Blood in the Eye*, George Jackson wrote,

> The purpose of the chief repressive institutions within the totalitarian capitalist state is clearly to discourage and prohibit certain activity, and the prohibitions are aimed at very distinctly defined sectors of the class and race sensitized society. The ultimate expression of law is not order—it's prison. There are hundreds upon hundreds of prisons, and thousands upon thousands of laws, yet there is no social order, no social peace.[113]

In 1971, the state killed George Jackson within San Quentin prison, and several months later the prisoners of Attica State Prison in New York rebelled against the conditions in the jail and in solidarity with the Soledad Brother. The retaliation against this uprising is still in popular memory.

The movement against the imprisonment of people on political grounds has tried to do at least two things: to raise awareness of the existence of *political* prisoners and to free this or that individual prisoner. The Committee to Free Angela Davis, for instance, was formed to galvanize people on her behalf, to raise slogans like "Free Angela Davis," and to fight for her freedom as a political act against the crackdown on dissent in general. Today's campaign to "Free Mumia" works on the same axis. The Jericho Movement takes the individual cases and makes a general political campaign around the issue of all political prisoners.[114]

The State of the Pen

Three former BPP members went to the Angola prison in Louisiana on robbery charges, with the belief that they would spend a short time in jail before being paroled. While in jail, Albert Woodfox, Herman Wallace, and Robert King Wilkerson founded the BPP of Angola, in 1971, to struggle against the terrible conditions within the jail. They reached out to white prisoners, tried to forge solidarity against the prison regime and fought the guards on the conditions within the Farm. One of the main complaints of the BPP was the systematic use of rape by the guards to discipline the population. Human Rights Watch, in 2001, criticized the widespread use of rape by guards for social control.

> Men in prison were subject to prisoner-on-prisoner sexual abuse, whose effects on the victim's psyche were serious and enduring. Victims of rape, in the most extreme cases, were literally the slaves of the perpetrators, being "rented out" for sex, "sold," or even auctioned off to other inmates.[115]

"It wasn't much help to go to the security," Woodfox notes, "because most of the security people were condoning that type of activity. They would benefit from it because they would get money or favors for allowing rapes to happen. Some of the guards themselves would be involved in the rapes."[116] In 1972, the guards framed the Angola 3 for the murder of a prison guard, saddled them with life sentences, and threw them in solitary confinement, but these three men continue to fight against the brutal conditions within prisons.

Most of those who are at work on prison reform come from one of these three communities: former inmates, families of those in jail, and religious groups such as the Quakers who are morally opposed to prisons. They record the horrid conditions in the jails and bring the truth to those of us who are immune to the violence done in our name.

Disenfranchisement

In 1998, the nonprofit Sentencing Project released an important report that detailed the widespread denial of the franchise to felons. The authors found that all but four states (Maine, Massachusetts, Utah, and Vermont) did not allow felons to vote, while two-thirds of the states did not allow those on probation to vote either. Almost four million US citizens, or one in 50 adults, are unable to vote. Almost a million and a half of them have completed their sentences, and a million and a half are black (13 percent of all black men cannot vote). Bush II won the presidency through Florida, a state where a third of black men cannot exercise their right to vote.[117]

The fight against this denial of the vote is being conducted on the legal and political front. Since the denial of the vote violates the civil liberty of the ex-felons, many of the organizations that tackle those questions are in the fray (including Human Rights Watch, Amnesty International, the Sentencing Project, and others). On the political front, prisoners' rights groups and Left organizations fight for the franchise with the knowledge that the prison complex is a warehouse of dissent, so the movement must ensure that these folk are able to be involved in the political fights of our time. Pressure from all these quarters caused several states to change their policies, so that Delaware (where once a felon faced a lifetime ban on the franchise) restored voting right to felons in June 2000, New Mexico did the same in March 2001, and so did Maryland in 2002. Cases are pending in Florida, a hotbed of discontent over the 2000 election.[118]

The New Abolitionists

While these are all important arenas of struggle, they fall short of the more general call for the abolition of all prisons. Many prisoner writers (such as George Jackson) and small ex-prisoner liberation groups (such as the Out of Control Lesbian Support Committee, the California Coalition for Women Prisoners, and the California Coalition for Battered Women in Prison) called for abolition long before the Crime Bill of 1993, and before the incarceration boom. In 1988, for instance, the first issue of the Canada-based *Journal of Prisoners on Prison* was dedicated to the notion of "prison abolition." Critical Resistance, a network of abolitionists formed in 1997, offered the most clear-headed description of "abolition":

- Abolition is a political vision that seeks to eliminate the need for prisons, policing, and surveillance by creating sustainable alternatives to punishment and imprisonment.

- Abolition means acknowledging the devastating effects prison, policing, and surveillance have on poor communities, communities of color, and other targeted communities, and saying, "No, we won't live like this. We deserve more."

- Abolitionists recognize that the kinds of wrongdoing we call "crime" do not exist in the same way everywhere and are not "human nature," but rather determined by the societies we live in. Similarly, abolitionists do not assume that people will never hurt each other or that people won't cross the boundaries set up by their communities. We do imagine, however, that boundary crossings will happen much less often if we live in a society that combines flexibility with care to provide for, and acknowledge, people's needs. To do that, we must create alternatives for dealing with the injuries people inflict upon each other in ways that sustain communities and families. Keeping a community whole is impossible by routinely removing people from it.

• An abolitionist vision means that we must build models today that can represent how we want to live in the future. It means developing practical strategies for taking small steps that move us toward making our dreams real and that lead the average person to believe that things really could be different. It means living this vision in our daily lives.

A crucial part of this statement is the portion, "abolitionists do not assume that people will never hurt each other or that people won't cross the boundaries set up by their communities." In April 2000, radical activists held the Color of Violence: Violence Against Women of Color conference at the University of California, Santa Cruz. An oversubscribed event, the conclave raised the problem of violence against women, particularly within communities of color. While there is considerable, but not adequate, discussion of violence against white women, the organizers felt, there is a general invisibility over the problem of violence by men of color against women of color. Activist Andrea Smith notes that the domestic violence movement first began as a community transformation struggle, but then devolved to psychiatric and legal strategies. The reduction of the struggle meant, "Mainstream anti-violence advocates are demanding longer prison sentences for batterers and sex offenders as a frontline approach to stopping violence against women." For communities of color, this approach is not palatable because "the criminal justice system has always been brutally oppressive toward communities of color."[119] As Angela Davis put it in the keynote address:

> One of the major questions facing this conference is how to develop an analysis that furthers neither the conservative project of sequestering millions of men of color in accordance with the contemporary dictates of globalized capital and its prison industrial complex, nor the equally conservative project of abandoning poor women of color to a continuum of violence that extends from the sweatshops through the prisons, to shelters, and into bedrooms at home.[120]

Having raised the problem, Davis posed a question to organizers:

> We want to continue to contest the neglect of domestic violence against women, the tendency to dismiss it as a private matter. We need to develop an approach that relies on political mobilization rather than legal remedies or

social service delivery. We need to fight for temporary and long-term solutions to violence and simultaneously think about and link global capitalism, global colonialism, racism, and patriarchy—all the forces that shape violence against women of color. Can we, for example, link a strong demand for remedies for women of color who are targets of rape and domestic violence with a strategy that calls for the abolition of the prison system?[121]

Davis and Critical Resistance, therefore, do not simply call for an abolition of prisons in an idealistic vein.[122] CR's program against prisons, the police and the Crime Bill is a window into how to struggle to transform the system and yet be aware of the need for security:

If our vision is to eliminate the need for prisons, policing, and surveillance, we must have a clear idea of what we need to make our communities safe and secure. We must make those alternatives realistic and we must be able to begin building them today. We need community alternatives that keep people out of the hands of police and out of prisons and jails, while addressing the fears that people live with on a daily basis. We can do that by building our communities and ending a reliance on, and belief in, law enforcement as the only solution. Here are just a few examples of what those alternatives might include:

• Community-based economic resources: Current cooperative economic models provide us with one set of strategies to build our communities. We can create a means for providing meaningful work—and training for that work—to all. This work and training can provide for our housing, food, and clothing, and should contribute to the well being of the community.

• Community-based education models: We have examples of small, charter, and alternative schools that have been successful in showing us alternative means of educating our community. Community-based schools can offer education to anyone who wants it (youth and adults). Education can be free, participatory, and aimed toward sustaining the kinds of social environments we want to create. They can also model the community forms we want in their teaching practices. Our schools can tailor the learning process to the needs of the students and can involve the adult community in learning and teaching so schools are not isolated from the rest of the community.

• Community forums: Some current restorative justice models from around the world provide us with examples of how community mediation and problem solving is used to resolve conflicts and keep our communities safe. We must create a means of dealing with people who hurt each other (physically, mentally, emotionally, materially). We can establish community forums to address grievances people have regarding each other and as a means of resolving those conflicts. Such formations could include community councils that mediate between individuals/groups, community elders to whom community members could go to for advice and counsel, age-, issue-, and interest-specific groups for building community ties (youth groups, artists' circles, support groups, study groups, etc.), and community-based strategies for keeping individual community members from harming themselves or others and to provide disincentives for repeating such actions. Above all, these groups can grow from the community and their direction and scope should come from the people involved in them and whom they affect.

• Community services: Current community-based organizations provide us with good examples of how services may be provided. We must provide services to those who have difficulty providing for themselves. Such strategies can emphasize not only taking care of those who need the most help, but finding ways to help people get through these systems and come out with both what they need and their humanity and dignity intact. These models can also include working with people who currently provide such services to design workshops, trainings, and ongoing support and resources that go beyond providing individual advocacy and services, and emphasize gaining independence from those systems.

• Medical care: Current neighborhood clinics and free clinics provide us with good examples of strategies for making free health care available to all. Such services can include basic health (preventative, checkups, acupuncture, etc.), health crises (major medical emergencies, terminal illness), dental and visual health, and mental health (both routine counseling and therapy as well as crisis care and care for the mentally disabled, etc.).

Many of the strategies discussed above are already in place. They are not fantasies, but real life examples of community building and growth.[123]

Discussions, lawsuits, film festivals, actions, and outreach characterize the work of Critical Resistance. In many ways, its work mirrors that of the Prison Moratorium Project founded in 1995, whose signature has been to marry prison abolition work with hip-hop culture (with its *We Remember Attica* hip-hop teach-ins in 1996, its Education,

Not Incarceration program from 1997, its War on Drugs, War on Us, high school program from 1999, its *No More Prisons* music CD, its Not With Our Money campaign from late 2000, its anti–Sodexho Marriott campaign on college campuses, and finally its Stop the Disappearances movement with DRUM against the illegal detentions after 9/11).

To abolish prison, as Critical Resistance recognizes, is to abolish the dispensation that we live under in general, the world of the CEO class on the one side and the contingent on the other, the world of the fat cat and the world of the hard hat, of surplus and deficit.

1   Angela Y. Davis, *If They Come in the Morning: Voices of Resistance* (New York, 1971), p. 25.
2   Martin Luther King, Jr., "Declaration of Independence from the War in Vietnam (April 1967)," *Ramparts*, May 1967, pp. 33–37. The best introduction to the *socialist* side of Dr. King is in Michael Eric Dyson, *I May Not Get There With You: The True Martin Luther King Jr.*, New York: Free Press, 2000. Chapter 3 of the book offers the context of King's position on Vietnam and imperialism.
3   Dyson, *I May Not Get There With You*, p. 112.
4   Steven Holmes, "Clinton Tells Hispanic Group It Must Combat Urban Crime," *New York Times*, November 23, 1993.
5   Peter Mattheissen, *Sal Si Puedes (Escape If You Can): Cesar Chavez and the New American Revolution*, Berkeley: University of California Press, 2000, p. 280.
6   Robert Scheer, "The River of Hypocrisy Runs Wide and Deep," *Los Angeles Times*, August 1, 1995.
7   After the Stuart case, Boston mayor Raymond Flynn created a commission under attorney James St. Clair to investigate the department. The St. Clair Commission report, *Report on the Boston Police Department Management Review Committee*, released on January 14, 1992, acknowledged the department's racist response to Stuart's claims.
8   Kevin Cullen, "Stuart dies in jump off Tobin Bridge," *Boston Globe*, January 5, 1990, and Kevin Cullen and Mike Barnicle, "Probers suspect Stuart killed wife," *Boston Globe*, January 10, 1990.
9   Robert Perkinson, "Civil Liberties: Oklahoma Fallout," Z, July/August 1995.
10   I urge you to turn to Daniel Levitas's *The Terrorist Next Door: The Militia Movement and the Radical Right*, New York: Thomas Dunne/St. Martin's Press, 2002 for details on the fascist bands that dot the US landscape. On the suspension of rules for those held as terrorists, see Barbara Olshansky, *Secret Trials and Executions: Military Tribunals and the Threat to Democracy*, New York: Seven Stories Press, 2002. I have written about the problem of McCarthyism in "The Green Menace: McCarthyism after 9/11," *The Subcontinental*, vol. 1, no. 1, 2003.
11   Kurt Eichenwald, "White Collar Defense Stance: The Criminal-less Crime," *New York Times*, March 3, 2002.
12   Jonathan D. Glazer, "Mad as Hell: Hard Time for White-Collar Crime," *New York Times*, July 28, 2002.
13   I have explicated the logic of the political disagreements in *War Against the Planet*.
14   *US News & World Report*, December 30, 1968.
15   William S. Buckley, "On the Right," *National Review*, May 5, 1970.
16   *Report of the National Advisory Commission on Civil Disorders*, New York: Bantam Books, March 1968.

17 For an excellent overview of the issues, see Kim Strosnider, "Anti-Gang Ordinances After *City of Chicago v. Morales*: The Intersection of Race, Vagueness Doctrine, and Equal Protection in the Criminal Law," *American Criminal Law Review* no. 39, Winter 2002.

18 Dirk Johnson, "2 Out of 3 Young Black Men in Denver Are on Gang Suspect List," *New York Times*, December 11, 1993.

19 Steven Stycos, "Legislator cleared in trial exposing a dozen brutality complaints against Officer Merandi," *Providence Phoenix*, June 21, 1996.

20 President W. J. Clinton, "Memorandum on Fairness in Law Enforcement: Memorandum for the Secretary of the Treasury, the Attorney General, the Secretary of the Interior," June 9, 1999.

21 Even this data is not necessarily useful, as politicians influence how the numbers are collected. Fox Butterfield, "Some Experts Fear Political Influence on Crime Data Agencies," *New York Times*, September 22, 2002.

22 David Harris, *Driving While Black: Racial Profiling on Our Nation's Highways*. American Civil Liberties Union Special Report, June 1999.

23 US Government, Office of Civil Rights, *Who is Guarding the Guardians? A Report on Police Practices and Civil Rights in America*, Washington, DC: OCR, November 2000.

24 "I hereby direct you to review the use by Federal law enforcement authorities of race as a factor in conducting stops, searches, and other investigative procedures. In particular, I ask that you work with the Congress to develop methods or mechanisms to collect any relevant data from Federal law enforcement agencies and work in cooperation with State and local law enforcement in order to assess the extent and nature of any such practices. I further direct that you report back to me with your findings and recommendations for the improvement of the just and equal administration of our Nation's laws."

25 Christian Parenti, *Lockdown America: Police and Prisons in the Age of Crisis*, London: Verso, 1999, p. 9. For an insightful look at the origins of the "war on drugs," see Edward Jay Epstein, *Agency of Fear: Opiates and Political Power in America*, London: Verso, 1990.

26 Most of the correctional statistics used in this chapter are from the Bureau of Justice Statistics Correctional Surveys, the National Probation Survey, the National Prisoner Statistics, Survey of Jails and the National Parole Survey. A summary of the numbers, until 1990, is available in Patrick Langan, "America's Soaring Prison Population," *Science*, no. 251, March 29, 1991, pp. 1568–1573.

27 Agreement on this point is stunningly universal. From the Right, John Dilulio is pretty forthright in his widely cited article, "Against Mandatory Minimums," *National Review*, May 17, 1999, and at length in the report by Anne M. Piehl, Bert Useem, and John Dilulio, *Right Sizing Justice: A Cost-Benefit Analysis of Imprisonment in Three States*, New York: The

Manhattan Institute, 1999. That same year, from the Left, Marc Mauer published his useful book, *Race to Incarcerate*, New York: The New Press, 1999. The leading criminologist Michael Tonry comes to similar conclusions in his *Malign Neglect: Race, Crime and Punishment in America*, New York: Oxford University Press, 1995. In May 2000, Human Rights Watch released a comprehensive survey of racism and incarceration, *Punishment and Prejudice: Racial Disparities in the War on Drugs*, New York: Human Rights Watch, vol. 12, no. 2 (G), 2000.

28   All data is from the Bureau of Justice Statistics.

29   Marc Mauer, *Young Black Men and the Criminal Justice System: A Growing National Problem*, Washington, DC: Sentencing Project, 1990.

30   I invite the reader to visit my book *Fat Cats and Running Dogs*, pp. 164–166, where I offer some details on the Citibank-Salinas connection. For more on the role of the CIA, see Alexander Cockburn and Jeffrey St. Clair, *Whiteout: The CIA, Drugs and the Press*, London: Verso, 1998.

31   Barry R. McCaffrey, "Race and Drugs: Perception and Reality, New Rules for Crack Versus Powder Cocaine," *Washington Times*, October 5, 1997. The article in the *Journal of Alcohol and Drug Education* (1995) was entitled "Drug Use and African Americans: Myth Versus Reality" and it was written by Burston, Jones, and Robert-Saunders.

32   Salim Muwakkil, "The Criminal Just-Us System," *In These Times*, April 19, 1993, pp. 26-27.

33   "US Appeal's Judge's Sentences That Defy Mandatory Guidelines," *New York Times*, August 29, 1993. The case is *US v. Hawley* (984 F. 2d 252) in the Eighth Circuit, 1993.

34   "Sentencing in the Federal Courts: Does Race Matter? The Transition to Sentencing Guidelines, 1986–1990: Summary," Washington, DC: Bureau of Justice Statistics, 1993.

35   David Baldus, Charles Pulaski, and George Woodworth, "Monitoring and Evaluating Temporary Death Sentencing Systems: Lessons from Georgia," 18 *UC Davis Law Review* 1375, 1985 and *Idem.*, "Comparative Review of Death Sentences: An Empirical Study of the Georgia Experience," 74 *Journal of Criminal Law and Criminology* 661, 1983.

36   Speech at Annual Dinner in Honor of the Judiciary, American Bar Association, 1990, *The National Law Journal*, February 8, 1993.

37   Jeffrey Pokorak, "Probing the Capital Prosecutor's Perspective: Race and Gender of the Discretionary Actors," 83 *Cornell Law Review* 1811, 1998.

38   David Baldus and George Woodworth, "Race Discrimination in America's Capital Punishment System Since *Furman v. Georgia* (1972): The Evidence of Race Disparities and the Record of Our Courts and Legislatures in Addressing This Issue," Report for the American Bar Association, 1997, or "Race Discrimination and the Death Penalty in the Post-*Furman* Era: An Empirical and Legal Analysis with Recent Findings from Philadelphia," 83 *Cornell Law Review* 1638, 1998.

39 For an excellent analysis of the *McCleskey* case, see Chaka M. Patterson, "Race and the Death Penalty: The Tension between Individualized Justice and Racially Neutral Standards," *Texas Wesleyan Law Review*, vol. 2, no. 1, Summer 1995 as well as the ubiquitous, Baldus, Pulaski, and Woodworth, "Law and Statutes in Conflict: Reflections on *McCleskey v. Kemp*," *Handbook of Psychology and Law*, ed. Dorothy Kagehiro and William Laufer, New York: Springer-Verlag, 1992.

40 Backed by evidence of racism in the judicial system, a movement against the death penalty seems to be in formation in the US. In 1997, the generally liberal state of Massachusetts almost reinstated the death penalty under pressure from right-wing politicians. On the heels of the Louise Woodward case, public demonstrations prevented the passage of the Massachusetts reinstatement by one vote (Ms. Woodward was an English au pair who was charged with the murder of an infant, but public outcry stayed the hand of the court and she was let off with time served—that is, the time of her trial where she was found guilty of murder). One could be more sanguine about this if the ultimate punishment were not death. In April 1999, the US opposed the UN Human Rights Commission's moratorium on executions (India abstained). State-sanctioned racist murder, it seems, will not cease.

41 Libero Della Piana, "From the Cold War to the War on Crime," *Third Force,* November/December 1994, p. 8.

42 Sam Vincent Meddis and Deborah Sharp, "Prison Business is a Blockbuster," *USA Today*, December 13, 1994.

43 The best summary of this material is in George Lipsitz, *The Possessive Investment in Whiteness*, Philadelphia: Temple University Press, 1998, Chapter 1.

44 Tamar Lewin, "Low Pay and Closed Doors Confront Young Job Seekers," *New York Times*, March 10, 1994.

45 In 2002, data shows that "the unemployment rate for college graduates has risen as much since early last year as it has for high school dropouts. Joblessness among whites has increased by about the same amount, in proportional terms, as it has among blacks and Hispanics." David Leonhardt and Daniel Altman, "With Few Jobs Being Created, Pain Is Felt Far and Wide," *New York Times*, October 13, 2002.

46 Richard Barnet, "The End of Jobs," *Harper's*, September 1993, p. 48. Between 1982 and 1988 (the "magical" Reagan years), 15 million new jobs were created and most of these jobs were in the service sector (which has since borne many of the cuts alongside manufacturing).

47 Glenn C. Loury, "The Moral Quandary of the Black Community," *The Public Interest* 79, Spring 1985, p. 12.

48 Much of this work is the result of the New Chicago School, mainly from students of William J. Wilson such as Sudhir Venkatesh (see his two papers, "Getting Ahead: Social Mobility Among the Urban Poor," *Sociological Perspectives*, vol. 37, no. 2, 1994, and "The Social Organization of Street Gang Activity in the Urban Ghetto," *American Journal of Sociology*, vol. 103, no. 1, July 1997) and Loic Wacquant, "America as Realized Social Dystopia: the politics of urban disintegration," *International Journal of Contemporary Sociology*, vol. 34, no. 1, 1997. The philosopher Charles Mills points out that the term used to designate the class of the contingent, the "underclass," operates in popular discourse in such a way as "a class which is not a class, a social entity which is asocial." Charles W. Mills, "Under Class Under Standings," *Ethics*, vol. 104, July 1994, p. 858.

49   William Julius Wilson, *When Work Disappears: The World of the New Urban Poor*, New York: Random House, 1996, p. xiii.

50   Manning Marable, *The Crisis of Color and Democracy*, Monroe: Common Courage, 1992, pp. 18–19.

51   Angela Y. Davis, "Masked Racism: Reflections on the Prison Industrial Complex," *ColorLines*, vol. 1, no. 2, Fall 1998, p. 12 and p. 13. For an extension of her crucial arguments about prisons and capitalism, see "From the Prison of Slavery to the Slavery of Prisons: Frederick Douglass and the Convict Lease System" and "Racialized Punishment and Prison Abolition," *The Angela Y. Davis Reader*, Ed. Joy James, Oxford: Basil Blackwell, 1998.

52   Gregory Winter, "Trading Places: When Prisons Substitute for Social Programs," *ColorLines*, vol. 1, no. 2, Fall 1998, p. 22.

53   Amnesty International's excellent report is entitled *Not Part of My Sentence: Violations of the Human Rights of Women in Custody*, AI, 1999.

54   Nell Bernstein, "Left Behind: Tens of Thousands of Children Have a Parent Behind Bars. What Are the Social Costs of Their Loss?" *Mother Jones*, July 10, 2001.

55   My data is from Howard N. Snyder and Melissa Sickmund, *Juvenile Offenders and Victims*, Washington, DC: Office of Juvenile Justice and Delinquency Prevention, 1999.

56   Barry Feld, "Criminalizing the American Juvenile Court," 17 *Crime and Justice* 197 (1993), p. 251. Barry Feld's monograph, *Bad Kids: Race and the Transformation of the Juvenile Court*, New York: Oxford University Press, 1999, should be compulsory reading for anyone who pretends to make *public* policy.

57   "Youth Curfews on the Rise," *Associated Press*, November 30, 1997.

58   Human Rights Watch, *World Report 2001*, New York: HRW, 2001. From a decade before, one might want to see Amnesty International, *Allegations of Police Torture in Chicago, Illinois*, London: Amnesty International, 1990. When George Bush the Elder spoke of bombing Iraq because of an Amnesty International report on torture of Kuwaitis, a few of us marched in Chicago with copies of this document, recently

released, with the slogan, "If Kuwait is Area 1, Chicago is Area 2," Area 2 being the police station of the brutality at the intersection of 91st Street and Cottage Grove Avenue. It was not the best slogan, but it had good intentions.

59 Kelsey Kaufman, *The Brotherhood: Racism and Intimidation Among Prison Staff at the Indiana Correctional Facility-Putnamville*, Greencastle, Indiana: Russell J. Compton Center for Peace and Justice, De Paul University, 2001.

60 Eve Goldberg and Linda Evans, "The Prison Industrial Complex and the Global Economy," Berkeley: Prison Activist Resource Center.

61 Hongda (Harry) Wu, *Laogai: The Chinese Gulag*, Boulder: Westview Press, 1992.

62 Harry Wu, "A Chinese Word to Remember—*Laogai*," *Washington Post*, May 26, 1996.

63 James Seymour and Richard Anderson, *New Ghosts, Old Ghosts: Prisons and Labor Reform Camps in China*, New York: M. E. Sharpe, 1998.

64 Muriel Cooper, "Add Justice to Shopping List: Harry Wu helps kick off UFCW Wal-Mart drive," *AFL-CIO News*, December 1, 1995.

65 In 1999, the US government began an investigation of Wen Ho Lee, a scientist at the US government's Los Alamos laboratory. The FBI charged Lee with giving nuclear secrets to China, even as Lee, a long-time employee of the government, denied all charges. Finally, after bluster from the government, the General Accounting Office showed that the main agents in the field offered incomplete testimony to railroad Lee. Vernon Loeb, "FBI Official Misled Congress About Lee, GAO Says," *Washington Post*, June 29, 2001.

66 Dexter Roberts and Stan Crock, "Is It Cold Enough for You?" *Business Week*, March 29, 1999, p. 40.

67 Letter from Henry Gonzalez (representative of the 20th district, Texas) to Carol Hallett, commissioner of US Customs, March 18, 1992. The contours of the debate are laid out in Gary Martin, "Gonzalez flails use of Mexican 'slaves,'" *San Antonio Express-News*, March 29, 1992.

68 Christian Parenti, *Lockdown America*, p. 217.

69 Ken Silverstein, "America's Private Gulag," *Counterpunch*, June 1, 1997.

70 Vince Beiser, "How we got to two million," *Mother Jones*, July 10, 2001.

71 For more on Halliburton, see my *Fat Cats and Running Dogs*, pp. 62–66.

72 Paulette Thomas, "Making Crime Pay: triangle of interests creates infrastructure to fight lawlessness," *Wall Street Journal*, May 12, 1994.

73 With the increasing number of life sentences in jails, some people are speculating that soon prisons will have to build geriatric wards which will need more government funded medical personnel.

74 Eric Schlosser, "The Prison Industrial Complex," *Atlantic Monthly*, vol. 282, December 6, 1998.

75   Meddis and Sharp, "Prison Business," quotes Meredith De Hart of the Census Bureau.

76   There are a host of other firms that I have not taken up in detail: Cornell, Esmor, Pricor, Management & Training Corp., Correction Services Corp., Dominion Correction Services, Maranatha Corrections, Tuscolanta Corrections.

77   Philip Mattera and Mafruza Khan, *Jail Breaks: Economic Development Subsidies Given to Private Prisons*, Washington, DC: Good Jobs First, 2001. "The actual rate," they underscore, "is very likely higher, but cannot be determined because state corporate income tax credits are not disclosed."

78   DBL was the company that made "junk bonds" a household word in the 1980s, under the stewardship of Michael Millken. The story on Pricor was summarized by *Covert Action* in fall 1993, drawing from William P. Barrett, "I Guess We Look Stupid," *Forbes*, February 3, 1992, and Kyle Pope, "Prison Sellers Fail in Texas, Take Pitch East, Suits Pursue Backers of Florida Jail Deal," *Houston Chronicle*, March 3, 1992.

79   For example (and again, thanks to *Covert Action* for the citations), Rhoda Hillberg, "They Built It, But Inmates Didn't Come: Minnesota Town's Private Prison, Built to Create Jobs, Attracted No 'Clients,'" *Los Angeles Times*, February 23, 1993; Richard Witt, "Crime Doesn't Pay Off for Irwin County Jail: Rental Prison Holds Hard Lessons in Finance," *Atlanta Journal and Constitution*, February 7, 1993.

80   Silverstein, "America's Private Gulag."

81   Ibid.

82   Alex Friedmann, "Prison Privatization: the bottom line," *Corpwatch*, August 21, 1999.

83   Parenti, *Lockdown America*, pp. 221–25.

84   Friedmann, "Prison Privatization."

85   Goldberg and Evans, "The Prison Industrial Complex."

86   Telephone conversation with Larry Walsh of the RICI, December 16, 1994.

87   The information on Arizona comes from *Corrections Digest*, November 17, 1993. I am grateful to Jenni Gainsborough of the National Prison Project (ACLU) for her help with information. The late Kathy DeLeon, who served nine months in federal prison, told me that she did not make more than pennies for her work. She died in custody, not long thereafter.

88   The case, decided on November 1, 1993, is *Hale v. Arizona*, 93–353.

89   Parenti, *Lockdown America*, pp. 230–31.

90   Parenti, *Lockdown America*, p. 232, and Cynthia Young, "Punishing Labor: Why Labor Should Oppose the Prison Industrial Complex," *New Labor Forum*, no. 7, Fall/Winter 2000, p. 41.

91   Goldberg and Evans, "Prison Industrial Complex."

92   Lucia Hwang, "Working for Nothing: The Failure of Prison Industry

Programs," *Third Force*, vol. 4, no. 3, July/August 1996 and Parenti, *Lockdown America*, pp. 230–235.

93 Young, "Punishing Labor," p. 47.

94 For more details on the campaign and on MPLU, contact Michael Lee, Communications Officer of the MPLU, at 2435 E. North St., PMB 255, Greenville, SC 29615 or by email, convict78@hotmail.com.

95 GM, meanwhile, is in a crisis of its own. On June 5, 1998, workers at GM's Flint Metal Center went on strike; six days later their comrades from the Delphi East components plant in Flint, Michigan, joined them. By mid-June, 9,200 United Auto Workers (UAW) members were on strike against GM. They had idled 23 assembly plants and 94 parts plants, with just over 100,000 additional workers off work. GM operations in the US, Mexico, Canada and Singapore had been halted. Further, in North America, 83 percent of GM's production was on hold. GM controls 31 percent of the world's automobile share. UAW went on strike with two demands on the table: (1) That GM reneged on a 1995 promise to upgrade the Flint plants with a capital infusion of $500 million. The company put in $120 million and then used the rest to bargain with UAW. GM wanted UAW to decrease its control over certain aspects of the production process (safety rules, etc). Instead of putting capital into an older plant, GM wanted to shift its production site to Mexico (where it would build a new mechanized factory and use the cheaper, non-union, Mexican labor). (2) That GM use contract labor for its low-tech work, a process that cost UAW 2,500 jobs. With no common language on these issues, the talks went nowhere. There was a time a few decades ago when GM controlled close to half the world's automobile market. By the late 1990s, its share went down to 31 percent, but this did not hurt GM's capacity to earn enormous profits. In 1995, the company posted an annual profit of $6.9 billion (four times more than the gross national product of Nicaragua). In the third quarter of 1997, GM's profits totaled $1.1 billion (with $423 million or 40 percent earned from North American operations). This profit was earned by at least three means: (1) a reduction of man-hours required to assemble cars by 62 percent (from 39 hours to 24 hours) and a general increase in the speed of the plants; (2) a decrease in the workforce of 150,000 US workers from 1979 to 1990 (compensated by lower-wage workers in Mexican *maquiladoras* or sweatshop factories); (3) a use of profits for dividends to shareholders and as salaries to management rather than for reinvestment in the deteriorating physical plant of US factories. For the workers the situation was bleak. Since the late 1970s, UAW lost over 550,000 members. "Those workers who were laid off," says Sean McAlinden of the University of Michigan, "disappeared into nothingness—they got nothing." This strike represented the frustrations of the workers against the globalization of capital. UAW President Stephen Yokich congratulated GM for its 1995 record profit, but complained that management did not give proper credit to the union for its role in enhancing the bottom line. In an excellent example of collaboration between workers and management, UAW asked for just a little bit more of the pie rather than challenge the unequal basis of labor and capital. UAW lost the action.

96   Alisa Solomon, "Detainees Equal Dollars. The Rise of Immigrant Incarcerations drive a prison boom," *Village Voice*, August 14–20, 2002. Solomon's many writings on immigrant detention, long before 9/11, provide a road-map for the lay reader. I have relied upon it extensively for this section.

97   Keep in mind that by mid-2002, the rate of inmates increased by only a percent, but this number does not count those who are held in detention. Fox Butterfield, "1% Increase in US Inmates is Lowest Rate in Three Decades," *New York Times*, July 31, 2002.

98   Alisa Solomon, "Locked Up in Limbo," *POZ*, September 1999, pp. 82–86.

99   Alisa Solomon, "Yearning to Breathe Free," *Village Voice*, August 8, 1995; "Wackenhut Detention Ordeal," *Village Voice*, September 1–7, 1999; "A Dream Detained," *Village Voice*, March 24–30, 1999; "Sweet Release," *Village Voice*, June 8, 1999.

100 Tram Nguyen, "Detained or Disappeared?" *ColorLines*, vol. 5, issue 2, Summer 2002.

101 Marika Litras and John Scalia, "Immigration Offenders in the Federal Criminal Justice System, 2000," Washington, DC: BJS, 2002 (NCJ-191745).

102 Alisa Solomon, "Wackenhut Detention Ordeal."

103 The details are in my *Fat Cats and Running Dogs.*

104 John Sullivan and Matthew Purdy, "In Corrections Business, Shrewdness Pays: A Prison Empire," *New York Times*, July 23, 1995.

105 US Immigration and Naturalization Service, *The Elizabeth New Jersey, Contract Detention Facility Operated by Esmor, Inc.: Interim Report*, July 20, 1995.

106 David Gonzales, "Jail Uprising Leaves Many Sad and Bitter," *New York Times*, June 25, 1995.

107 Human Rights Watch, *Locked Away: Immigration Detainees in Jails in the United States*, New York: HRW, September 1998. HRW's evidence came from interviews and from three news reports: Christine Gardner, "Defense Argues for US Guards in Trial Over Illegal Immigrants," *Reuters*, March 3, 1998; "Detained Immigrant Recalls Rough Treatment at Union County Jail," *Associated Press*, February 2, 1998; Ronald Smothers, "Immigrants Tell of Mistreatment by New Jersey Jail Guards," *New York Times*, February 6, 1998.

108 Teresa Mears, "Detainees Held by INS say Jails Rife with Abuse," *Boston Globe*, August 2, 1998, and Human Rights Watch, *Locked Away*.

109 The furor around the spurious book *The Bell Curve* illustrates the reactionary urge to justify inequality by an argument for natural differences Charles Murray and Richard Herrnstein, *The Bell Curve. Intelligence and Class Structure in America*, New York: The Free Press, 1994, but for several useful critical essays, *The Bell Curve Wars: Race, Intelligence and the Future of America*, ed. Steve Fraser, New York: Basic Books, 1995.

110 In a speech in Minnesota, Gingrich told the GOP faithful that the Constitution calls for "life, liberty and the pursuit of happiness," and that "it doesn't call for a federal entitlement to happiness. It doesn't say a federal department of happiness. There's no quota or set-aside for happiness." "Gingrich Accuses Clinton of Avoiding Recommendations," *Minnesota Daily*, February 8, 1996.

111 Angela Davis, "From the Prison of Slavery to the Slavery of Prison: Frederick Douglass and the Convict Lease System," *The Angela Y. Davis Reader*.

112 Susan Rosenberg, "Female Political Prisoners and Anti-Imperialist Struggle," *Journal of Prisoners on Prison*, vol. 2, no. 2, Spring 1990. There are two extraordinary collections being edited by Joy James: *Imprisoned Intellectuals: America's Political Prisoners, Liberation and Rebellion*, Lanham, MD: Rowman and Littlefield, 2003, and *Abolition: Incarceration, Enslavement and Rebellion*, Albany: SUNY Press, forthcoming.

113 George Jackson, *Blood in My Eye*, Baltimore: Black Classics Press, 1990, pp. 99–100.

114 To reach the Jericho Movement, contact the National Organizing Committee at P. O. Box 650, New York, NY 10009, 212-502-1143, www.thejerichomovement.com.

115 Human Rights Watch, *World Report 2001*, New York: HRW, 2001.

116 Materials on the Angola 3 are available at www.angola3.org.

117 Jamie Fellner and Marc Mauer, *Losing the Vote: The Impact of Felony Disenfranchisement Laws in the United States*, Washington, DC: Sentencing Project, 1998.

118 Patricia Allard and Marc Mauer, *Regaining the Vote: An Assessment of Activity Relating to Felon Disenfranchisement Laws*, Washington, DC: Sentencing Project, 2000.

119 Andrea Smith, "Colors of Violence," *ColorLines*, vol. 3, no. 4, Winter 2000–2001.

120 Angela Davis, "The Color of Violence Against Women," *ColorLines*, vol. 3, no. 3, Fall 2000.

121 Davis, "The Color of Violence." The All-India Democratic Women's Alliance has been at work for almost two decades on community transformation as a means to struggle against misogynist violence. Elisabeth Armstrong's forthcoming work on the subject will address this theme at length. See, "From Hands to Mouths: AIDWA and the Politics of Funding," *ANNALS: Journal of Political and Social Science*, forthcoming.

122 Rick Sauve offers a caveat against the utopianism of the idea of abolition, but it seems to me that CR's program is far from utopian and close to what Sauve calls the "dismantling of this monstrosity." "Prison Abolition: The Need for Decriminalization," *Journal of Prisoners on Prison*, vol. 1, no. 1, Summer 1988.

123 www.criticalresistance.org/whatisabolition.html.

WORKFARE

I'm a woman. I'm a black woman. I'm a poor woman. I'm a fat woman. I'm a middle-aged woman. And I'm on welfare. In this country, if you're any one of these things you count less as a human being. If you're all those things, you don't count at all. Except as a statistic. Welfare's like a traffic accident. It can happen to anybody, but especially it happens to women. As far as I'm concerned, the ladies of NWRO [National Welfare Rights Organization] are the front-line troops of women's freedom. Both because we have so few illusions and because our issues are so important to all women—the right to a living wage for women's work, the right to life itself.

—Johnnie Tillmon, 1972[1]

ON THE OUTSKIRTS OF CLINTONVILLE, 1999

In Philadelphia, within sight of the Liberty Bell, a group of working-class folk without homes set up a tent city to protest the war against the poor. They were part of the Kensington Welfare Rights Union (KWRU), a group formed in April 1991 to fight the Pennsylvania-wide cuts in welfare supports for the unemployed contingent working class. Following tent cities, marches, and finally a Freedom Bus tour (Freedom from Unemployment, Hunger and Homelessness), the KWRU occupied the land beside the Liberty Bell to protest Clinton's "welfare reform" bill of 1996. Their tent city was named "Clintonville."

In Boston, Massachusetts, a professor at Brandeis University submitted a review of Nobel-laureate Robert M. Solow's *Work and Welfare* to the *Times Literary Supplement*. The essay, "Clinton's Leap in the Dark" appeared in 1999, as plans for Clintonville germinated among KWRU organizers. In the article, the professor, Robert Reich, former

secretary of labor during Clinton's first term as president, explained the
horror felt by the liberals in the Democratic Party by the Welfare Bill of
1996.[2] Reich wrote:

> When during his 1992 presidential campaign, Bill Clinton
> vowed to 'end welfare as we know it' by moving people
> "from welfare to work," he presumably did not have in mind
> the legislation which he signed into law in August 1996. The
> original idea had been to smooth the passage from welfare to
> work with guaranteed healthcare, childcare, job training and
> a job paying enough to live on. As a result former welfare
> recipients would gain dignity and independence, and society
> as a whole would have the benefits of their labors.

Furthermore, Reich noted, "The 1996 legislation contained none
of these supports—no healthcare or childcare for people coming off
welfare, no job training, no assurance of a job paying a living wage, nor,
for that matter, of a job at any wage. In effect, what was dubbed welfare
'reform' merely ended the promise of help to the indigent and their
children which Franklin D. Roosevelt had initiated more than 60 years
before." So far, the tenants of Clintonville would agree with this
confederate of Clinton.

But welfare organizers, such as the KWRU, hit a stone wall with
the national media as well as in the corridors of power. No one cared to
hear criticism of the bill.

The White House, meanwhile, was jubilant about the bill. Clinton
reserved his glee for an August 1999 welfare-to-work conference in
Chicago, when he argued that all states had fulfilled their quotas of
getting people off welfare to work, with 35 percent of welfare recipients
with jobs by the end of 1998. Behind Clinton, a slew of governmental
and nongovernmental studies showed, however, that the scenario did
not merit such praise. In early August, the Urban Institute reported that
most women who left welfare went into the low-wage sector, with a
third in straits of hunger, with 40 percent unable to pay rent and with
two-thirds without health insurance.[3] Another Urban Institute study
and a report from the General Accounting Office, both published in
1999, showed that as the poor dropped out from Food Stamp
eligibility, the demands on charity food banks increased in proportion.
Seven and a half million people left the Food Stamp program between
April 1996 and 1999, and, as the GAO noted, the drop in child

participation "dropped more sharply than the number of children living in poverty, indicating a growing gap between need and assistance."[4] Struck by the multitude of reports such as these, Senator Paul Wellstone raised his voice against welfare "reform," only to find the media and the experts deaf to his announcement:

> There's been a flurry of credible reports suggesting that all is not well with welfare reform yet President Clinton and Vice President Gore continue to claim that welfare is "working." What they overlook is why, at a time when the welfare rolls have been cut in half and the economy is booming, we now are finding that millions more children are going to bed hungry each night; demand for emergency food assistance is growing; millions of poor families are dropping off the Food Stamp rolls faster than economic indicators would predict; and former welfare recipients are losing their medical coverage, cannot make the rent and utilities, and are unable to afford child care. These are not the results of successful reform. The welfare rolls may have been cut in half, but not poverty.[5]

Robert Reich walked the same road as Wellstone on this one:

> We have no way of knowing how many of these people are in permanent jobs paying a living wage, or are in temporary jobs paying so little that they have to double up with other family members and leave their children at home alone during the day, or are living on the street. And we may never know, even after the economy slides into recession, and the ranks of the unemployed begin to grow once again. The sad truth is that America has embarked on the largest social experiment it has undertaken in this half of the twentieth century without even adequate base-line data from which researchers can infer what has happened, or deduce what will happen, to large numbers of poor people who no longer receive help.

Then, he paused, and justified the need for a Clinton-type reform, although he would have removed people from welfare with a soft landing. Most American women with young children, he argued, work, and "many of them are struggling to make ends meet." They are without healthcare and daycare, two important ingredients for a wage worker's life. Given that they work and have no support, Reich noted, "It has seemed increasingly unfair for poor non-working mothers to receive welfare benefits." The unfairness was heightened, Reich argued, because "a highly visible portion of these beneficiaries (although not a majority) was black or Hispanic." Why did the government need to conduct welfare "reform"? Two reasons, said Reich: (1) Because there are more working poor in the country and if they can work, and not get support, it was "politically untenable" to provide welfare to some; (2) "Being 'tough' on welfare thus seemed to be a matter of imposing discipline on a group of people who are morally lax and undeserving, relative to the increasingly hard-pressed working families just above them." In other words, the contingent and working class had to be treated equitably, whether employed or not, and these new mechanisms would help discipline the entire class of low-wage and no-wage workers. Reich, one of those who disavowed the pressure of policy creation based on demographic support, nevertheless touted the line that welfare creates a racist form of jealousy among white workers and the administration must undercut that by ending "welfare as we know it."

From Reich, then, we get an adequate confession of the reasons for welfare "reform," despite the full knowledge of the misery it created. The issue here is not that the government did not know what it was doing, that one more study, just one more, might convince people of the inherent cruelty of new policy. *They knew that welfare "reform" meant grief.* However, to appeal to the (white) working class, the Clinton Democrats felt that they had to shrug off their social democratic commitments to the multi-ethnic working class in general. Furthermore, if prisons provided one means to discipline the contingent class of workers, welfare "reform" provided one more way to "discipline" (this is now Reich's term as well) the "morally lax" *underclass.* The strategy of welfare "reform" was not to provide independence to the people, it was to ensure that those without any hope of getting a good job would be disciplined by the private sector and starvation, or else go to prison if they took any action against the state. This is a far cry from freedom.

A BRIEF HISTORY OF WELFARE

In January 1935, the US Congress, at the initiative of FDR, passed the Social Security Act to provide relief to the impoverished, unemployment insurance to the laid off, as well as social insurance schemes for retirement and disability. The omnibus act set in place a two-tier system of social benefits: for those within the world of work, the benefits of retirement and disability insurance provided a genuine comfort, while the working poor could only take refuge in highly punitive forms of charity through programs such as Aid to Dependent Children (ADC) and other forms of relief.[6] Furthermore, there was another two-tier[7] system, this within ADC, as Linda Gordon notes: "Blacks were systematically deprived of access to ADC benefits." The charity side of the Social Security Act did not mean that the state acted benevolently toward the working poor; rather, the state adopted policies to monitor, regulate, and discipline the working poor, who had to succumb to these techniques if they wanted the check from the government. The state manipulated assistance to the wiles of macroeconomic conditions: when there was a need for contingent and low-wage work, the managers of ADC and other charity programs suspended aid to drive people to work, set rates much below wage rates (following the principle of "less eligibility"), used residency requirements to shunt newcomers when it suited them, or else argued that the mother of the dependent child had a lover who could care for the child ("midnight raids" by the government to check on ADC recipients were part of the story of the disciplinary procedures of the state).[8]

In 1961, the US government allowed two-parent families with an unemployed father to avail themselves of the newly renamed Aid to Families with Dependent Children (AFDC). Two years later, the federal government created the Medicaid and Food Stamp programs that disbursed medical and food assistance to those on AFDC, as well as others. In 1964, the Congress passed the Economic Opportunity Act—legislation intended to be the centerpiece of the government's "unconditional war on poverty." These programs sent considerable money into the segregated zones of the poor, and, as Frances Fox Piven and Richard Cloward argued, "For a time these programs did not so much moderate unrest as provide the vehicles through which the black ghettos mobilized to demand government services. They activated a new leadership structure in the ghettos and they also activated masses of black poor."[9]

One of those who began to receive welfare, became political through the mechanisms of social control set up by the state (such as the "midnight raids"), and then helped form the LA-based Aid to Needy

Children–Mothers Anonymous (ANC–Mothers Anonymous) in 1962 was Johnnie Tillmon. Raised in a rural Arkansas family of sharecroppers, Tillmon moved to California, worked in a series of jobs despite a host of illnesses, raised six children on her own, and then, when too sick to work, she turned to the government who had till then gladly received her taxes, but failed to live up to its social contract with dignity. Once she was organized, Tillmon's political consciousness moved swiftly:

> People just started talking. We found out that all over the country the attitudes of the general public and the welfare department, were the same toward anybody on welfare. The people from New York got treated by the social workers and the other people the same as they did in Mississippi. In the past, most of us had been so ashamed that we were on welfare that we wouldn't even admit it to another welfare recipient. But as we talked to each other, we forgot about all the shame, and as we listened to the horrible treatment and conditions all over the country, we could begin thinking about the idea that maybe it wasn't us that should be ashamed.[10]

Tillmon, Dovie Coleman, Dorothy Dimascio, Edith Doering, Ruby Duncan, Kate Emmerson, Bertha Hernandez, Etta Horn, Catherine Jermany, Frankie Jeter, Marion Kidd, Margaret McCarthy, Alice Nixon, Carmen Olivio, and Beulah Sanders found George Wiley, a Syracuse University chemistry professor who quit his job to lead the newly formed National Welfare Rights Organization (NWRO) in 1967.[11] These women, with Wiley and a host of other organizers and allies such as Madeleine Adamson, Barbara Bowen, Richard Cloward, Gary Delgado, Marcia Henry, Hulbert James, Rhoda Linton, Bill Pastreich, Wade Rathke, Mark Splain, Tim Sampson and the Reverend Paul Younger, pushed the federal government with a novel approach to welfare rights.[12]

The anti-poverty programs legitimized the demand for welfare, turning it, at least in the eyes of the contingent class, into a right and not charity. The rhetoric of the Civil Rights movement underscored the power of the state and its ability to defraud people of their just desserts. In his famous address at the March on Washington (August 28, 1963), for example, Martin Luther King, Jr., censured the United States for its failure to live its Constitutional creed. He said:

> Instead of honoring this sacred obligation, America has
> given the Negro people a bad check; a check which has come
> back marked "insufficient funds." We refuse to believe that
> there are insufficient funds in the great vaults of opportunity
> of this nation. And so we've come to cash this check, a check
> that will give us upon demand the riches of freedom and the
> security of justice.[13]

Some may believe that this is metaphoric, but many would have
instinctively found here a programmatic call for economic justice *from
the state.*

After a study of welfare programs, Piven and Cloward published a
charter for social action in the *Nation* called "A Strategy to End
Poverty" (it appeared on May 2, 1966, although in circulation for at
least six months prior to publication), just as almost 2,000 people in
Ohio marched from Cleveland to Columbus on a welfare rights march.
The Piven-Cloward plan did not go after the broad structural forces
that produced the condition of the contingent, but it demanded that
those without hope of a job earn a guaranteed income. With this as a
goal, Piven-Cloward felt that mass-based organization was not as
important as mobilized disruption of the system by the poor across the
country. If the poor demanded welfare according to the government's
own criteria, the welfare rolls would expand, begin to impact state
budgets and therefore bring the question of poverty to the forefront of
the electoral battles. In other words, rather than organize those in
poverty, "to mobilize for a welfare disruption, families would be
encouraged to demand relief."[14] This became the principle strategy of
the NWRO, at least from 1967 to 1972. In the early 1960s, less than a
million people had been on the welfare rolls; by 1972, three million
demanded welfare to the tune of $5 billion—a victory for the
movement, at any rate, as well as a step toward the national
conversation on poverty envisaged by NWRO.

That was not to come. In 1968, President Nixon proposed the
Family Assistance Plan (FAP) designed to cut social welfare, and
instead to provide a family of four with a guaranteed annual income of
$2,600 (Daniel Patrick Moynihan's Guaranteed Annual Income came
to only $1,800). Far below the poverty line, NWRO resisted it with a
campaign called "Live on a Welfare Budget," a challenge to the families
of Congressional leaders to do their best on this low income. NWRO

had already discussed the issue of a guaranteed annual income, and it had placed this important demand in its platform. Reflecting on NWRO's demand, Tillmon wrote:

> We put together our own welfare plan, called Guaranteed Adequate Income (GAI), which would eliminate sexism from welfare. There would be no "categories"—men, women, children, single, married, kids, no kids—just poor people who need aid. You'd get paid according to need and family size only and that would be upped as the cost of living goes up.[15]

In 1969, NWRO's membership totaled 22,000—the apex of the movement. A lack of liberal support for welfare rights (support = cash), several tactical errors by NWRO, and a leadership crisis crippled NWRO's ability to be effective as Nixon set the seeds for a lurch to the Right.[16] When Nixon announced his "welfare reform" agenda, NWRO was not capable of a riposte—it had mobilized people to sign up for welfare, but as Nixon's rules put pressure on the states to treat those on welfare as criminals, NWRO did not have the organizational capacity to respond. In 1970, the federal government turned over administrative power to the states to monitor welfare recipients. If a state showed that more than three percent of those who took welfare had been ineligible, it would have to pay a fine to the government. Rather than get to the stage of a fine, the states became strict with welfare recipients, cut back the disbursements and gained needed fiscal relief—on the backs of the indigent. Despite several Supreme Court decisions on behalf of the broadest welfare payouts from 1968 to 1970, the courts refused to establish a constitutional "right to life" (or to follow the broad entitlements enacted in the International Declaration of Human Rights, 1948—refused by the United States and many other states around the world).[17]

In 1972, Nixon offered the slogan "Workfare, not Welfare," where he returned the emphasis of federal welfare programs from the side of a guaranteed income to a disciplinary procedure to drive the contingent class toward low-waged, unskilled work. Even back in 1961, when the state allowed money to go to families if the father lost his job, the state had to deny assistance to the family if he refused to work "without good cause." The next year Congress created the Community Work and Training (CWT) program to train the indigent toward work. The 1964 Economic Opportunity Act included CWTs. The government included the emphasis on work to increase the labor market productivity of the poor. The contingent class lived in poverty, the government's main economic advisers argued, because they either worked too little or else they had no skills to earn them sufficient money. CWT programs would increase their skills and discipline them into hard work.[18] Along this grain, in 1968, the government required states to create a program called Work Incentive (WIN) for "appropriate" welfare recipients, especially unemployed fathers.

A series of measures in the Reagan years framed "poverty" through the lens of "welfare to work." Not enough to be arrested by the growth of the poor, public policy now had to concentrate on getting the contingent to waged work. The Omnibus Budget Reconciliation Act (1981) asked states to require welfare recipients to do job training, job searches, and apprenticeship while they drew funds; the Job Training Partnership Act (1982) and the Tax Equity and Fiscal Responsibility Act (1982) allowed states to *require* job searches as a criteria for funds; Family Support Act (1988) created the Job Opportunity and Basic Skills (JOBS) program to push welfare recipients into waged work, with medical assistance as well as childcare for a year after AFDC ends. Long before Clinton, "welfare to work" had become the mantra of public policy framers.

Indeed, long before we heard about "ending welfare as we know it," welfare as a social wage had already deteriorated. "The rollback of means tested benefits began in the early 1970s," reflects Frances Fox Piven. It took "the form of allowing inflation to erode the real value of benefits, by one-third between 1970 and the mid-1990s, while politicians began the assault on welfare mothers for their sexual and work behavior."[19] In the two states that housed more than half of those who signed up for welfare, the assaults from Governors Rockefeller (New York) and Reagan (California) demonstrated the government's anti-woman, anti-poor administrative response. As early as 1961, in his political campaign against Barry Goldwater, Nelson Rockefeller noted that he did not condone "the use of public assistance to encourage idleness." Even as he tried to forge a middle ground between a gutless liberalism and a heartless conservatism, to speak, for instance, of government help for those "truly in need," the Right scored him as a liberal and he failed to make any political headway.[20] In 1972, he would not make any such mistakes. Rockefeller hired a millionaire as inspector general to write a report about "welfare fraud" in the state, a provocation that then allowed him to "refuse welfare benefits to any newcomer to New York State who could not find decent housing or health care."[21] Not only did Ronald Reagan conduct similar maneuvers, but also in 1976, while on the campaign trail for the presidency, he made up a story about a black woman from Chicago's South Side:

> [She] has eighty names, thirty addresses, twelve Social Security cards, and is collecting veteran's benefits on four non-existing deceased husbands. And she is collecting Social Security on her cards. She's got Medicaid, getting food stamps, and she is collecting welfare under each of her names.

When asked to name the woman, Reagan demurred, and a hive of investigative reporters descended on the South Side, to no avail. David Zucchino, who won a Pulitzer Prize for his journalism, spent time with two mothers on welfare in Philadelphia and showed that the Reagan myth of the "welfare queen" was far off the mark.[22] Finally, in Nevada, the Department of Welfare went after "welfare cheaters" in late 1971. The state of Nevada put its entire department toward an audit of welfare recipients, screened the paperwork of a community generally without accountants and lawyers, and knocked a fourth of them off its rolls. Welfare "reform," again, predated Clinton; indeed it came with welfare itself.

In 1972, NWRO's leader Johnnie Tillmon captured the sexist formulas of welfare, how it was designed *from the start* to regulate, discipline, and control the lives of the contingent class:

> Welfare is like a super-sexist marriage. You trade in a man for the Man. But you can't divorce him if he treats you bad. He can divorce you, of course, cut you off anytime he wants. But in that case, he keeps the kids, not you. The man runs everything. In ordinary marriage, sex is supposed to be for your husband. On AFDC, you're not supposed to have any sex at all. You give up control of your own body. It's a condition of aid. You may even have to agree to get your tubes tied so you can never have more children just to avoid being cut off welfare. The man, the welfare system, controls

your money. He tells you what to buy, what not to buy, where to buy it, and how much things cost. If things—rent, for instance—really costs more than he says they do, it's too bad for you. He's always right. That's why Governor [Ronald] Reagan can get away with slandering welfare recipients, calling them "lazy parasites," "pigs on the trough," and such. We've been trained to believe that the only reason people are on welfare is because there's something wrong with their character.[23]

To discipline the contingent class, the state exercised two options: incarceration and welfare. The welfare state emerged in the 1930s, when turbulence in the world of finance left a third of the population without waged work and a large section of the rest with depleted bank accounts. As a safety net, the government provided welfare legislation that took care of unemployed single (mainly widowed) white women with children and unemployed, hungry people.[24] The government gradually extended benefits to people of color, drawing in a larger number of people who became irrelevant to the transformed, "jobless" economy. Those who came to these benefits found themselves not necessarily relieved of their burdens, as their lives became regulated by a state anxious to get them, via the training programs, retooled for the next economic expansion. Welfare, for the state, was always a warehouse for the surplus as well as a vocational school on the cheap to keep workers ready for when low-end jobs became available.[25]

To do all this, welfare remained a remarkably cheap option for the state. In 1992, when talk of "welfare reform" filled the airwaves, the Congressional Research Service estimated that the two largest items of the welfare budget comprised only two percent of the combined state and federal budgets (split evenly between AFDC and Food Stamps). If all forms of assistance were included (such as veteran benefits, school lunches, student Pell Grants, and aid to the charity sector), then the welfare budget still only drew just over ten percent of the state and federal budgets.[26] Even this was grossly exaggerated by escalating medical costs since the 1980s (for the Medicare and Medicaid programs that provide subsidized care). According to the US Congress, federal assistance in the early 1990s was lower than that provided in 1970.

The government (and both parties) went after those on welfare for criminality and greed, just as corporate giants went on untrammeled with their crimes and their welfare—the tax shelters and breaks, the fraud and the pork.

"THE WORST THING BILL CLINTON HAS DONE"[27]

In 1996, by the initiative of President Bill Clinton, "welfare as we know it" ended.

On the campaign trail in 1992, Clinton read the work of Harvard University's public policy luminaries Mary Jo Bane and David Ellwood who found that most people who entered the welfare system did not stay for very long. Drawing from this finding, Ellwood proposed to "divide and conquer" those on welfare. The state should enforce "time limits" on welfare use, this to target those who stayed on welfare, at the same time ensuring that those who used welfare as a means of transit should not be affected.[28] Clinton, apparently, was enthused by the idea of "time limits" and on the campaign trail, he began to use the phrase, "No one who can work should be able to stay on welfare forever" (the phrase appeared in his campaign book, *Putting People First*).[29] Clinton followed the Democratic Leadership Council's 1990 declaration, "We believe the purpose of social welfare is to bring the poor into the nation's economic mainstream, not maintain them in dependence."[30] While this sounds reasonable, it means that the contingent class not be allowed a social net, but they must be forced into active work in the low-wage sector—where the most job growth took place in the Clinton years. When in power, Clinton appointed Bane and Ellwood to the Department of Health and Human Services where they, along with Clinton's axe-man Bruce Reed, began to develop a welfare "reform" proposal.

In a book published in 1994, Bane and Ellwood wrote that if people had child support, medical insurance, and good paying jobs "there would be far less need for welfare." In other words, they began with the premise that people wanted to work, that those on welfare did not fail because of some intrinsic reason, but because the system did not enable them to live with dignity. With structural assistance (childcare, etc.), "Single parents could realistically support themselves at the poverty line if they were willing to work half-time, even at a job paying little more than the minimum wage. If they were willing to work full-time, they could move well above the poverty line." If the private sector did not provide the good jobs, and "if the government is not willing to provide cash support forever, it must provide full- or part-time jobs." If the jobs enabled people to support themselves, "then the notion of a time-limited transitional assistance program for both single-parent and two-parent families makes sense. A rich set of training and support services ought to be included as part of the benefits. But the cash program would be of limited duration."[31] Bane and Ellwood's entire program relied upon an ensemble of government-backed services, such as childcare, medical care, unemployment insurance, and living wages.[32] Without these, welfare "reform" would be tantamount to social cruelty.

In 1996, a California Democrat, Representative Matthew Martinez, put his name to the Jobs Creation and Infrastructure Restoration Act (HR-950). The bill, pushed by the National Labor Community Coalition for Public Works Jobs, called for the creation of a $250 billion fund toward emergency public works programs over a five-year period. The government would not only provide full-time jobs to those who formed the contingent class, but they would be hired to help rebuild the infrastructure in those zones that they inhabited. These state-hired workers would rebuild schools, homes, parks, and transportation systems. The Martinez bill could have been one of the avenues used by the Clinton administration had it been serious about the support mechanisms for those who were being kicked off the welfare rolls. The Bane-Ellwood team could have added specific language for childcare and medical insurance to the bill and, with Democratic support, Congress would have had to debate the philosophical differences between neoliberalism and socialism. At a protest on October 18, 1997, while the Martinez bill came up for the second year, the United Farm Workers' Dolores Huerta noted, "You would think that with welfare deform that a public works jobs bill would be a priority. But it's not! Congress and President Clinton should be putting this bill first instead of last."[33] In fact, the Clinton approach was not to debate the bill, but to undercut the movement by commandeering Martinez. Bribed with an extension of the $1.4 billion Long Beach free-way into Martinez's district, Clinton earned his vote on the fast-track authority for trade deals, ended his fealty to the jobs bill, and pushed him into a corner so that he emerged a few years later as a Republican.[34]

When the Republicans won the mid-term Congressional elections in 1994, Ellwood resigned from his job. The night of long knives for welfare recipients had begun.[35] Under the illusion that what Ellwood foresaw would not come true, Bane remained and was joined in the welfare policy group by Peter Edelman (husband of Marion Wright Edelman of the Children's Defense Fund). When Clinton went ahead and signed the welfare "reform" law sent to him by Congress (Personal Responsibility and Work Opportunity Reconciliation Act, or PRWORA), both Bane and Edelman resigned from government in protest (as did Wendell Primus, also on the welfare team). Edelman, in disgust, told the press, "I have devoted the last 30-plus years to doing whatever I could to help in reducing poverty in America. I believe the recently enacted welfare bill goes in exactly the opposite direction."[36]

AFDC ended, and TANF (Temporary Aid to Needy Families) was born. The welfare bill provided $16.5 billion in block grants to states to manage their TANF recipients. Those on TANF could receive federal assistance for a total of 60 months for their lifetime, most are required to work while in receipt of the funds, and the states could set their own rules for the program. Between 1996 and 2000, the TANF caseloads declined by more than 50 percent. *That means, in these few years, six million people lost access to government assistance.*

Why did Clinton sign the welfare "reform" act of 1996? Certainly, the liberal position (time limits plus state supports) lost the argument to the Right, whose ideologues played on fears of "black pathology" and of "women's license" to gain the upper hand among the mainly white men who run the government. In 1984, a rather obscure and not professionally well-regarded scholar, Charles Murray, published a screed against welfare called *Losing Ground: American Social Policy, 1950-1980*; Murray's book followed, but overshadowed, George Gilder's 1981 anti-welfare classic *Wealth and Poverty*, Ronald Reagan's favorite book. In 1994, Murray returned to center stage with a shabby book (co-authored with Richard Herrnstein) called *The Bell Curve*, in which he argued that the welfare-fed "underclass" would cause the collapse of American civilization:

> The underclass will become even more concentrated spatially than it is today. The expanded networks of day care centers, homeless shelters, public housing, and other services will always be located in the poorest part of the inner

city, which means that anyone who wants access to them will have to live there. Political support for such measures as relocation of people from the inner city to the suburbs, never strong to begin with, will wither altogether. The gaping cultural gap between the habits of the underclass and the habits of the rest of society will make it increasingly difficult for children who have grown up in the inner city to function in the larger society even when they want to.[37]

Murray and Herrnstein called the process underway in America, "dysgenesis," the opposite of eugenics, and defined by a racist anthropology in the early part of the 20th Century as the general decline of the genetic materials of humans because of such things as "race-mixing" and the development of cultural pathologies.[38] George Gilder also returned to the scene, with books and interviews, magazine articles and testimonials before Congress. In 1994, in an interview, he was asked about the "pathologies" of welfare, and he responded:

Essentially, welfare benefits are far better than low-wage, entry-level jobs. Welfare gives benefits far superior to entry-level jobs because they yield valuable leisure time for the recipient. Thus it usurps the male role as chief provider and undermines the foundation of families. His provider role is absolutely central to the family; if the state replaces the male provider, you don't have families. The welfare state cuckolds the man. That is why we have eighty percent illegitimacy rates in the inner cities. The welfare state has been far more destructive to the black family than slavery was.[39]

There is an obsession in these texts against the social capability and sexual autonomy of the black woman. The data becomes irrelevant when the rhetoric is charged up:

- Black girls, age 15–17: 90 percent have no children.
- Black girls, age 18–19: 76 percent have no children.
- Black single mothers: 75 percent hold jobs and were outside the welfare system in 1995.
- Black children in single-parent households: 34 percent.

Furthermore, in 1995, there were more whites on AFDC than blacks, most people had between one (43 percent) and two (30.7

percent) children, only a handful were teenagers (7.6 percent), and most remained on welfare for under two years (19 percent less than seven months, 15 percent between seven months and a year).[40]

The Heritage Foundation's Robert Rector and the National Fatherhood Initiative's Wade Horn joined Gilder to champion the need for "marriage promotion" as a panacea for poverty. This despite the fact that a GAO study in 1987 (that looked at over a hundred studies of welfare from 1975) noted, "Research does not support the view that welfare encourages two-parent family breakup."[41] The Right, with no grounding in the data, rushed ahead with its racist and misogynist assassination of the welfare state. And Clinton was there with them all the way.

Several studies point to Clinton's tendency to seek political power rather than hold the line on ideology (what has been called "triangulation").[42] If the theory of "triangulation" is about deceit and guile, others argue that Clinton, Blair, and others of their ilk embody the "third way," neither socialist nor conservative. This "third way" must capitulate to the permanence of capitalism, and then decipher ways to make the market just.[43] At least this second argument has the merit of allowing Blair/Clinton to come to the table in defense of an ideology and not just to hold onto their seats. These explanations are useful, but they are incomplete.

The issue is not so much why did *Clinton* sign the act, but why did welfare "reform" come to be in 1996? For most of the 20th Century, the dominant form of capital was that held and deployed by industrialists. Industrial concerns worried about a relatively qualified and totally disciplined workforce. Governments used fiscal policy to maintain steady unemployment to discipline labor and to feed the surplus population in case it was ever needed for production. From the 1970s to the 1990s, mobile finance capital took predominance in the world and produced what we now call globalization. Reagan's structural adjustment of US manufacturing began a process in the 1980s that set in motion a demand for low-paid labor—both to work in the service industries, but also to undercut the union shops in the newly started small, industrial sector. Clinton's feint against welfare freed up the reserve army from its barracks into the battlefield of wage work, where one of the important results was to put pressure on the wages of the service sector. Welfare "reform" is not the willful result of vicious politicians, but is a condition of globalized capitalism and a failure of nerve among the liberal wing of the mainstream parties to temper the pressure from business for cheap labor. The old way to discipline the surplus population through the carrot (welfare) and the stick (incarceration) has begun to lose its shine, and the state flailed about in search of a new method for social control.

WAR AGAINST THE POOR

What's wrong with welfare "reform"? Before we get into the details of the defects in the 1996 law, it is pressing to underscore the cruelty of the bill. While only 15 percent of the population at large reports to the government that they or their children are disabled, among TANF recipients, the figure is 44 percent. A US government General Accounting Office study in 2002 found that "the recipients with impairments were half as likely to exit TANF as recipients without impairments." Nevertheless, those with a disability and on the TANF rolls *had* to find jobs at a rate much higher than those with a disability and not on TANF. "Regarding other potential sources of income," the GAO noted, "leavers with impairments were more likely than leavers without impairments to report having no income from personal earnings, household earnings, or SSI [Supplemental Security Income—a federal program to assist those low-income individuals who are elderly, blind, or disabled], but they also were more likely to receive Food Stamps and Medicaid."[44] A state that does not offer the maximum opportunity for those with various physical and psychological impairments, if it can afford it, is an uncivilized and cruel state.

This is not all. There are a host of problems with TANF, and here they are.

McJobs

TANF created the means for states to push welfare recipients off the rolls and into workfare jobs. Indeed, one of the main tests for the success of the welfare reform has been the decline in the number of those who now accept TANF. The Department of Health and Human Services reports, however, that less than a quarter of those who leave the welfare roll did so because they found a job, while 56 percent left for "unknown" reasons. "People disappear from the rolls because they are 'sanctioned' for missing appointments or because they can't find childcare, or they are 'diverted' from applying in the first place," reports Gary Delgado, executive director of the Applied Research Center, a movement think-tank. "Most of those leaving TANF have found their way into the gender ghettos of service, sales and clerical work where they are earning barely above the minimum wage."[45]

Sandra Robertson, executive director of the Georgia Citizen's Hunger Coalition, concurs. Data from the welfare rolls means little. "We don't care what those numbers are," she notes. "They don't reveal much. We want the legislature to measure the success of welfare reform by the economic conditions of the families." By all accounts, and Georgia is as stark as any state, those who once lived on AFDC and other state support programs experience old times in the New Economy.[46] Or take Wisconsin, home to Tommy Thompson. In 1985–86 the state disbursed welfare payments to nearly 300,000 recipients, but by 1999 it sent checks to only 35,000 people.[47] Where have the poor gone? Economist Randy Albelda notes, "Society cannot expect single mothers to enter low-wage labor markets and exit poverty."[48] They don't exit poverty, so they take refuge in the impoverished private charity sector. As the number of Food Stamp recipients dropped by 40 percent, the lines at the soup kitchens grew progressively longer, this according to Pat Gowens, executive director of Milwaukee's Welfare Warriors.[49] Poverty remains, but the poor have been banished from state care.

If those on workfare enter the low-wage sector because there are few other jobs for them, their entry displaces other workers from these jobs and, crucially, depresses wages further. The Department of Labor guidelines for TANF workers makes it clear that they cannot work for less than minimum wage, but since many TANF workers hold jobs as part of their "training" period, they are "not entitled to the minimum wage." These trainees are not meant to displace "regular employees."[50] While it is very hard to ensure that this does not occur for each individual job, macroeconomic studies show, "Economic analysis indicates that workfare is likely to have a substantial, negative effect on the broader workforce—and particularly on the lowest-wage, most disadvantaged workers."[51]

A good test case for welfare reforms' decisive impact against the contingent class is New York City. Here, Mayor Rudy Giuliani ruthlessly went after the unionized workforce in the early 1990s, then, with welfare reform, flooded the tight, barely unionized labor market with 130,000 workfare workers through the Work Experience Program (WEP) between February 1995 and December 1996.[52] Like Clinton, Giuliani praised the drop in the welfare rolls and the rate of job growth among those formerly on AFDC. However what he did not address, and what the media remained silent about, was that the WEP workers did the same jobs as former unionized workers for less pay, and whatever pay they did receive was subsidized by tax dollars. The WEP workers at the low end toil for around $1.80 per hour, or $3,600 per year rather than about $20,000 per year for a unionized worker (also an outrageously low salary). The WEP workers earned about a third less than the poverty line, and only 14 percent of WEP workers ended up with a paid job.[53] Community Voices Heard, a workfare rights group in New York City, showed in their innovative report that the average WEP recipient in 1999 earned no more than $5,724 per year (inclusive of all benefits, including Food Stamps), for about 22 hours of work a week. They could work no more, because this was the threshold for workfare workers. Since most of these jobs were during the day, and since these are the high-surveillance, low-wage jobs, it was impossible to seek out alternative employment while on the clock. And it was equally impossible to gain job training, because New York's WEP program insists that the recipients do their time, before they can get the skills.[54]

If this were not bad enough, discrimination rears its head as TANF recipients enter the workforce. A survey published in 1999 showed that 54 percent of welfare recipients struggled with racism and sexism, with disability discrimination, and other sorts of harassments.[55] A third of black TANF recipients found a job, whereas more than half the whites entered the low-wage swamp. As Susan Gooden of the Center for Public Administration at Virginia Tech puts it, "In general, blacks earn less than whites, are less likely to be employed full-time and are overrepresented in lower paying occupations."[56] Partly this is so because more blacks and Latinos live within the walls of wageless cities, and since decent jobs are in short supply, it is no surprise that TANF recipients from the world of color do not have a high employment rate. If the government retooled transportation networks, perhaps this would not be the case. Furthermore, people of color are paid less than whites, so that the jobs are even less attractive for them than for whites.

Who Will Keep the Kids?

If a parent is forced to take a low-wage job, who will take care of the kids? Norma Calderón, of People Organized to Win Employment Rights (San Francisco, CA), said at a welfare rights hearing in Washington, DC, on February 5, 2002:

> While I was in workfare, I spent $150 a month on childcare. I sent in reimbursement requests, but never received anything. I went to the Children's Council to ask for benefits, but they were denied. I would like to work full-time, but without childcare, I can't. What am I going to do with my children when my wages are so low that I can't afford childcare and I don't have family members here who can help me? Welfare didn't provide adequate childcare either. I don't want to be forced to leave my children unattended while I'm at work, or to place them in unsafe or inadequate childcare. I know that I'm not alone because I have spoken with many other mothers who are in the same situation. The system makes it difficult to get out of poverty and to survive. There are thousands of families that don't have jobs that allow us to make enough money to provide for our children.

Calderón's account sums it up for millions of women who have to balance childcare with waged work. Activist Grace Chang notes:

> When wages and household subsidies are cut, women as wives and mothers adjust household budgets often at the expense of their own and their children's nutrition. As public health care and education vanish, women suffer from lack of prenatal care and become nurses to ill family members at home.[57]

Impoverished women stretch their bodies to provide their own services.

In a remarkable book, economist Nancy Folbre offers a strong critique of our economic culture that casts from view the vast amount of reproductive work done by women, just as it lifts up waged work as the only positive feature in our world.[58] Women had been able to provide the labor of the "invisible heart" in the era when the "family wage," thanks to union pressure on management, allowed a male breadwinner to finance the livelihood of a family. With the "family wage" now a thing of the past, political scientist Nancy Fraser notes, conservatives crack down on women with a contradictory message: they say that men must be the primary breadwinner, even the "family wage" earner, in an era when the one-income household has become impossible, *and* they say that women must go out and get a job. "Punitive, androcentric, and obsessed with employment despite the absence of good jobs, [neoliberal policies of the conservatives] are unable to provide security in a postindustrial world."[59] The rhetoric of workfare serves in great measure to pervert the idea of "work" itself. When the working class women of color work hard to raise children, those in power call them lazy, just as the magazine industry loudly applauds the sexist push to drive (mainly white) middle-class women away from the public sphere and into the arms of their children. Work, for the poor, is reduced to wage work, and working class mothers are expected to feel useless if they are not out there in numbing jobs for subhuman wages.[60]

Childcare is only one aspect of the lack of state supports to help transition welfare recipients into the waged work force. From Chicago, we learn that many TANF recipients who fell off the rolls lost their homes and are now in homeless shelters. Forty-four percent of homeless families in the shelters told researchers that they had lost cash assistance benefits, while 85 percent of those in the shelters said that they had experienced some level of the welfare "reform" cuts.[61] From Los Angeles, we hear that 60 percent of those in the family shelters found the "welfare bureaucracy…unresponsive in providing supportive services that would stabilize their lives." Among these services, the homeless families numbered childcare, transportation, job training, and homes.[62] From Tennessee, we find that almost 30,000 families who have been cut off from the welfare rolls are "lost in the bureaucratic maze, unable to obtain the assistance promised them, and struggling to keep jobs while keeping up with rigid program requirements." Without decent public transportation and childcare, many former recipients report that they face "the termination of a participants' benefits for failure to attend class, keep an appointment with a caseworker, or hold a full-time job."[63] From Albany, New York, news comes that only two percent of those on TANF are enrolled in the Transitional Childcare Services provided by the state—the bureaucratic maze bewilders recipients, but also documented cases of racist discrimination prevent recipients from learning about the meager transition services offered by the state.[64] Community Voices Heard reports that New York City's municipal authorities failed "to address the needs of families reaching their time limits," and "benefit reductions due to sanctions have caused roughly 54 percent of survey respondents to fall behind on their rent payments, 44 percent to be unable to afford food costs, 36 percent to have their utilities cut off, and 21 percent to lose their health benefits."[65]

A study from Boston shows us that a living wage for a family of three would be about $3,263 per month. To earn this money, the adult would have to hold a job that earns $17.47 per hour, already far above minimum wage. In Boston, an expensive city, childcare costs would be $985 per month—almost a third of the expenses.[66] In 1999, a third of working women across the country earned wages at or below the poverty level, significantly more than the share of men (20.7 percent) at that level. We are in the Purgatory of the Service Economy, where "temporary work" is the new euphemism for indentureship in the workforce, where no one can watch the kids while TANF workers are at work, where the state puts the kids in foster care because of that—childcare in a punitive economy.

Theft of Children

The removal of children from the family is not an unlikely scenario. When Newt Gingrich was the Speaker of the House, he tendered a proposal to bring back the poorhouse and state children's facilities, to return us to the days of Oliver Twist.

In Utah, the state has already started to take away children from TANF recipients who cannot find a job and need TANF. Bonnie Macri, executive director of Jedi for Women in Salt Lake City, Utah, tells a chilling tale. If a woman cannot get a job after the 36 month TANF limit, then the state of Utah takes her children away and puts them up for adoption (Utah decided on the strict 36 month cut-off, while Connecticut is the strictest state with only 21 months of TANF). The state admits that about 2,000 children have been removed from their mothers, while Jedi thinks this is a deflated figure. Rebecca Gordon of the Applied Research Center summarizes the story of Utah based on a survey of TANF recipients:

> Welfare caseworkers inform Family and Child Services a
> month after a TANF family reaches its lifetime benefit

limit. Within a month, Family and Child Services makes an unannounced visit to the family's home to determine its fitness as a place for children. One respondent's weeping son was removed from her home with no investigations whatsoever, because at the moment when the visitor from Family and Child Services arrived, she was tending his bloody nose. Another was told she didn't have enough canned goods in her pantry, not too surprising a situation as her welfare benefits had been terminated. Her children were taken, too. Still another woman lost her children on laundry day. She'd had her kids throw their dirty clothes down to the foot of the stairs so she could bag it up and take it to the Laundromat. The FCS worker walked in, observed the pile of clothes and promptly removed the children from this "unfit" home. Perhaps the saddest case was that of a woman who had managed to leave an abusive situation, only to lose her children because she "allowed" them to see her being beaten up. In most of these cases, it was the loss of benefits that precipitated a visit from FCS and subsequent breakup of the family unit.[67]

Only a short while after Jedi took up this issue, over 300 families joined them because they had personally lost children to welfare reform.[68] Gwendolyn Mink shows that Department of Health and Human Services adoption numbers rose from 28,000 in 1996 to 46,000 in 1999, and then holds, "The adoption law hovers within the TANF regime as the regime's final solution to independent motherhood."[69]

Reading, Writing, Racism

The rhetoric of workfare and of dignity through work falsely raises the hopes of families who feel trapped by the constraints of economic injustice. Janet Robideau of Indian Peoples' Action in Montana finds that many Native American women turn to workfare programs as a means to get paid. To earn well, many try to break out of the gender ghetto through post-secondary education. But, Indian Peoples' Action found that a number of their members worked hard to complete their degrees through state-assisted childcare and scholarship programs only to lose access to these resources on the last stretches toward their degrees. They are "cut off at the knees," says Robideau. "It's like giving someone a car with three wheels."

Racism, furthermore, blocks access to the small amount of education money available.[70] Helen Nickens of Grassroots Organizing from Mexico, Missouri, spoke at the February 5, 2002, briefing on Capitol Hill:

> The county director and other agencies who are supposed to help people in need denied services to me because I am of color. Neighbors of mine who are poor, white, and receive welfare benefits and other services are aware of the way people of color are treated differently. Because I am an African American woman, they do not inform me about educational opportunities, real job training, or other support services. If they are not ignoring us or pretending we don't have real racial concerns then they are harassing us and turning their noses up at us.

Susan Gooden's study of welfare recipients in Virginia shows that whereas the black recipients had better educational qualifications than whites, not one caseworker encouraged black folk to go to school. Meanwhile, just over 40 percent of whites said that caseworkers asked them to go to school and better their prospects for jobs. Instead, the caseworkers pushed blacks toward drug and background tests to raise more such racist barriers for them.[71]

As the assault on public education intensifies across the country, fewer funds go toward decent educational opportunities for the TANF recipients. Those who are immigrants and who do not have English as a first language experience the "English Only" classrooms, harassment, and inconsiderate behavior from TANF caseworkers, and an impossible task in the job market without the language supports so crucial for adaptation to a foreign land, or in a land that does not respect multilingualism. Make the Road By Walking, a community organization in Brooklyn, conducted a study of welfare recipients, 65 percent of whom found it impossible to communicate with their caseworkers because the city did not provide translation services in the TANF offices. "Language has caused me so many problems," said Donatilla P., one of those surveyed. "I can't even describe them all."[72] From Idaho, we hear that "limited English-speaking people" do not get counseling for the TANF application process, and because of enrollment delays they often do not get transitional facilities, like childcare.[73] Hostility to immigrants, as well as lack of concern for language education and translation, leads to a decline in immigrant access to Food Stamps (as documented in Santa Clara County, California) and healthcare (as documented for New York City).[74]

There is no childcare reimbursement for the evening hours spent in school, little care that education cannot be time-bound, and certainly no concern that education alongside wage labor and parenthood is well nigh impossible. The government claimed at the time that there just were no funds available for these "social" programs, while the welfare bill provided $250 million in federal matching funds for states who inserted "abstinence only" into the school curricula. Education, then, did get funds, but not toward the generation of skills for those on TANF; rather, the funds taught a type of sex education that is not only unrealistic (that is, which does not deal with HIV-AIDS, condoms, sexual parity, and joy rather than rape and violence), but which does not stand muster in a bill on its own. Instead of education for those on TANF, the state insisted, under the heading "education," that the schools teach conservative values to all students.

The Man Don't Take No Mess

The TANF regime comes with a full array of surveillance mechanisms as well as procedures for the caseworkers to "sanction" the recipient. Each recipient has an "individual responsibility plan" that has to be followed, and if anything is awry, the caseworker is allowed to sanction the recipient by cutting off benefits for a period of time, or for good. Gary Delgado and Rebecca Gordon of the Applied Research Center show that sanctions are used as a disciplinary mechanism, that "they are the primary reason that welfare rolls have declined," that more than half of those on TANF knew the rules, but less than half had been told about the appeals process if they are denied benefits, and that blacks face the highest rates of sanctions, not for any other reason than the racist lens through which the program is administered.[75] "Race casts a much longer shadow than any of the other factors considered in this analysis over the state adoption of get-tough welfare reforms," writes political scientist Sanford Schram. Indeed, the states that adopted the toughest sanctions regimes housed the largest population of blacks, and in those states, blacks by far received the cruelest treatment from caseworkers.

Where African American single mothers predominated on the rolls, the chances were much higher that the state would choose stricter policy options. And those policies were more likely to affect African American mothers than their white counterparts. Race mattered at least twice over when it came to imposing the get-tough policies of welfare reform.[76]

In Alameda County, California, the state has jailed thousands of people whom they charge with "welfare fraud." Faced with two felony counts (one of fraud and the second of perjury), many low-income people plead guilty and thereafter find it hard to get a job with a criminal record. Frequently, the county charges the recipient with fraud when the problem is an accidental overpayment by the state.[77] Angela Chung of People United to Build a Better Oakland (PUEBLO) points out in 1996, "We know that a lot of money was given to Alameda County to develop an aggressive welfare fraud policy." The county gets incentives from the state to find those who commit fraud, a clear indication that the goal is not to increase employment but to find new ways to discipline urban populations. Eighty-four percent of those who seek assistance in Alameda County are people of color, and Alameda has the highest percentage of blacks in California. That the state has targeted this county for its feverish prosecution of welfare errors bespeaks the racism of the entire apparatus.

Tie You Up in Knots

TANF, version '96, was about "work" and the creation of personal responsibility through the regulation of a job. TANF, version '02, is about marriage, about the production of a fantasy two-parent family that produces normal children and, thanks to a variant of the "family wage," is able to live with dignity. TANF '96, however, did say in its preamble, "Marriage is the foundation of a successful society," and it did allocate almost $650 million to states if they reduced "out-of-wedlock" births and abortions. The federal government rewarded states if they acceded to conservative measures of social engineering, rather than if they took care of the poor in a civilized manner. If the state backs away from the regulation of corporations, it does not seem chary of regulating the lives of the poor.[78]

If Clinton pushed marriage, Bush the Younger and his Marriage

Czar, Wade Horn (assistant secretary for children and families in the Department of Health and Human Services), are eager to deny any services to unmarried mothers, and therefore to *force* women of the contingent class to marry. In 1997, Wade Horn, along with Andrew Bush, wrote in a report for the neoconservative Hudson Institute:

> As state officials launch new welfare reforms, they must not lose sight of the larger issues of fatherhood and marriage. The problem is that strategies for promoting fatherhood and marriage are, to a very large extent, in conflict with those that seek to help single mothers achieve self-sufficiency through work. Indeed, a welfare system that helps single mothers become employed, but ignores the need to promote fatherhood and marriage, may serve only to enable unmarried women to rear children without the presence of the father.[79]

Without a doubt, one earner in a family makes survival difficult. This is not the reason why Bush-Horn want to see TANF women in marriages. They have a patriarchal agenda whose premise is that moral values can only be imparted to society if women are married to men, and if the man is the head of a household (the idea of "Fatherhood"). The Bush administration's Responsible Fatherhood Act is the major attempt to discipline those on TANF further by pushing women to marry at the state's insistence, despite the fact that in many communities, the state has locked up large numbers of men for drug-related, nonviolent crimes.

A major challenge to the Bush-Horn plan was that it would force women to remain in abusive relationships or else to return to abusive spouses if they had already fled them. Sixty percent of women on the TANF rolls have been in relationships where violence has been a factor. In response to this line of argument, Horn told the media, "Government can help [couples] manage conflict so that it doesn't escalate into violence. We don't want to be a federal dating service. Nor do we want to force people to get married or push couples into abusive relationships."[80] Certainly the Bush-Horn proposals do not force people to get married, but they give them an impossible choice: either marry and receive the TANF benefits, or struggle to survive without any state-funded social net.

In Montana, the rules to make the poor marry deepen the oppression of women who are in difficult situations, as well as of lesbians whose partnerships are not recognized by the marriage promotion advocates. "I was married to my ex-husband for thirteen years," testified Mary Caferro of Working for Equality and Economic Liberation (Helena, Montana) on February 5, 2002.

> We had four children, and he made a good income but was very abusive and an alcoholic. I stayed in the marriage, feeling that I couldn't put my children into a situation that was economically unstable. I knew that if we split up we would live in poverty. I stayed in the marriage, afraid that I wouldn't have the support to leave, and putting what I thought were my children's needs in front of my own safety. The abuse was extreme. When things escalated and it became unsafe for my children too, I found the strength to leave him. I saved my family's life. That is why I am not married. I want to get married again because I love, care, and respect the person. Not because I am being coerced by the government with the threat of my children's benefits being cut off.

This experience drew from Mary the following strong analysis:

> Marriage promotion is not about solving poverty. Marriage promotion is about controlling women by using racist rhetoric and restrictive policy. Single parents have been touted as being responsible for all social evils of society today. This dehumanizing myth serves to foster the stereotype of the welfare queen and further instill shame and guilt on our mothers.

Sociologist Mimi Abramovitz makes two more excellent points in her preface to a movement study on marriage promotion. She writes of the double standard of Bush-Horn, and of the Bush-Horn fear of women's liberation:

> The marriage promotion program also suffers from a troublesome double standard. While forcing poor women on welfare to marry regardless of their needs and interests, its supporters vehemently oppose stable non-matrimonial relationships and same sex bonds. The pro-marriage campaign also implies that economic dependence on men is better for women than economic dependence on the state. Of course, access to outside income, be it wages or cash aid,

has the potential to increase a woman's autonomy and to increase her bargaining power at home and at the job. Perhaps this is why welfare reform cuts benefits, pushes women into low wage jobs, and promotes marriage![81]

States' Rights! Corporate Rights!

Clinton's welfare bill set a new standard within the US for "devolution." The federal government had been the font of social welfare, but with the welfare bill, administrative decisions now devolved to the statehouse. Each state was now entrusted to set eligibility requirements, time limits, and benefit levels. This meant that there is no federal standard, there is no yardstick by which to measure the various programs and their effectiveness and the various federal regulatory agencies (Office of Civil Rights, Department of Labor) are at sea with the enormous apparatus of TANF. With no federal guidelines and oversight, some regions adopted novel approaches to decrease the TANF rolls: Selma, Alabama, for instance, located its welfare office five miles outside town, outside the reach of public transport.[82] Delgado and Gordon of the Applied Research Center argue:

> Devolution has reintroduced the tyranny of states' rights. Whether it is a question of guaranteeing access to public transportation, securing funds for public schools that serve poor children—through Title I of the Elementary and Secondary Education Act—or guaranteeing employment rights through the Americans with Disabilities Act, the federal government has acted in arenas where individual states either cannot or will not do so.[83]

Furthermore, states feel pressure to cut welfare rolls to save money, mainly because there has been no nationwide preparation for any emergency, such as a depression and consequent rush for social services by the impoverished. Instead of fighting to create a fund for this emergency, states are pinching pennies to roll over TANF money for any eventuality.[84]

The federal government has not only devolved power to the arbitrary control of the states, it has also given up its service provision role to private corporations. Welfare services have now entered the private sector, the profit sector, to bilk the poor to achieve targets at their expense. Maximus, Inc., one of the private social service firms, lied to get a contract in Colorado and earned many complaints for racist discrimination in Milwaukee, Wisconsin; America Works, Inc., has been charged with drawing $1 million from New York State for putting people in jobs, something they did not do; Curtis and Associates asks those eligible for welfare to fill out long, complex forms, and if they cannot do so, it denies them coverage (all the while collecting money from the state).[85]

Despite all these reasons why welfare "reform" is flawed, the bill was passed in 1996, it has been celebrated, and now, as reauthorization is on the table, there are many that want to push its draconian policies even further. The workfare program, however, cannot deliver quality jobs, a colossal failure best represented by the increase in petty crime (and in the prison population). "The real issue," says Peter Edelman, who resigned from the Clinton administration in 1996, "isn't welfare. It's poverty." But poverty is not a problem of the federal government in the age of structural adjustment. The problem of poverty is abandoned in favor of the state's obsession with its debt rating. In May 1999, Alan Greenspan noted, "The arithmetic of foreign debt accumulation and compounding interest costs does indicate somewhere in the future that, unless reversed, our growing international imbalances are apt to create significant problems for our economy."[86] One way to cut funds was to kill social welfare and to set people free to work in the low-wage sector. On October 1, 1999, the *Wall Street Journal* reported a modest gain in income in the US, but it was forced to acknowledge the words of Rose Woolery, a working mother: "This country is still for those who have money. For the people who don't have it, you're not going to get it."[87] Those who "have it," "get it" from the US's corporate welfare program. From 1996 to 2000, ten of the global corporations received a $50 billion tax break from the US Treasury, with Microsoft taking in a $12 billion tax break (with no tax paid in 1999 despite $12.3 billion in profits), General Electric took away $12 billion in tax welfare and Ford earned "relief" of just over $9 billion. In 1999 and 2000, WorldCom paid no taxes even though it took in profits of $15.2 billion, General Motors paid no tax for three of the last five years, again despite profits of $12.5 billion, while Enron paid no taxes for the past four years despite $1.8 billion in reported profits.[88] For 2002, the US military took home $360 billion, a 14 percent increase on the 2001 budget, the size of the increase ($44 billion) itself greater than the annual defense budgets of Japan ($41 billion), Great Britain ($35 billion), Russia ($29 billion), Germany ($23 billion), China ($14.5 billion) and North Korea ($1.3 billion). For 2003, the Pentagon wants an additional $30 billion and the president's budget proposes an additional six percent increase over the 2002 disbursement.[89] All this for the military-corporate alliance, but nothing for social development.

BUSH'S LEAP OF FAITH

George W. Bush's political agenda is essentially ABC: Anything But Clinton. From Kyoto to Korea, this has been the general approach of the administration on everything except welfare. On welfare, the Bush and Clinton agenda is similar. In his 1999 campaign book, *A Charge to Keep*, Bush followed the Clinton position that "Too much government fosters dependency." He wrote:

> The new culture said if people were poor, the government should feed them. If criminals are not responsible for their acts, then the answers are not in prisons, but in social programs. People became less interested in pulling themselves up by their bootstraps and more interested in pulling down a monthly government check. A culture of dependency was born. Programs that began as a temporary hand-up became a permanent handout, regarded by many as a right.[90]

This Clintonian analysis translated into unoriginal policy suggestions: time limits on welfare benefits and workfare, with no consideration for the education or any support network for those on welfare.

In early 2002, reports from across the country showed that the welfare rolls begin to rise as inequality increased in the year of 9/11. The modest increase (one percent) took place in two-thirds of the states.[91] In big cities, however, the welfare rolls continued to slide, despite the widespread lack of jobs and overcrowded food banks. "The people running non-profit, community-based feeding agencies overwhelmingly indicate that people kicked off welfare are coming to them for help because they do not have jobs," said Joel Berg, executive director of the New York City Coalition Against Hunger.[92] With the scorecard for TANF in hand, Congress began to consider reauthorization of the law (as stipulated in 1996) in the early months of

2002. In May 2002, the House passed Bush's version of welfare "reform," not unlike the 1996 bill, but with stricter work requirements, a little more money for childcare, and more talk of marriage as an obligation. In September 2002, more than half the Democrats in the Senate called upon the majority leader, Tom Daschle, to begin a debate on welfare, to extend the 1996 law for another three years, and to add more money for childcare.[93] The Senate dithered, Bush extended the program till the end of 2002, and the fight continued over childcare and work requirements. Then, on February 13, 2003, the House once more passed its draconian version of welfare reform, with strict work rules for those who want welfare, with more pressure to push people to work rather than toward education. "In 1964, Lyndon Johnson declared a war against poverty," said Representative Pete Stark (Democrat from California). "Today, my Republican colleagues and the President have declared a war against the poor."[94] Bush took the Clinton insistence upon work above all else to its logical limit: now work is everything, education is irrelevant.

While Clinton eagerly sought to send the social welfare aspects of government to the states and to private agencies, Bush welcomed the role of religious organizations, the "armies of compassion" to tender welfare. "A compassionate society," said President Bush, "is one which recognizes the great power of faith. We in government must not fear faith-based programs, we must welcome them."[95] When critics said that his faith-based approach violated the constitutional barrier between the church and state, Bush said:

> Participation in faith-based programs must be voluntary, and we must make sure secular alternatives are available. But government should welcome the active involvement of people who are following a religious imperative to love their neighbors through after-school programs, childcare, drug treatment, maternity group homes, and a range of other services. Supporting these men and women is the next bold step of welfare reform.[96]

Even here, there is nothing spectacularly different from the Clinton years, because the 1996 law offered faith-based organizations an opportunity to bid for welfare contracts under a provision called "Charitable Choice." The law even allowed these organizations to offer religious services alongside secular assistance. To champion "faith-based charity" is a convenient way to shrink the state's social welfare aspect without the appearance of callousness. The Bush domestic ploy resembles the demand made on states across the globe over the last two decades to cut back on social welfare and give that sector over to "nonprofit" or "nongovernmental" organizations, including religious institutions.[97]

Part of the Bush angle is to use the "faith-based initiatives" as a way to provide cover for the racism of welfare reform. In 2002, he regularly visited black churches to offer his promotion of the form of institutional religion over the content of religious charity. "We've got to recognize," he told a predominantly black congregation in Milwaukee, "there are some people in our country who wonder whether the American experience is meant for them. It's one thing to make sure that we are secure, but we also have got to understand that in our plenty, there are pockets of despair and hopelessness."[98] The message sounds compassionate, but because of the draconian policies from the administration it did not fool anybody. Reverend Timothy McDonald is the president of the African American Ministers Leadership Council, a group of 60 ministers spread over 30 states. The Bush administration, he argues, "is trying to buy the allegiance of the black church. And that is to the advantage of the Republican Party, because the black church has been a major thorn in their side." Theresa Thomas Boyd, a pastor at the nondenominational Christian Church Matters of the Heart, says that the Bush initiative "is a buy off, but to me it's more of a brainwash. The buy off is the money, and the brainwash is that there's always a different, underlying agenda."[99]

When some Democrats wanted to hold the line on these two issues, Bush exploded, saying that any change on his position "would hurt the very people we're trying to help."[100] As the GOP takes control of Washington, and the Democrats slither around in search of a new skin, the contingent class is going to pay a heavy price. "We're trying to help those people," Bush said, but it is *those very people who want to help themselves....*

NON-REFORMIST REFORM: THREE APPROACHES TO LIBERATION

In 1996, the forces of humanity did not stand up against the Clinton-Gingrich alliance, and the welfare bill went through without much fuss. The unions did little, the welfare rights movement was in disarray, and the feminist movement let down the side.[101] Shortly after

TANF came into force, the welfare movement rose from the ashes, fiery and ready for the fight. The welfare fights that I profile below do not fit into what Andre Gorz calls "reformist reforms" that simply maintain the status quo and shore up the system, but they go along the grain of "non-reformist reforms," ones that in a cumulative fashion tend toward social transformation.[102] If we go back to Rosa Luxemburg's careful thoughts on the subject, "non-reformist reform" refers to those social changes that not only produce new forms of social engagement, but also put the extant social structure into crisis: welfare, in the Piven-Cloward formula, has the tendency to call into question the liberal hypocrisy of the system, but it also provides the material basis for the further mobilization and organization of the working poor toward fundamental social transformation.[103] Too many on the US Left abjure "reforms," and too many of those in the reform industries are uninterested in a Left agenda—a dialectical unity of these two opposites is what is needed in our current conjuncture. Not just any "reforms," but mainly "non-reformist reforms."

As more and more people are released from prisons (just as others move into them, or else those out will be recycled in) and with the absence of social assistance, the only way the state has to keep the reserve army of labor in check is by lockdown conditions in urban areas. The anti-police brutality fight is one part of the struggle, but in a defensive way; the welfare fight gets at the same problem but in a proactive way. The fight for welfare liberation is an offensive one.

Tax the Rich in Connecticut

In mid-2000, the Campaign to End Child Poverty in Connecticut sent a delegation to meet with the Democratic leadership in the state house. As we entered the main lobby, we began to feel awkward. The Connecticut State House is opulent and aristocratic, with the lobbyists gathered like sharks in the stairwell, and under a very high ceiling state representatives trade in their personal oddities for their considerable power. Committees deign to hear certain bills and fast-track others, as the mentality of a clique keeps outsiders apprehensive.

The Connecticut Teachers' Union, with its considerable muscle, organized a meeting for the Campaign, and representatives from Vecinos Unidos and the Communist Party (CP) spent half an hour trying to convince the leadership of the Democratic Party to support the Campaign to End Child Poverty's Bill no. 5461 (End Child Poverty Social Investment Fund). Vecinos Unidos, being a welfare rights group, is a natural at this sort of campaign, but neither the teachers' union nor the Communist Party are newcomers to the politics of Connecticut's poor. The CP in New Haven, for instance, has been instrumental in most major campaigns from below, from the Civil Rights movement (including the Black Panther Party work and the defense committee for Bobby Seale, for instance) to the fight against homelessness and poverty. In the 1980s, the People's Center, the home of New Haven's CP, became the drop-in center for the city's homeless. There, the CP, along with Yale University's Hunger and Homelessness Action Project and the Yale Law School Legal Aid Program, organized the destitute into a political movement to reopen and expand the city's shelter program. The current (2002) tent city in New Haven Green is a legacy of the CP's work in the city.[104] In 1999, statistical data released by the state of Connecticut showed that not only did the state have a high rate of the nation's wealthy, but it also housed a high rate of the impoverished. To celebrate the eightieth anniversary of the CP, the organizers of the party planned a Concert to End Child Poverty. At the pre-concert rally, several leaders of local groups talked about a campaign on this theme, and at a meeting the next week, the Campaign to End Child Poverty was born. Over 30 organizations joined up, including unions, faith groups, welfare rights groups, and community organizations. The years of activity that preceded 1999 went into the strength of the group.

With that behind us, a year later, in mid-2000, our delegation sat with the leadership of the state's Democratic Party in the statehouse. We made our pitch: Connecticut has the highest disparity in income and wealth in the US. A tenth of all Connecticut's children live below the official poverty line. In the cities, among the youth of color, the figure rises to over 30 percent. Unimaginable grief comes from a lack of resources. How can a relatively deprived child be expected to have the same opportunities as those who are privileged? Our popular prejudice in favor of equal opportunity is mocked by our social conditions. Connecticut used to be one of the most generous states, yet with a paltry social welfare program. Before 1996, while a family of three in Mississippi earned $120 per month, the same family in Connecticut took home a check for $600 or more. The social safety net has disappeared. This is unconscionable and the delegation urged the elected officials to support the Social Investment Fund. Smiles all around.

Then, two of the women from Vecinos Unidos testified on the harshness of life without social assistance. The Urban Institute calls Hartford, the home of these women, one of the kindest to people on public assistance, but even here the conditions are atrocious. The women mentioned the renewed, anti-feminist glamorization of domesticity for elite white women, just as women of color are being treated as criminals for tending to their children.

It is powerful stuff. The elected officials interrupt periodically to say that this problem or that problem can be dealt with by this piece of an extant law or by that social agency. To them the problems are those of access and not of disenfranchisement: if only the women knew of the support structure that the good government of Connecticut has already given its people! But the women are adamant: yes, we've tried to get the child-care benefits, but we've been told we don't qualify because of this, that, and the other thing. And the official says, call my office I'll sort it out. Another woman says she can call your office, but what about the thousands of other women who don't know they can do that. We need civics classes and better trained state workers, says the official. Frustration sets into the conversation.

Eventually little came of the meeting. The representatives said that they supported the spirit of the bill, but they could not see what the specifics might be. How do you spend the money, they asked? The Campaign to End Child Poverty has worked for several years with lawmakers to craft legislation that offers children a healthy and just future. The bill calls for a two percent tax on the portion of income above $200,000 per year (only the money above this amount will bear the tax). This tax or social levy would only affect three percent of the population and it would raise $600 million. The bill does not say how the money will be spent, but the Campaign does offer many ideas. The assault on welfare left thousands of families in Connecticut, as elsewhere, without the means to live with dignity. The Campaign wants families to receive a cash payment, this so that the recipients are allowed the dignity to spend the money as they wish (the state used to dictate how the funds are spent via Food Stamps, and so forth). Furthermore, the Campaign sets aside funds for the creation of social services that cannot receive funds because of a draconian "spending cap" passed by the conservative state legislature. There is even talk of a neighborhood corps of civics workers whose role it is to go door to door and check in with families to see if they can provide any social capital to help engender change.

The Campaign targets children for a strategic reason: the media and power elite stigmatize poor women (often women of color), and any program that targets them is sure to fail. Obviously any program that targets children will enable the destiny of all people, not just children. The status of Connecticut's children is stark and the Campaign offered a good strategic wedge to break open discussion on welfare by an appeal to a generally vacuous moral liberalism.

A year later, in the spring of 2001, 500 academics from Connecticut signed a petition on behalf of the Campaign and its bill. The Campaign organized a press conference to highlight this development as well as to publicly turn over the signatures to the sponsors of the bill. Two legislators came to the conference. Tina King, a member of the Campaign, harangued the statehouse for its indifference. With a child in her arms, she said, "I'm standing as an American citizen ready to fight for my rights." Only one reporter came to the event, Dan Levine of the *Hartford Advocate*.[105] The struggle continues….

"You Only Get What You're Organized to Take"

In 2000, the Republican Party chose to hold its political convention in Philadelphia, Pennsylvania. Eager to win the North for a team from the South (Bush) and the West (Cheney), the Republicans also wanted to showcase the new form of development in America so dear to the heart of those in power: the fancy downtown. Downtown Philadelphia, like most large US cities, experienced "white flight" from the end of World War II to the present. Even in the 1990s, the population of Philadelphia declined by just over four percent, and it would have been more had the city not attracted Latinos and Asians to keep the numbers up.[106] The population in Bucks County and Montgomery County that border Philadelphia grew by ten percent. To attract those who took their tax dollars elsewhere as consumers (and some as residents), the city spent vast sums of taxpayer dollars to "revitalize" downtown. Millions of dollars went toward a convention center, surrounded by new, expensive hotels and shops, all financed with bond issues and taxes. On top of this, the city managers wanted to build a $1.2 billion (or more) baseball stadium in the area that now houses a 150-year-old Chinatown. The city (and state) felt comfortable spending money on corporate welfare, but their plan for the poor was quite different.[107]

Professor Dennis Culhane of the University of Pennsylvania's School of Social Work has produced a most depressing body of work. From a reading of some of the papers in his considerable oeuvre, it becomes clear that Philadelphia is a city in crisis, with a large homeless population drawn from neighborhoods battered by structural adjustment. Almost 70 percent of those who use the shelters of Philadelphia, the "city of brotherly love," had once lived in working-class neighborhoods now assaulted by a loss of jobs and services. These are the neighborhoods with abandoned homes (30,000 across the city) and stores, high rates of police brutality and violence, and a collapse of the social democratic institutions, such as schools and representative democracy.[108] A quarter of those who live in Philly struggle below the federal poverty line; a third of the children in the city live south of success. In Kensington, Philly's poorest neighborhood, only a fifth of the population turns out to exercise its franchise.

The city had a plan for the poor: to discipline them with an overwhelming police dragnet known as Operation Sunrise. The neighborhoods known as Kensington and Fairhill once housed the Irish working class that worked in the many manufacturing plants whose carcasses are still visible here and there. As black migrants moved into the city, the Irish and other whites fled with the jobs, although those also disappeared in the 1970s as the economy shifted focus. In Kensington, whites remain in a majority, with the median income less than $26,000. Almost half of those 70,000 who now live in Kensington-Fairhill survive below the poverty line. The managing director of Philadelphia, Joseph Certain, complained about drug use in the neighborhood, characterizing the situation as a "neighborhood emergency," and said that 1998's Operation Sunrise was a "military regimen" to rejuvenate the area.[109] How does police violence solve a problem whose roots are in this: only 21 percent of those in Kensington earn income via employment, the rest are unemployed; only 31 percent had access to trade school or college, while the rest barely finished high school; even though close to three-quarters of the residents in Kensington had bank accounts, there are no banks in the area…? What does Operation Sunrise do to create the long-term means for security and prosperity among the people in Kensington? Nothing.

The new mayor, John Street, talked of demolishing blight and attracting the New Economy to the city, to create a "Philacon Valley." Rather than turn over abandoned homes to the homeless, he began to demolish them and turn them over to developers. The future is not a home for everyone, but one more Jump Street USA—a city-financed $50 million retail complex in the Temple University area to rival Harlem in New York City. The Jump Street project took place when Street was the head of the City Council. His predecessor, Mayor Rendell, said of the project, "People in North Philadelphia [people of color] are dying to go to the movies here instead of going downtown [where the white suburbanites visit]. They are dying to eat in some first-class restaurants right here, instead of going downtown. This is going to be a true destination."[110] The people are *dying* all right, whether to see a movie or eat at a first-class restaurant is another question.

If we're talking rights in Kensington, there's one place that walks the walk: the Kensington Welfare Rights Union (KWRU). Born in 1991 from a conversation between five "welfare mothers," KWRU is innovative in its approach to welfare rights and effective in getting its message out to the world.[111] KWRU draws on the abolitionist heritage (with its new Underground Railroad—a network of individuals who support KWRU), but for its ideological sustenance, mainly on the human rights tradition. If the campaign in Connecticut drew on the "Tax the Rich" line, the KWRU position is "Human Rights for All." The horizon for KWRU is the Universal Declaration of Human Rights from December 10, 1948, adopted by the General Assembly but not by individual states mainly because the USSR and its allies felt chary about the freedoms of association and expression, whereas the USA refused to agree to the rights to housing, income and a job, education, medical care, and other basic needs.[112] Even as the US did not agree with this broad declaration of human needs, the KWRU in 1997 began a campaign to document human rights violations based on the horizon set by the world community in 1948.

KWRU's use of the human rights framework is not unique; indeed most welfare rights' groups riff off the Declaration as they formulate their demands. The distinctive aspect of KWRU's work is at the strategic and tactical level. According to Willie Baptist (the education director at KWRU), if we accept that the liberal reformers from above have failed to liberate the poor, that charity is not the solution, then the welfare recipients must liberate themselves. When the working class held jobs, they were able to pay dues to sustain their own organizations (unions), but among the contingent there is no surplus income for organization building. So how does KWRU operate? One of KWRU's main slogans is "You Only Get What You're Organized to Take." Here is Willie Baptist on the slogan:

> We don't advocate going around taking things all the time, but when it comes to families who are being displaced with no other recourse, when there's empty buildings just sitting there complete with plumbing, or an empty church with plumbing and heating, and there's people sitting there with families and kids, who have no other options but to die or go into the church, we go into the church.

When KWRU did this, and a group of priests objected, those within the church said, "We talked to God, and God told us that we shouldn't let the families die on the streets." This shamed the priests into allowing the people shelter.

> The basic position of the poor is where we have to take our destiny into our own hands and put ourselves into relationship with others who see their self-interest tied to us, whether social workers, labor leaders, students, or people in the religious community, and win the bulk of the American people to a program that affects their lives as well as ours.

KWRU organizes people to *take* what they need, forms these sites into bases (called Human Rights Houses) to expand the struggle, and then pursues a political campaign from this base. A Freedom Bus Tour, a Poor People's Summit, a University of the Poor, and the Poor People's Human Rights Campaign form the various parts of the political campaign of KWRU. It is significant, however, that Willie Baptist and Mary Bricker-Jenkins (both senior KWRU leaders), note that the campaign does not "and has not prescribed specific programs, opting instead to emphasize the imperative of organizing a mass base for change, to 'win people's hearts and minds' to the notion that economic justice is both necessary and possible."[113]

KWRU plays a very important role in Philadelphia and the theories that emanate from its virtuoso practice have stimulated discussions across the country. However, there are some points that remain open for debate. For example, what does it mean for KWRU not to prescribe specific programs or reforms in its political work? Does this mean that KWRU does not have a legislative agenda, a program for the transformation of the state and for state power? If this is so, then why bother with the indictment of the state for human rights reforms? If the state is to be abjured, why bring it into the picture at all? What is not clear from KWRU is how must the welfare rights movement understand the state. What is clear, however, is that KWRU is a phenomenal organizer of the contingent class and it encourages people to become leaders, turn to a progressive set of values and take the country back. As KWRU leader Cherri Honkala put it:

> To bring this movement to everybody out there, we in this room have to see ourselves as leaders. We have got to get people out of their intoxication in every sense of the word, to get people to put down the drugs, the alcohol, the television, and the despair. If we can inspire them to get involved, then we can win the fight because we are the majority of the people and we can truly take our country back.[114]

The New Millennium Freedom Riders

"It is outrageous to hold a conference that excludes the very people being talked about," said Mark Toney, executive director of the Center for Third World Organizing (CTWO). In Washington, DC, policy wonks gathered for the New World of Welfare conference in early February 2001. Organized by the University of Michigan's Ford School of Public Policy, the conclave sought to frame the policy debate for the reauthorization of the federal welfare laws in 2002. But the organizers failed to include the voices of those on welfare or those who are on the frontlines of welfare reform.[115]

Toney and about 100 other grassroots organizers fought their way into the conference and registered their displeasure at the undemocratic way decisions are formulated in the US. They came to DC to put the political elite on notice: we are here, we can speak, and we won't allow you to make policy behind closed doors. They didn't do much direct action, the sorts of things that one sees at recent international monetary conferences recently. Rather their very presence as a bloc, their questions, their interventions, their intelligence, all this was a shock to those who have got so very used to being managers of the republic.

The speakers invited to formulate the debate came from the ideological Right: Charles Murray, Jason Turner (the controversial welfare commissioner for New York City), "scholars" from the American Enterprise Institute and Heritage Foundation (notably Robert Rector) and finally, Tommy Thompson, the US Secretary of Health and Human Services. Faced with word of the "disruptions," Thompson withdrew himself "due to safety concerns." When the grassroots talk back, the establishment senses the Bastille.[116]

Indeed, the New World of Welfare conference illustrates the problem with how this nation formulates "public" policy. The elite meet in expensive hotels (this was the prison profits–soaked Marriott),[117] far from the rabble, and formulate policy based on all manner of prejudices to suit the interests of Wall Street (and sometimes Main Street). But this time the grassroots sprouted, much to the discomfort of the suits.

Little protest occurs without meticulous preparation. This one came to us courtesy of GROWL, Grassroots Organizing for Welfare Leadership, a national platform of 50 grassroots organizations convened by CTWO. Founded two decades ago, CTWO has made quite a name for itself in the world of anti-racist justice. It is well known for its MAAP program, which began a decade ago as the Minority Activist Apprenticeship Program, but in 2001, changed the M to Movement. Activists of color learn CTWO's ideology-based direct action philosophy and then do six week-long internships with allies across the country. Apart from this, CTWO is also on the map as a leading part of the National Organizers' Alliance and the former publisher of *ColorLines* magazine.

In 1999, CTWO brought together organizations from across the country that either work on the issue of welfare justice or whose working class constituencies had begun to feel the effects of the ruthless welfare "reform" measure. These 50 groups come from places as distinct as New York City, Oakland, Miami, and Boise, but each of them brings their special experience of poverty. While groups such as Fifth Avenue Committee (Brooklyn, New York) or Direct Action for

Rights and Equality (Providence, Rhode Island) are community-based, working-class membership organizations, other groups offer technical support (such as San Francisco's We Interrupt This Message or Oakland's Applied Research Center), while yet other groups are labor formations (for example, Miami Workers' Center). This vast and energetic coalition of groups announced the formation of GROWL in May 2000 as a means to intervene in the welfare debate with a framework that is based on anti-racist justice, gender equity, sexual liberation, and class struggle.

GROWL moved forward with another outrageous act, a national briefing for lawmakers on the issue of welfare reauthorization from the grassroots! It was scheduled for September 11, 2001, and people from across the country trudged to DC to tell the lawmakers what's what. That date, unfortunately, was a disaster, and the meeting was postponed until February 5, 2002. After an immense amount of organization and planning, the meeting came off and it set a tone in DC: Don't make policy without listening to the people who have to live with those laws (if you listen to Enron executives to make energy policy, perhaps you should listen to the oppressed when you make oppression rules!). Of course there are no illusions that a hearing changes minds, but such a political act both steels those who face their mendacious representatives and it reminds these elected leaders that the base is neither disorganized nor passive. About 200 people gathered in a Capitol Hill hearing room to listen to the testimonies. "You'll rarely see a Capitol Hill policy briefing that moves the audience to tears," said Frances Fox Piven, a co-moderator of the briefing. "We heard remarkable stories that should challenge policy makers to take a serious look at the flaws in our country's welfare system." Much of the material in this chapter comes from that briefing, as well as from the materials prepared by GROWL over the past two years. "GROWL is the voice of those who are directly impacted," says Sandra Robertson, of the Hunger Coalition. "We are representatives of those whom we are fighting for. We are our own voices. That is minimal in other coalitions and networks. But for GROWL, this is pivotal." Unquestionably, GROWL's uniqueness lies in its genuine grassroots flavor. But, as this Left ensemble makes clear, the issue is not just that the people be allowed to speak, but that the radical analysis of working-class conditions is organized into the debate. The "welfare debate has been hijacked by the

Right," says Toney. "No one says welfare reform is wrong," explains former GROWL coordinator Dana Ginn Parades. "It increases poverty, rips families apart. What's that got to do with family values?"

What is the purpose of GROWL, of the national network of these impressive grassroots organizations? GROWL is about power, about power secured in the struggle to win concrete gains from the formally democratic system as well as to push the quantitative gains towards a qualitative transformation. Parades laid out the dispute with the government's framework in the following manner:

> [The government's] framework declares that "work"—meaning paid work outside the home, no matter how demeaning or poorly compensated—must be the highest value in our society. So when poor people care for their families or get an education, they are not viewed as "working." The dominant philosophy holds that childcare or education are not important enough to support with a strong safety net. GROWL challenges this philosophy from a grassroots perspective by conducting research to influence policy makers, building effective networks of grassroots and support organizations, and providing trainings and consultations to increase grassroots capacity.[118]

How does GROWL propose to reframe the debate on welfare?

- Consolidate a progressive political alliance. If the local organizations can join their place-based power into a nationwide force and if they conduct a full-scale attack on the Right's view of welfare, then perhaps they can move the discussion on social assistance to include class inequality, homelessness, illness, starvation, and immobility and to fight for economic equity, homes, healthcare, food, transportation.
- Document how welfare "reform" perpetuates racism, sexism, and xenophobia. If the justice framework is not open about the specific mode of attack utilized by the Right, we will miss the race, gender, and national questions raised by welfare "reform" and by "welfare as we know it."
- Expand the definition of work. Waged work is not the only kind of labor, as childcare, cultural work, and other social contributions must be seen as worthy of income support.

- Build a collective vision. Fight to value justice, creative expression, and social interactions over the anomie of welfare "reform."

Human rights is part of the framework, but rather than assume that we are fighting for inalienable rights in a state whose character is a given, the groups within GROWL are on the road to entirely refashion the relationship between the state and the citizen. We need to think of new organizational forms for social interaction and the GROWL campaign, if it does retain the virtuosity of its members, will go in that direction. GROWL is, then, about organization as well as ideological and political struggle. "What we want for citizens in our state cannot be won unless we get national legislation," says Robertson, and Toney adds, "unless we change the global conditions of exploitation that are based on racism." GROWL recognizes that its fights are about this reform and that reform, but it is more than the sum of each of these local battles. In Montana, Native peoples felt that they were being singled out for attack, says Robideau, but GROWL shows us how "we are not alone, that there is a pattern, a systematic attack against working people of color." GROWL organizes the heart and soul of the surplus population to fight back against the systematic attack on them, but also to try to imagine in their struggle a better world. "We're here and we're not alone," says Robideau. "Together we're going to change this world. If you're in the way, get in step, because we're coming."

1   Johnnie Tillmon, "Welfare is a Women's Issue," *Ms.*, 1972.

2   All quotations are from Robert B. Reich, "Clinton's Leap in the Dark: How the plight of the "next to poor" has distorted the reform of welfare," *Times Literary Supplement*, January 22, 1999.

3   Pamela Loprest, *How Families that Left Welfare are Doing: A National Picture*, Washington, DC: Urban Institute, 1999.

4   GAO, *Food Stamp Program: Various Factors Have Led to Declining Participation*, Washington, DC: GAO, 1999; Sheila Zedlewski and Sarah Brauner, *Are the Steep Declines in Food Stamp Participation Linked to Falling Welfare Caseloads?* Washington, DC: The Urban Institute, 1999; Hunger Action Network of New York State, *The Reality of Hunger: A Survey of Emergency Food Program Utilization in NYS between November 1995 and November 1999*, Albany: HAN-NYS, 2000; Northwest Federation of Community Organizations, *Food Stamps Out Hunger: Hunger in the West and What Governors and Congress Can Do About It*, Seattle: NFCO, 2001; Oregon Action, *Hunger Pangs: Oregon's Food Stamp Program Fails to Deliver*, Portland: OA and Seattle: NFCO, 2000, and Oregon Action, *Still Not Making the Grade: AFS Gets a 'C' from Families Seeking Food Stamp Benefits*, Portland: OA and Seattle: NFCO, 2001.

5   "Wellstone Challenges White House Assertion of Welfare Reform 'Success Story,'" Press Release from Senator Paul Wellstone's office, August 3, 1999.

6   Excellent overviews of the "two tier" system can be found in G. John Ikenberry and Theda Skocpol, "Expanding Social Benefits: The Role of Social Security," *Political Science Quarterly*, vol. 102, no. 3, 1987, and John Myles, "Postwar Capitalism and the Extension of Social Security into a Retirement Wage," one among many useful essays in *The Politics of Social Policy in the United States*, edited by Margaret Weir, Ann Orloff, and Theda Skocpol, Princeton: Princeton University Press, 1988. I am following the very useful 1979 summary from Frances Fox Piven and Richard Cloward, *Poor People's Movements*, pp. 264–361. For a passionate account of the life of the contingent class and welfare, see David Hilfiker, *Urban Injustice: How Ghettos Happen*, New York: Seven Stories Press, 2002.

7   Linda Gordon, *Pitied But Not Entitled. Single Mothers and the History of Welfare*, Cambridge: Harvard University Press, 1994, p. 276.

8   For example, Lucy Komisar, *Down and Out in the USA: A History of Public Welfare*, New York: Franklin Watts, 1977, pp. 75–77. Komisar's general approach mirrors that of Anthony Platt's *The Child Savers: The Invention of Delinquency*, Chicago: University of Chicago Press, 1969. Platt denounces the paternalistic studies of child welfare and adopts a Marxist view of welfare as social control. Elizabeth Wilson's *Women and the Welfare State*, London: Tavistock, 1977, takes the Platt approach one step further. From a feminist standpoint, she argues that welfare policy is more than

"just a set of services it is also a set of ideas about society and family."
The state, then, forms the working-poor American family.

9   Piven and Cloward, *Poor People's Movements*, p. 271. Charles Payne reports
     that the anti-poverty money enabled activists to start getting a paycheck,
     that not only did most of them not get co-opted, but "they went on
     agitating inside their new organizations, often against their own bosses."
     *I've Got the Light of Freedom: The Organizing Tradition and the Mississippi
     Freedom Struggle*, Berkeley: University of California Press, 1995, p. 358.
10   Mary Lynn Kotz and Nick Kotz, *A Passion for Equality: George A. Wiley
     and the Movement*, New York: Norton, 1977, p. 199.
11   Linda Gordon's fantastic study offers us a prehistory of NWRO in the
     mutual benefit societies, church groups, womens' clubs and in the
     National Association of Colored Women, from the 1890s to the 1930s.
     Pitied But Not Entitled, chapter 5.
12   For a fuller discussion of NWRO, see Andrea Sachs, "The Politics of
     Poverty: Race, Class, Motherhood and the National Welfare Rights
     Organization, 1965–1975," Minneapolis: University of Minnesota Ph.
     D., 2001; Lawrence Ballis, *Bread or Justice: Grassroots Organizing in the
     Welfare Rights Movement*, New York: Heath, 1974; Robert Fisher, *Let the
     People Decide: Neighborhood Organizing in America*, New York: Twayne,
     1984; Larry Jackson and William Johnson, *Protest by the Poor: The Welfare
     Rights Movement in New York City*, New York: Lexington, 1974; Kotz and
     Kotz, *A Passion for Equality*; Jacqueline Pope, *Biting the Hand that Feeds
     Them: Organizing Women on Welfare at the Grassroots Level*, New York:
     Praeger, 1989; Guida West, *The National Welfare Rights Movement: The
     Social Protest of Poor Women*, New York: Praeger, 1981.
13   Martin Luther King, Jr., "I Have A Dream," *A Testament of Hope*, p. 217.
14   Piven and Cloward, *Poor People's Movements*, p. 284.
15   Tillmon, "Welfare is a Women's Issue."
16   Piven and Cloward, *Poor People's Movements*, tell the broad story well.
     Guida West shows us how the black women on welfare fought to gain
     control of an organization dominated by middle-class black men (like
     Wiley) and middle-class white men (like Tim Sampson and Bert De
     Leeuw). It was not simply a matter of identity, but also of how the issues
     came to be cut. Against Nixon's Family Assistance Plan (FAP), West tells
     us, "The male dominated staff gave top priority to goals that reinforced
     the 'intact' and traditional family (where both father and mother are
     present), ignoring the fact that the majority of NWRO's members
     represented female-headed households." West, *The National Welfare
     Rights Movement*, p. 86.
17   The most significant case was *Goldberg v. Kelly* (392 US 254, 1970) in
     which the justices accepted that welfare is a form of property that could
     not be withheld without due process. However, *Rosado v. Wyman* (397 US
     413, 1970), *Dandridge v. Williams* (397 US 471, 1970), and *Wyman v. James*

(400 US 309, 1971) put limits on the state's responsibility to provide welfare, allowed the state to restrict welfare, and, from the last case, allowed the state to violate the privacy of welfare recipients.

18   For instance, Robert Lampman, *The Low-Income Population and Economic Growth*, Washington, DC: Congressional Joint Economic Committee, Study Paper no. 12, 1959; Vincent Burke and Lee Burke, *Nixon's Good Deed: Welfare Reform*, New York: Columbia University Press, 1974.

19   Frances Fox Piven, "Globalization, American Politics and Welfare Policy," *Lost Ground: Welfare Reform, Poverty and Beyond*, Eds. Randy Albedia and Ann Withorn, Cambridge: South End Press, 2002, p. 31. Also, Sanford F. Schram, *Words of Welfare: The Poverty of Social Science and the Social Science of Poverty*, Minneapolis: University of Minnesota Press, 1995, pp. 77–97 offers a useful overview of how statistics work in the top-down side of welfare policy.

20   Lisa Levenstein, "From Innocent Children to Unwanted Migrants and Unwed Moms: Two Chapters in the Public Discourse on Welfare in the United States, 1960–1961," *Journal of Women's History*, vol. 11, no. 4, Winter 2000.

21   Piven and Cloward, *Poor People's Movements*, p. 333.

22   David Zucchino, *The Myth of the Welfare Queen*, New York: Touchstone Books, 1999.

23   Johnnie Tillmon, "Welfare is a Women's Issue." The point about getting the tubes tied is not idle. In 1990, the *Philadelphia Inquirer* proposed the enforced use of the contraceptive Norplant to prevent women on welfare from bearing children. D. Kimelman, "Poverty and Norplant: can contraception reduce the underclass?" *Philadelphia Inquirer*, December 12, 1990. Vanessa Williams, then president of the Philadelphia chapter of the National Association of Black Journalists called the editorial "a tacit endorsement of slow genocide." Clarence Page, "Hope Best Way to Fight Poverty," *Oregonian*, December 31, 1990. AFDC recipients had an average of 1.9 children, with the median period of receipt of AFDC only 23 months.

24   The notion of the "blameless widow" is central to this stereotype upon which politicians made policy. Gordon, *Pitied But Not Entitled*, chapter 2.

25   If this theory appears too conspiracy-oriented, one need only read the basic texts of neoclassical economics. In 1958, A. W. Phillips argued for a negative, or inverse, relationship between the rate of inflation and unemployment. That is, when unemployment remained low, wages skyrocketed and vice versa. In the late 1960s, Edmund Phelps and Milton Friedman made a more sophisticated model called "expectations augmented Phillips curve," where they disaggregated the short and long term expectations of workers, but in the end argued for a "natural rate of unemployment." Embarrassed by the baldness of the phrase,

economists now refer to the "natural rate" as NAIRU, "non-accelerating inflation rate of unemployment." The two central papers on this are Edmund Phelps, "Phillips Curves, Expectations of Inflation and Optimal Employment Over Time," *Economic*. NS 34, no. 3, 1967 and Milton Friedman, "The Role of Monetary Policy," *American Economics Review*, vol. 58, 1968. If there must *naturally* be an unemployed population, it would be relatively deskilled, in need of surveillance, and occasionally hired to discipline the rest of the population.

26   Congressional Research Service, "Cash and Non-Cash Benefits for Persons with Limited Income: Eligibility Rules, Recipient and Expenditure Data, FY 1990–92," Washington, DC: CRS, 1993 (Report 93–832 EPW).

27   Peter Edelman, "The Worst Thing Bill Clinton Has Done," *Atlantic Monthly*, no. 297, March 1997.

28   David Ellwood, *Divide and Conquer: Responsible Security for America's Poor*, New York: Ford Foundation, 1987, and Mary Jo Bane and David Ellwood, "Slipping into and out of poverty: the dynamics of spells," *Journal of Human Resources*, vol. 21, no. 1, Winter 1986.

29   The line also appeared in the 1992 Democratic Platform, "A New Covenant with the American People," in Part two, entitled "Responsibility."

30   E. J. Dionne, *They Only Look Dead: Why Progressives Will Dominate the Next Political Era*, New York: Simon & Schuster, 1996, p. 69.

31   Mary Jo Bane and David Ellwood, *Welfare Realities: From Rhetoric to Reform*, Cambridge: Harvard University Press, 1994, pp. 157–58.

32   Clinton's first draft of welfare "reform," the "Work and Responsibility Act" of 1994 proposed that work must pay, assistance must be limited to two years, the state must enforce child support payments, and the state must provide education and the support structure to enable people to go to school. For a good introduction to the legislative process and the Washington blather, see Anne Marie Cammisia, *From Rhetoric to Reform: Welfare Policy in American Politics*, Boulder: Westview, 1998.

33   Evelina Alarcon, "Rallies Boost Martinez Jobs Bill," *People's Weekly World*, October 25, 1997.

34   Margot Hornblower, "Pork and the Fast Track," *Time*, February 9, 1998.

35   Ellwood would later regret that "time limits" remained on the agenda, without the social support. David Ellwood, "Welfare Reform as I Knew It: when bad things happen to good policies," *American Prospect*, no. 26, May–June 1996; Frances Fox Piven and David Ellwood, "Controversy," *American Prospect*, no. 27, July–August 1997.

36   Barbara Vobejda and Judith Havemann, "2 HSS Officials Quit Over Welfare Changes," *Washington Post*, September 12, 1996.

37   Murray and Herrnstein, *The Bell Curve*, p. 524.

38 Biologists and psychologists have repudiated this argument, such as in *Intelligence, Genes and Success: Scientists Respond to the Bell Curve*, Eds. Devun, Fienberg, Resnick and Roeder, New York: Springer-Verlag, 1997, and *Inequality by Design: Cracking the Bell Curve*, Eds. Fischer, Hoot, Jankowski, Locas, Swidler and Yoss, Princeton: Princeton University Press, 1996.

39 "Freedom From Welfare Dependency: An Interview with George Gilder," *Religion and Liberty*, vol. 4, no. 2, March–April 1994.

40 Committee on Ways and Means, US House of Representatives, *Overview of Entitlement Programs*, Washington, DC: Congress, 1994.

41 Frances Fox Piven and Richard Cloward, "The Historical Sources of the Contemporary Relief Debate," *The Mean Season: The Attack on the Welfare State*, Eds. Fred Block, Richard Cloward, Barbara Ehrenreich and Frances Fox Piven, New York: Pantheon, 1987, pp. 58–62.

42 This is the general tenor of Christopher Hitchens's gossipy *No One Left to Lie To: The Triangulations of William Jefferson Clinton*, London: Verso, 1999, and of Robert Reich's *Locked in the Cabinet*, New York: Vintage, 1998.

43 Anthony Giddens, the prophet of the "third way," wrote, "The new mixed economy looks instead for a synergy between public and private sectors, utilizing the dynamism of markets but with the public interest in mind." *The Third Way: The Renewal of Social Democracy*, London: Polity, 1999, pp. 99–100. After Enron, this emperor has no clothes.

44 GAO, *Outcomes for TANF Recipients with Impairments*, Washington, DC: GAO, no. 02-884, 2002, p. 2. Also Winifred Collier-Bolkus, "The Impact of the Welfare Reform Law on Families with Disabled Children That Need Child Care," Wilmington, DE: Widener University, Ph.D., 2000.

45 Gary Delgado, "Racing the Welfare Debate," *ColorLines*, vol. 3, no. 3, Fall 2000.

46 Washington State, headquarters of the Microsoft New Economy, is no paradise. The Northwest Federation of Community Organizations finds that about 40 percent of all jobs in the region pay less than the living wage for a single adult, while 75 percent pay less than a living wage for a single adult and two children. Northwest Federation of Community Organizations, *Northwest Job Gap Study: Searching for Work that Pays*, Seattle: NFCO, 1999. Washington Citizen Action found that 300,000 families in Washington State live below the federal poverty line. Washington Citizen Action, *The Washington Economy: Working But Not Making a Living*, Seattle: WCA and NFCO, 2000.

47 Lying with statistics is well-known to the BJP government in India: The government revised the poverty line in such a way that in Pune district the number of poor families fell from 59,340 to 34,000, while in Yeravada, the decline was stunning, from 12,000 to 261. This is either magic or mendacity.

48 Randy Albelda, "Fallacies of Welfare-to-Work," *Lost Ground*, p. 84.

49 Four studies from Milwaukee Women and Poverty Public Education Initiative lay out the facts clearly: *W-2 Community Impact Study* (WPPEI, 1998 shows that recipients turn to family and friends to bear the cost of survival); *Myth and Reality: The Experience of W-2 in Wisconsin* (WPPEI, 2000, shows that the Wisconsin program left the poor without any transitional services, in poverty); *The Status of Employment Opportunity for W-2 Participants in Central City Milwaukee* (WPPEI, 2000, shows that out of all W-2 participants with a job, only one in six earns an income above the poverty line); and *Voices from the Community* (WPPEI, 2001, lets us listen in as W-2 recipients document racism and harassment at the welfare office, and a lack of income and housing as impediments to freedom).

50 "Labor Protections and Welfare Reform," Washington, DC: Department of Labor, 1997.

51 Chris Tilly, *Workfare's Impact on the New York City Labor Market: Lower Wages and Worker Displacement*, New York: Russell Sage Foundation, Working Paper no. 92, 1996; Lawrence Mishel and John Schmitt, *Cutting Wages by Cutting Welfare: The Impact of Reform on the Low-Wage Labor Market*, Washington, DC: Economic Policy Institute, 1995. For an overview of the workfare issue, see Jamie Peck, *Workfare States*, New York: Guildford, 2001.

52 Karen Carrillo, "Welfare Warfare," *Third Force*, January/February 1997, pp. 10–11.

53 Hunger Action Network of New York State, *Assessing the Effectiveness of Welfare-to-Work Programs in New York State: Recommendations for Economic Security*, Albany: HAN-NYS, 2001.

54 Community Voices Heard, *New York City's Public Sector Sweatshop Economy*, New York: CVH, 2000. For an update on WEP, see Kim Phillips-Fein, "The Education of Jessica Rivera," *Nation*, November 25, 2002.

55 National Partnership for Women and Families, *Detours on the Road to Employment: Obstacles Facing Low-Income Women*, Washington, DC: NPWF, 1999.

56 Susan Gooden, *Examining Racial Differences in Employment Status among Welfare Recipients*, Oakland: Applied Research Center and GRIPP, 1997, and "The Hidden Third Party: Welfare Recipients Experience Employers," *Journal of Public Management and Social Policy*, no. 5, Summer 1999; Institute for Research on Poverty, *What's Working? Where Do We Go From Here?* University of Wisconsin, IRP, 1999.

57 Grace Chang, *Disposable Domestics*, Boston: South End Press, 2000.

58 Folbre, *Invisible Heart*.

59 Nancy Fraser, *Justice Interruptus: Critical Reflections on the "Post-Socialist" Condition*, New York: Routledge, 1997, p. 43.

60   For an argument in favor of a revaluation of "work," see Gwendolyn
     Mink, *Welfare's End*, Ithaca: Cornell University Press, 2002.
61   Chicago Coalition for the Homeless, *Families Hardest Hit: Effects of Welfare
     Reform on Homeless Families*, Chicago: CCH, 2000.
62   Los Angeles Coalition to End Hunger and Homelessness, *Welfare to
     Worse: The Effects of Welfare Reform in Los Angeles County, 1998–2000*, Los
     Angeles: CACEH&H, 2000.
63   Tennessee Justice Center, *Who's Off First? A Look at the Impact of "Families
     First" and the Effects of Welfare Reform in Tennessee*, Nashville: TJC, n. d.
64   Hunger Action Network of New York State, *Bridging the
     Gap—Transitional Benefits: What Are They? An Overview and Survey of 15
     Counties*, Albany: HAN-NYS, n. d.
65   Community Voices Heard, *Time Limits or Time Bomb? Assessing New York
     City Welfare as the Five-Year Time Limit Approaches*, New York: CVH, 2001.
66   Jean Bacon, Laura Russell, and Diane Pierce, *The Self-Sufficiency Standard:
     Where Massachusetts Families Stand*, Boston: Wider Opportunities for
     Women, 2000.
67   Rebecca Gordon, *Cruel and Unusual: How Welfare "Reform" Punishes Poor
     People*, Oakland: Applied Research Center, 2001, p. 27. For one family's
     moving story, see Akiba Solomon, "*Saved* by the System: Why are so many
     kids of color taken into the child welfare system?" *ColorLines*, Fall 2002.
68   This is the contemporary version of a historical problem in the US, as
     shown by Linda Gordon, *The Great Arizona Orphan Abduction*,
     Cambridge: Harvard University Press, 1999.
69   Gwendolyn Mink, "Violating Women: Rights Abuses in the Welfare
     Police State," *Losing Ground*, p.103.
70   The centrality of race to the welfare story is well documented in Ken
     Neubeck and Noel Cazenave, *Welfare Racism: Playing the Race Card Against
     America's Poor*, New York: Routledge, 2001.
71   Susan Gooden, "All Things Not Being Equal: Differences in
     Caseworker Support Towards Black and White Welfare Clients,"
     Harvard Journal of African American Public Policy, vol. IV, 1998, and "Race
     and Welfare: Examining Employment Outcomes of White and Black
     Welfare Recipients," *Journal of Poverty*, vol. 4, no. 3, 2000.
72   But Make the Road By Walking does in their fine report, *System Failure:
     Mayor Giuliani's Welfare System is Hostile to Poor and Immigrant New Yorkers*,
     Brooklyn: Make the Road By Walking, 1999. This is also the finding of
     the Coalition for an Accountable and Respectful HRA, *A Tragedy of
     Errors: The New York City Human Resources Administration Fails New York's
     Neediest Residents*, New York: Make the Road by Walking, New York City
     AIDS Housing Network, and Urban Justice Center-Human Rights
     Project, 2000, as well as by CAAAV: Organizing Asian Communities,
     *Eating Welfare: a youth conducted report on the impact of welfare on the Southeast
     Asian community*, New York: CAAAV, 2000.

73 Idaho Community Action Network and Northwest Federation of Community Organizations, *Left Alone: State Barriers Prevent Idaho Parents from Accessing Child Care Program*, Boise: ICAN and NFCO, 2000.

74 Services, Immigrant Rights and Education Network, *Immigrant Family Access to Food Stamps in Santa Clara County: A Preliminary Assessment*, San Jose: SIREN, 2000, and New York Immigration Coalition, *Welfare Reform and Health Care: the wrong prescription for immigrants*, New York: NYIC, 2000.

75 Gary Delgado and Rebecca Gordon, "From Social Contract to Social Control: Welfare Policy and Race," *From Poverty to Punishment: How Welfare Reform Punishes the Poor*, Oakland: Applied Research Center, 2002, p. 39. The point about sanctions being the main reason for the decline in the welfare rolls comes from a study by two conservatives, Robert Rector and Sarah Youssef, *The Determination of Welfare Caseload Decline*, Washington, DC: Heritage Foundation, 1999. For context on the racism of the administration sector, see Maya Wiley, "Getting Our Due: Enforcing Fairness in the Welfare System," *From Poverty to Punishment*.

76 Sanford Schram, "Race and State Welfare Reform Choices: A Cause for Concern," *From Poverty to Punishment*, pp. 100–01.

77 PUEBLO's Living Income Project, *Criminalizing the Poor: the human casualties of welfare reform, the unjust prosecution of welfare overpayment in Alameda County*, Oakland: PUEBLO, 2000.

78 I have relied for this section on Martha F. Davis, "Legislating Patriarchy," *From Poverty to Punishment* and Daniel HoSang, *Failing Our Families: A State-by-State Report Card on Family Supports Under Welfare Reform*, Oakland: Center for Third World Organizing, 2002.

79 Wade Horn and Andrew Bush, *Fathers, Marriage and Welfare Reform*, Indianapolis: Hudson Institute, 1997.

80 Lawrence O'Rourke, "Bush Welfare Plan will push love, marriage," *Sacramento Bee*, February 25, 2002.

81 Mimi Abramovitz, "Foreword," *Failing Our Families*, p. 10.

82 Gordon, *Cruel and Unusual*, p. 18.

83 Delgado and Gordon, "From Social Contract to Social Control," *From Poverty to Punishment*, p. 36.

84 GAO, "Challenges in Saving for a 'Rainy Day,'" Washington, DC: GAO, 2001.

85 Bill Berkowitz, "Welfare Privatization: Prospecting Among the Poor," *From Poverty to Punishment*.

86 Alan Greenspan, "The American Economy in a World Context," thirty-fifth Annual Conference on Bank Structure and Competition of the Federal Reserve Bank, Chicago, May 6, 1999.

87 Jacob Schlesinger, "Charting the Pain Behind the Gain: Wages Barely Budged Over Decade," *Wall Street Journal*, October 1, 1999.

88   "Surge in Corporate Tax Welfare Drives Corporate Tax Payments Down to Near Record Low," Citizens for Tax Justice, April 17, 2002, and details in *Fat Cats and Running Dogs.*

89   James Dao, "Pentagon Seeking A Large Increase in Its Next Budget," *New York Times,* January 7, 2002. The budget figures are from "US Military Budget climbs to $360 billion," Council for a Livable World, Washington, DC, 2002.

90   George W. Bush (with Karen Hughes), *A Charge to Keep: My Journey to the White House,* New York: HarperCollins, 1999, pp. 229–30.

91   Alexandra Marks, "Spike in welfare rolls reignites debate over safety net," *Christian Science Monitor,* February 7, 2002.

92   Leslie Kaufman, "Economy Dips While Welfare Drops in Cities," *New York Times,* August 31, 2002.

93   Robert Pear, "50 Senators Ask Daschle for Debate on Renewing Welfare Law," *New York Times,* September 12, 2002.

94   Robert Pear, "House Endorses Stricter Work Rules for Poor," *New York Times,* February 14, 2003.

95   Frank Bruni and Lauri Goodstein, "Bush's Favorite Project: Helping Religious Groups Help the Needy," *New York Times,* January 26, 2001.

96   Bush, *A Charge to Keep,* p. 232.

97   In Pakistan, for instance, the US government egged on the World Bank as it helped crush public institutions in the 1980s. By 1995, the year of the downfall of the Pakistani rupee, the UN reported that almost two-thirds of the adults in the country suffered from illiteracy, and among women, the number rose to three-quarters. The very rich send their children to expensive private schools and then overseas for education, but the rest of the population must make do in the *madrassas,* the faith-based schools often funded by Saudi money and generally the purveyors of conservatism. Despite the well developed critique of Taliban-like policies in Pakistan, in October 2000, US policy analyst and former State Department man Stephen P. Cohen wrote, "Some madrassas, or religious schools are excellent." "Others," he wrote, "are hotbeds for jihadist and radical Islamic movements," but these, he emphasized, are only about 12 percent of the total and they "need to be upgraded to offer their students a modern education." *Wall Street Journal,* October 23, 2000.

98   Julie Mason, "Bush's Strategy to Win Black Votes Bypasses NAACP," *Houston Chronicle,* July 12, 2002.

99   Barbara Miner, "Politics Trumps Religion: Bush's Faith-Based Initiative," *RaceWire,* Oakland: Applied Research Center, October 2002.

100   Robert Pear, "Particulars Slow Compromise on Extension of Welfare Law," *New York Times,* October 15, 2002.

101   "Welfare Organizers Strategy Roundtable," *Third Force,* May/June 1995; Gwendolyn Mink, "Feminists, Welfare Reform, and Welfare Justice," *Sojourner,* October 1998.

102 Andre Gorz, *A Strategy for Labor*, Boston: Beacon Press, 1964, pp. 6–8, noted in Schram, *Words of Welfare*, p. 193.

103 Richard Cloward and Frances Fox Piven, "A Strategy to End Poverty," *Nation*, May 2, 1966.

104 For some background, see Jess Champagne, "Left at the Center," *New Journal*, April 24, 1998.

105 Edward Ericson and Dan Levine, "The Scoop: Making a Difference," *Hartford Advocate*, April 5, 2001.

106 Martha Moore, "Amid suburban push, a surprise from Philly," *USA Today*, March 11, 2001.

107 For an excellent expose on how stadiums are a part of corporate welfare, see Joanna Cagan and Neil DeMause, *Field of Schemes: How the Great Stadium Swindle Turns Public Money into Private Profit*, Monroe: Common Courage Press, 1999.

108 Dennis Culhane (with Wong, Eldridge, Koppel and Metraux), *An Evaluation of the Homelessness Prevention Program in Philadelphia*, Philadelphia: Office of Housing and Community Development, 1999; Culhane (with R. Kuhn), "Patterns and Determinants of Shelter Utilization Among Homeless Adults in New York City and Philadelphia: A Longitudinal Analysis of Homelessness," *Journal of Policy Analysis and Management*, vol. 17, no. 1, 1997; Culhane (with Lee and Wachter), "Where the Homeless Come From: A Study of Prior Address Distribution of Families Admitted to Public Shelters in New York City and Philadelphia," *Housing Policy Debate*, vol. 7, no. 2, 1996; Culhane (with Lee), "Locating the Homeless: A Philadelphia Case Study," *GeoInfo Systems*, July 1995.

109 Andrea Fine, "Philadelphia Launches Dragnet to Rid the 'Badlands' of Drugs," *Christian Science Monitor*, July 7, 1998.

110 Herbert Lowe, "'Jump Street' Gets the Spotlight," *Philadelphia Inquirer*, June 7, 1998. Of the $85 million project called Harlem Center (on Lenox and 125th Street), Reverend Calvin Butts told Peter Noel, "Many pieces of land in Harlem have been undeveloped for years until recently. And one can count at least 400 jobs that have been created as a result of new construction." "I think we're beginning to claim the community," he pointed out. "You can't say 'reclaim' because we have never really owned Harlem. We are beginning to claim it." Butts's position drew fire from many African Americans, such as Reverend Al Sharpton: "My economic challenge to him was that if he really wanted to talk black economics, he ought to get us a black commercial bank so that we could lend brothers and sisters money to go into business and for mortgages. I did not ask him to give us a supermarket that Pathmark [a supermarket developer] is going to end up owning. Pathmark owning a supermarket in East Harlem is not economic development." Record Shack owner Sikhulu Shange told the *Village Voice* "the community businesses have been left out from day one. They give loans to the megastores, but not to us. Well we're not going to stand for that forever." To back up this small business sentiment, City Councilor Bill Perkins noted, "Gentrification is a two-edged sword. I'm glad to see Harlem USA [one of the megastore projects]; it's nice to have a mall. But that's not community investment. That's not building a future." Paul Keegan, "Who Owns Harlem?" *Inc*, August 1, 2000, and my "Racialization of Risk: Desi Developers on the A Train," *Little India*, July 2001.

111 I'm drawing on the excellent essay by Willie Baptist and Mary Bricker-Jenkins, "A View from the Bottom: Poor People and Their Allies Respond to Welfare Reform," *Losing Ground*, the KWRU website [www.kwru.org/educat/orgmod2.html], and especially from Willie Bishop, "On the Poor Organizing the Poor: The Experience of Kensington," February 1998.

112 The wide-ranging declaration was split in 1966 into the Convention on Civil and Political Rights and the Convention of Economic, Social and Cultural Rights. In 1976, as sufficient states ratified the convention, it went into effect. The US ratified the Convention on Civil and Political Rights in 1992, but has only signed and not ratified the Convention on Economic, Social and Cultural Rights.

113 Baptist and Bricker-Jenkins, "A View from the Bottom," p. 207.

114 Ibid, p. 206.

115 Most of my material comes from in-depth interviews (held in 2001 and 2002) with the staff of many of the GROWL organizations and from www.arc.org.

116 In 1966, when Sargent Shriver of LBJ's Office of Economic Opportunity held a news conference, 60 welfare recipients, mainly women of color, shouted him down. "Tell us where the poor are being helped," they chided him. Shriver left the building.

117 Jennifer Gonnerman, "Food Fight," *Village Voice*, April 14, 2000.

118 Dana Ginn Parades, "GROWL: Fighting Fierce for Welfare Rights," *CTWO Times*, vol. 3, no. 2, May/June 2000, pp. 1–3.

MOVEMENT

whose side are you on?
the side of the busstop woman
trying to drag her bag
up the front steps before the doors
clang shut i am on her side
i give her exact change
and him the old man hanging by
one strap his work hand folded shut
as the bus doors i am on his side
when he needs to leave
i ring the bell i am on their side
riding the late bus into the same
someplace
i am on the dark side always
the side of my daughters
the side of my tired sons.

—Lucille Clifton[1]

A few years ago, as the tumult of the anti-globalization movement struck the world, a young Lefty from New York City, Max Mishler, had an insightful observation. In his first year in college, he saw two sets of students who should be natural allies, but who barely communicated with each other. There are those who did community service, whether offering mentorship to students in the area, working at a soup kitchen, providing ESL assistance, building homes for Habitat for Humanity, sitting by the phones at a rape crisis center, or going door to door for a community service agency. Hard-working students such as these took time off from their busy schedules and often did this work as volunteers even as they carried one or two waged (or work-study) jobs to help sustain their time at college. The second lot of students joined political organizations, organized campaigns for social justice, attended marches and rallies, collected signatures for petitions, and did the everyday work of making the movement possible. There were, and are, of course, students who overlap between the two lots, but they are few and far between. Many political students look down at the reformism of the community service students, and the latter think the former are all blather and no action. Max felt that the community service students needed some politics and the political students needed to do some community service. These are dialectical opposites that need to be united.

These "political" youth helped push the US movement to join the planet's charge against global corporations. The 1999 anti-WTO protest in Seattle was the debut of this new thrust within the US, and it reappeared during the election campaign in 2000 (in Philadelphia and in Los Angeles), as well as at the IMF and World Bank meetings in Washington, DC, then in Quebec (during the deliberations over the Free Trade Zone of the Americas), and finally, in New York City (in a muted fashion during the 2002 World Economic Forum). These mobilizations momentarily pressured organized labor to revive coordination for international solidarity and environmental movements to temper their anti-productivism when confronted by peasants from the South. The long-term effects are less clear than the immediate show of camaraderie (although the personnel from the globalization movements formed the corps of the anti-war mobilizations in 2003). The mobilizations are indicative of the sentiment against capitalist globalization. Thousands of people travel long distances in this wasteland of mass protest to offer their bodies against the corporations and imperialism for a host of different reasons: frustration with the lack of democracy in the international agreements, anger at the lapse of environmental and labor regulation, general displeasure with corporate culture, and for a few, eagerness to participate in the construction of a movement against capitalism.[2]

In early 2001, journalist and activist Michael Albert took the temperature of the North American sector of the anti-globalization movement. While he celebrated the militancy of the post-Seattle civil disobedience, Albert pointed to a host of problems with this part of the movement for justice.

Stagnation on the Streets

If the North American anti-globalization movement signaled its re-emergence as a mass force at Seattle, the numbers of people at subsequent gatherings began to decrease, this before the year of 9/11. This is not to say that the mobilizations are a test of those who support the movement, because frequent mobilizations can only be carried forward by sections of the population that are mobile, people who can travel across the country for civil disobedience, get arrested, do jail time, then pay bail to take the bus to the next demo. There are many others who support the aims of a refashioned globalization, but who do not come out to the mass demonstrations. Those with children, those who need to maintain whatever jobs they find, those who have elders to care for, and others, are less able to travel to protest than the young, middle-class college students or hard-core activists whose lives are geared around political work. I've often felt that when we estimate the numbers at a protest we should multiply it by three or so to capture those who are there in spirit, but whose children are napping, whose parents need to be dropped off at an event, or whose bosses refused to allow them one more sick day. In her cogent reminder of why there was so little color in Seattle, movement intellectual Elizabeth Martinez notes:

> In personal interviews, activists from the Bay Area and the Southwest gave me several reasons for [people of color at Seattle being only about five percent of the total demonstrators]. Some mentioned concern about the likelihood of brutal police repression. Other obstacles: lack of funds for the trip, inability to be absent from work during the week, and problems in finding child care.[3]

Given that the contingent class is largely made up of people of color, the problems of contingency make the mobilization all the more difficult.

The problem is not simply the secular issue of getting the less mobile to the demos. "I worry," writes Albert, "that we may be creating seeds for an enlarging operational disconnect between the movement and certain types of organizing, and therefore between the movement and the uninvolved but potentially receptive public."[4] The "movement" has fashioned its own language, its own mode of communication (listservs on the Internet), and its own circles of trust—this is of course understandable in these hard times, but it does not facilitate outreach.

This is perhaps what Albert means by "operational disconnect." Those who demonstrate are certainly physically detached from the contingent class, a distance that has bred insularity in its disregard for the everyday reform fights that are an integral part of the struggle. Furthermore, the "movement" develops its militancy with no concern for the demands that might draw in the vast bulk of the population: there is no point in being ideologically right if you cannot at the same time translate those positions into the everyday struggles of the contingent (but more on that below).

What has happened is that "the movement" has come to be defined by "the mobilization," and this has major class implications for how the movement in general works. The "movement" draws people because it has become cool: at A16 (April 16, 2000), I met a group of high school friends in Washington, DC, who had borrowed the car of one of their parents, driven down for the weekend from Pennsylvania, and seemed happy to be *there, in the afterglow of Seattle*. Finally, one might say, the Left is getting cool, but this is not the kind of movement that will necessarily outlast its five minutes of fame. As Alexander Cockburn and Jeffrey St. Clair argue:

> Demonstrations flow out of organization and are only a tool in a political campaign or movement. Demonstrations didn't end the war in Vietnam. Demonstrations are only part, sometimes a small part, of long years of movement building and political campaigning at multiple levels. There can be a point when demonstrations achieve nothing, and if evident failures, are capable of demoralizing and trivializing any given campaign.[5]

The organizations of the contingent go to large demonstrations as well, but these are not the primary focus of the movement. Leaders of the contingent go to these demonstrations to revive their enthusiasm for much larger changes, build alliances across regions, learn about struggles elsewhere, and perhaps make unusual connections to put pressure on their local power structure.

Who is at the Frontline?

The veterans of the Seattle-type dynamic, Albert notes, have created "a culture that is hostile to the people who it's trying to organize. We're not going to have that whole aroused left get larger and larger until it involves 35 to 40 percent of the population, with the rest mostly just standing by the side and a few opposing it, if we are antagonizing most citizens."[6] The problem is deeper than this, because we are not simply organized as "citizens," but also as classes. In the eyes of the anti-globalization folks, the enemy is clear (IMF-World Bank-US Military) and the allies are clear (the People, those who come to the demonstrations), but the class reality of our times does not seem clear nor is there any apparent analysis of how the opposition must be clear about the class dynamics within it. Certainly there is a tradition within the US Left that argues on behalf of the students as a major revolutionary force, indeed that the white color wage-workers are also workers and therefore have parity alongside the working class.[7] Those who show up at the demonstrations, then, form the frontline of the struggle.

Barbara Epstein points out that most of the anti-globalization protestors within North America are more "attracted to the movement's culture and organizational structure than to anarchism as a worldview," indeed, that for many the main target is "corporate power, not capitalism." Anarchism, as style, she argues, is attractive to young people who feel burnt out by what they see as the failures of the Old Left and the New Left. Because of the lack of faith in these traditions and because of the lack of steam from organized labor, "many activists in the anti-globalization movement do not see the working class as the leading force for social change."[8]

All people, in a mass struggle, have to unite against the Dow Joneses, but certain people, the contingent, must be in the lead or else we will end up replicating the structures of power and privilege. The struggle is about the creation of leadership, it is about the generation of a program of social revolution from the bottom up. History shows us that any movement that starts white, ends white, and any movement that starts without a class focus, ends in the throes of conservative reaction, and furthermore, any movement of men pretty much descends into a boys' club. If we are not clear about the necessity of who is to lead and where the frontlines are located, we will not be able to enlarge the movement into the working class.

To my mind, then, the character of the demonstrations themselves holds within them the reason for the deracinated hostility of the mobilized. Those who go to the demonstrations think that they are at the forefront of the struggle, whereas the frontlines are held each day by the contingent class. In his 1956 essay, "Our Struggle," Martin Luther King, Jr., wrote, "Montgomery has demonstrated that we will not run from the struggle." Reflecting on this line, feminist scholar Elisabeth Armstrong writes:

> Using the definite article in "*the* struggle," [King] refers to the civil rights movement in its complex entirety; as a result, struggle takes on an added significance in the essay's title. "Our struggle" invokes both the battles against racial exploitation and oppression and the movement formed to sustain those battles. *Struggle*, in this heightened sense, alludes to the relationship between the consensus-building and instrumental activity of struggle and political organization. Struggle includes the process of how those minute and daily efforts inform the civil rights movement as a larger entity. Importantly, the term includes *how* that movement can then transform the disparate actions into substantive racial justice. Struggle, in this latter aspect, raises the question that wracked the later civil rights movement: What, organizationally, constitutes an expansive vision of racial justice?[9]

If the movement is not about the incremental work of struggle and if it relies upon the demonstration for succor and victories, then it loses the capacity to organize the contingent class, to build leaders among the contingent, to allow the contingent to lead us into a reorganization of society. The question, then, is not just about gaps that have opened up between those who demonstrate and those who don't, but between those who think they are at the frontlines when they toss the tear gas canisters back at the police and those who face routine political disenfranchisement, economic displacement, social disdain, and yet spend their days in their own forms of fight-back.

Build Capacity, Build Socialism

If activism is to show up and shut down this or that meeting, the only program one would need is a road map. Mike Albert, again:

> The absence of unifying goals, of shared long-term commitment, and of attention to communicating these forthrightly at every opportunity weakens not only our prospects of organizing usefully toward a distant end, but

also our near term efforts to reduce pain today. Today's activism, for want of revolutionary designs and spirit, is often ill-informed, frequently lacks integrity, and virtually never incorporates the kind of logic, solidarity, and spirit that can sustain long-term involvement by suffering constituencies.[10]

The "movement" is not unified in its lack of a program. There are those who come as parts of "interest groups" with well developed plans and programs of action: unions, environmental groups, communists, and feminists. Then there are those who are driven by a deeply anti-institutional tendency who do not wish to formulate a program, institutional procedures, or even a leadership: mainly the networks of anarchists, the libertarians, some greens. The coalition between the "Teamsters" and the "Turtles" is a fragile one, led mainly by their opposition to corporate power rather than in favor of this or that positive strategy. In this sense too, the movement is deeply limited, and indeed it is unclear whether it should be called a "movement" or simply a "mobilization."[11] The progressive pole in the US is certainly strengthened by the protests that have developed a veneer of the cool for youth: so that it is now socially important among progressive youth to protest rather than be cynical. However, the urge to protest is not the same as the urge to fashion another world.

An anti-globalization movement that is not rooted in the liberation of the contingent tends toward a dismissal of the state-form as the horizon of demands. "Today," wrote farmer activist José Bové, "people mobilize without wanting to take over state institutions, and maybe this is a new way of conducting politics. The future lies in changing daily life by acting on an international level."[12] The anti-state sentiment does not so much resemble the anarchist argument that the state form is corrupt and must therefore be smashed (a position that is endorsed by Lenin, but with a lag time); rather, what we see here is an argument for the *avoidance* of the state in the struggle for justice. Barbara Epstein writes of this strand:

> Anarchism has the mixed advantage of being rather vague in terms of its prescriptions for a better society, and also of a certain intellectual fuzziness that allows it to incorporate both Marxism's protest against class exploitation, and liberalism's outrage at the violation of individual rights. I

spoke with one anti-globalization activist who described the anarchism of many movement activists as "liberalism on steroids"—that is, they are in favor of liberal values, human rights, free speech, diversity—and militantly so.[13]

While we know that the WTO-IMF-WB is undemocratic, we don't get an account of how to make institutions accountable. The state, after all, is a formally accountable institution in a democracy and the people are within their constitutional rights to make demands on the state. It is important to lodge one's demands toward this institution to build capacity for the creation of a just global democracy. Michael Hardt in his analysis of the Porto Alegre summit makes an analytical distinction between those who work to "reinforce the sovereignty of nation-states as a defensive barrier against the control of foreign and global capital," and those who "strive toward a non-national alternative to the present form of globalization that is equally global."[14] While this may be so in the style of the slogans, it is not clear what the latter may look like in programmatic terms: what program demands can the latter make apart from get rid of the entire class of elites, *que se vayan todos!* The best of those who do not want to relinquish the state institutions as the horizon of accountable justice do believe in the creation of a "democratic globalization," and their programmatic demands strive to build state capacity toward such an eventuality. To do any less is to abdicate the field of political action.

Keeping Up With the Dow Joneses describes the political world of the contingent class and it makes the linkage between the local struggles within the US as well as the global shifts since the 1970s. That the members of the contingent class are survivors in the structural adjustment of the US is a direct link to those farmers and workers across the world whose howls of anger at the WTO-IMF-WB are now well known. We need to draw out these connections in our local battles, so that a fight against a dirty incinerator located near a working-class community of color in Providence, Rhode Island, is called "Another Bhopal" (as Direct Action for Rights and Equality did in 1994, the tenth anniversary of Union Carbide's reckless terrorism of the people of that Indian city); or an engagement against prison construction might be linked, via Cheney's firm Halliburton, with the base construction in Central Asia or China.

Programs are created in struggle, in the midst of the fight for everyday rights and toward the creation of capacity for the contingent.

In a debate with a fellow South African Leftist, Ruth First criticized the bend to

> revolutionary puritanism which is fluent on important
> notions of revolution, but which fails to make connections
> in political practice between immediate demands which
> mobilize, or more spontaneously ignite mass struggles, and
> the longer-term programmatic conception of the
> revolutionary alternative society.

If we wait around to draft the perfect program for struggle and blueprint for a future society, we will abandon the process of social change and sit on our hands. Programs develop from the heart of the struggle, as the fights sharpen points of contradiction and reveal new lines of advance. Furthermore, First argues:

> [T]he point about the practice of mass struggles, is that
> revolutionary programmes have to be won not only in the
> head, but in the streets, townships, factories and
> countryside, and by engaging in struggle, not abstaining
> from it because it does not start with a perfected long-term
> programme.[15]

Those among the contingent who are in organizations are at work building capacity for the class to make a push toward socialism. The fight for a living wage, against prisons, for a revaluation of work and welfare: these are the main avenues for the contingent class's battle for the resources to take the struggle deeper. Here there are concrete victories, there is the opportunity to organize people into power, and there is the hope that this drive, with a strong political ideology, will be able to stand up in this local sector against Wall Street and its allies.

1   Lucille Clifton, "Whose Side Are You On?" *Quilting: Poems 1987–1990*, Rochester: BOA, 1991, p. 18.

2   The voice of the North American movement is Naomi Klein. Her *No Logo: Taking Aim at the Brand Bullies*, New York: Picador, 1999 offers a clear analysis of the problems and of the demands of the renewed movement, and her *Fences and Windows*, New York: Picador, 2002 provides a useful summary of the texture of the movement itself.

3   Elizabeth Martinez, "Where Was the Color in Seattle? Looking for reasons why the Great Battle was so white," *ColorLines*, vol. 3, no. 1, Spring 2000.

4   Michael Albert, *The Trajectory of Change: Activist Strategies for Social Transformation*, Cambridge: South End Press, 2002, p. 12.

5   Alexander Cockburn and Jeffrey St. Clair, *5 Days that Shook the World*, London: Verso, p. 9.

6   Albert, *Trajectory of Change*, p. 45.

7   The literature is extensive, but anything from Marcuse would do. For a theoretical justification for this line, see Oscar Berland, "Radical Chains: The Marxian Concept of Proletarian Mission," *Studies on the Left*, September-October 1966 and Martin Nicolaus, "Proletarian and Middle Class in Marx: Hegelian Choreography and the Capitalist Dialectic," *Studies on the Left*, January–February 1967.

8   Barbara Epstein, "Anarchism and the Anti-Globalization Movement," *Monthly Review*, vol. 53, no. 4, September 2001.

9   Elisabeth Armstrong, *The Retreat from Organization: US Feminism Reconsidered*, Albany: State University of New York Press, 2002, pp. 91–92.

10 Albert, *The Trajectory of Change*, p. 119. John Lloyd's rather staid attempt to downplay the movement is correct, perhaps on one point, which is that while the movement says that "Another World is Possible," too frequently organizations and participants fail to seriously articulate what that world may look like. There is a "damn it all" tendency that is a privilege for the movement in certain sections of the overdeveloped world. John Lloyd, *The Protest Ethic: How the Anti-Globalization Movement Challenges Social Democracy*, London: Demos, 2001. Where Lloyd fails us is that he does not know the tenor of the anti-corporate, anti-imperialist struggle in the exploited zones of the world, not just in the former colonies and semi-colonies, but also within the overdeveloped world, among the working class of color.

11 Eric Mann, *Dispatches from Durban*, Los Angeles: Frontlines Press, 2002, offers an excellent overview of the limitations of our movement.

12 José Bové, "Revolting Choice," *Guardian*, June 13, 2001.

13 Epstein, "Anarchism."

14 Hardt, "Today's Bandung?" p. 114.

15 Ruth First, "After Soweto: A Response," *Review of African Political Economy*, January/April 1978, collected in Ruth First, *Voices of Liberation*, Ed. Don Pinnock, Pretoria: HSRC Publishers, 1997, p. 125.

INDEX

Public Policy Istitute, 55
Pulaski, Charles, 83
Puranic, Sandhya, 54
Putting People First (Clinton), 144

R

racism: criminalization as, 73–78,
    81–83; in government, 83–84,
    92–93, 125n40; in housing,
    58n10, 85; police and, xxi, 73,
    77–82, 170; prison and, xxi,
    88–93; slavery, xx, 48, 94; war
    on drugs, xviii, 17, 69, 80–83,
    90; in welfare system, 136–37,
    146–47, 151, 153–58, 162
rape, 91–92, 115–16
Rathke, Wade, 138
Raza, Ahmed, 110
Reagan, Ronald: on social issues,
    xvi, 29, 76, 141, 141–43;
    structural adjustment and,
    xv–xvi, xxvn4, 14, 86, 91, 148;
    unions and, 38
Rector, Robert, 148, 174, 185n75
Reed, Bruce, 144
Reich, Robert, 20, 25–26, 133–35
Rendell, Mark, 171
Report on Manufacturers (Hamilton),
    xx
reproductive rights, 142, 180n23
Republican Party, 77, 96, 146,
    164–65, 169
Responsible Fatherhood Act, 159
"Restore Teamster Power"
    (Russell), 65n103
Rhode Island Correctional
    Industries (RICI), 103–4
Rifkin, Jeremy, 61n51
right-wing, 12, 76, 97, 141–42,

146–48
Roach, Stephen, 4, 38
robber barrons, 10, 13–14, 16
Robertson, Sandra, 150, 175, 177
Robideau, Janet, 155, 177
Rockefeller, John D., 13
Rockefeller, Nelson, xviii, 141–42
Rodriquez, Cecilia, xxiii, 46
Roosevelt, Franklin D., xvi, 35,
    106, 134, 136
Rorty, Richard, 32
Rosenburg, Susan, 114
Ross, Andrew, 53
Russia, 163

S

Safe and Drug-Free Schools and
    Communities Act, 74
Sakhi for South Asian Women, 54
Sampson, Tim, 138
sanctions, 149, 153–54, 157–59,
    185n75
Sanders, Beulah, 138
Saudia Arabia, xx, 76
Scalia, John, 110
Scheer, Robert, 73
Schlosser, Eric, 100
Schram, Sanford, 157
Seale, Bobby, 167
Seattle, Battle of, 52, 190–91
Sen, Rinku, xxiii
Sentencing Project, 116
9/11 (September 11, 2001):
    economy and, 4, 10, 163;
    immigrants and, 44, 54, 109–10,
    121; military and, xvii, 18;
    politics and, 75–76
Service Employees International
    Union (SEIU), 1, 34, 39–40, 50

ABOUT THE AUTHOR

Vijay Prashad is associate professor and director of International Studies at Trinity College in Hartford, Connecticut. He is the author of the widely acclaimed *Everybody Was Kung Fu Fighting: Afro-Asian Connections and the Myth of Cultural Purity* (Beacon, 2001) and *Karma of Brown Folk* (Minnesota, 2000), both chosen as one of the 25 best books of the year (2001 and 2000 respectively) by the *Village Voice*. Other books by Prashad include *Fat Cats and Running Dogs: The Enron Stage of Capitalism* (Common Courage, 2002); *War Against the Planet: The Fifth Afghan War, US Imperialism, and Other Assorted Fundamentalisms* (Leftword, 2002); and *Untouchable Freedom: A Social History of a Dalit Community* (Oxford, 1999).

ABOUT SOUTH END PRESS

South End Press is a nonprofit, collectively run book publisher with more than 200 titles in print. Since our founding in 1977, we have tried to meet the needs of readers who are exploring, or are already committed to, the politics of radical social change. Our goal is to publish books that encourage critical thinking and constructive action on the key political, cultural, social, economic, and ecological issues shaping life in the United States and in the world. In this way, we hope to give expression to a wide diversity of democratic social movements and to provide an alternative to the products of corporate publishing.

Through the Institute for Social and Cultural Change, South End Press works with other political media projects—Alternative Radio; Speakout, a speakers' bureau; and Z *Magazine*—to expand access to information and critical analysis.

To order books, please send a check or money order to: South End Press, 7 Brookline Street, #1, Cambridge, MA 02139-4146. To order by credit card, call 1-800-533-8478. Please include $3.50 for postage and handling for the first book and 50 cents for each additional book.

Write or e-mail southend@southendpress.org for a free catalog, or visit our website at www.southendpress.org.

POINT LOMA NAZARENE UNIVERSITY

RYAN LIBRARY

RELATED TITLES FROM SOUTH END PRESS

Lost Ground:
Welfare Reform, Poverty, and Beyond
Randy Albelda and Ann Withorn, Editors.
ISBN 0-89608-658-5, $18

Raise the Floor:
Wages and Policies that Work for All of Us
Holly Sklar, Laryssa Mykyta, and Susan Wefald
ISBN 0-89608-683-6, $12

Criminal Injustice:
Confronting the Prison Crisis
Elihu Rosenblatt, Editor
0-89608-539-2, $18

Sweatshop Warriors:
Immigrant Women Workers Take On the Global Factory
by Miriam Ching Yoon Louie
ISBN 0-89608-638-0, $18

Disposable Domestics:
Immigrant Women Workers in the Global Economy
Grace Chang
0-89608-617-8, $18

Policing the National Body:
Race, Gender, and Criminalization
Jael Silliman and Anannya Bhattacharjee, Editors
ISBN 0-89608-660-7, $18

To order books, please send a check or money order to: South End Press, 7 Brookline Street, #1, Cambridge, MA 02139-4146. To order by credit card, call 1-800-533-8478. Please include $3.50 for postage and handling for the first book and 50 cents for each additional book.